'YOU WILL DYE AT MIDNIGHT'

'You will dye at midnight':
Threatening letters in Victorian Ireland

Donal P. McCracken

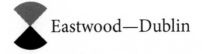
Eastwood—Dublin

This book is dedicated to
the memory of
Dr Seán Cheevers,
of Athenry and Durban

First published by Eastwood Books, 2021
Dublin, Ireland

www.eastwoodbooks.com
www.wordwellbooks.com
@eastwoodbooks

First Edition

Eastwood Books is an imprint of the Wordwell Group

Eastwood Books
The Wordwell Group
Unit 9, 78 Furze Road
Sandyford
Dublin, Ireland

ISBN: 978-1-913934-16-3 Paperback
ISBN: 978-1-913934-24-8 ebook

British Library Cataloguing in Publication Data.
A catalogue record for this book is available from the British Library.

Typeset in Adobe Garamond by Wordwell Ltd, Dublin.

Copy-editor: Heidi Houlihan

Cover design and artwork: Wordwell Ltd

Printed by: Sprint Print, Dublin

Contents

Preface

> I have been in the habit of receiving anonymus intonations of a
> somewhat similar description varying only as to the mode of death
> but also threatening my life ... I have become so accustomed to
> them that I scarcely read them.
>
> Daniel O'Connell, 25 May 1840

This book has emerged from research I began in the 1990s and early 2000s for
a biography of the famous Victorian Irish detective, John Mallon.[1] In that
process, I became aware not only that threatening letters were regularly sent to
the head of the G Division of the Dublin Metropolitan Police, but also that
threatening letters and notices were a much more widespread phenomenon in
Ireland, especially rural Ireland, in the 1880s. The contemporary elaborate
recording of crime and agrarian crime statistics, even if not always completely
accurate, gave a vivid indication about the extent of this extraordinary means
of intimidation. It is the saga of a society under strain and the use of the
threatening letter reflects a variety of emotions such as fear, frustration, self-
interest and, strangely enough, an intense feeling on the part of the author of
moral rectitude; a criminal act transmogrified into a legitimate act of war, be it
in support of the national cause or against one's neighbour.

The threatening letter was by no means a new phenomenon to Victorian
Irish society in the 1830s. Stephen Gibbons, in his interesting book *Captain
Rock, Night Errant: The threatening letters of pre-Famine Ireland, 1801–1845*,
reproduced 500 threatening letters of this earlier era, clearly illustrating that
the practice predates the wounding experience of the great Irish Famine of
1845 to 1850. It is important to recognise this because the phenomenon
cannot therefore be blamed solely on the collective psychological trauma of
the Famine and its consequences. The practice was well embedded in Irish
rural culture long before the potato crop failed. The evidence clearly suggests,
however, that the use of the threatening letter as a weapon of intimidation
did increase in the Victorian era. Why that was and how the phenomenon
manifested itself will be discussed. An anonymous letter is not, of course,
necessarily threatening. The Irish police forces were constantly receiving
information from individuals, sometimes in their pay and sometimes not.
Occasionally letters disclosing sensitive information to the authorities were
signed but Inspector Mallon made a point of removing such signatures at
times because he did not trust his superiors to be discreet and not expose his
informers' names unintentionally. He famously refused to tell the lord

lieutenant the source which led him to break the revolutionary assassination gang known as the Invincibles

The primary purpose of the real Irish Victorian threatening letter was to extort an action which the writer desired and which it was probable the recipient would resist. Generally speaking, the letter tended not to succeed in extracting that desired result, be it the evacuation of property, reversal of an eviction, providing employment to a named individual or cessation of a practice or policy, though there were some exceptions. The letter was frequently part of a wider process, however, which might involve other outrage crimes, such as shooting into houses, burning hayricks, hocking or maiming domestic animals and sometimes culminating in a physical attack on the letter's recipient. It might be supposed that class hatred was an element. In fact, class was usually merely coincidental and there are many examples of like-on-like intimidation, class-within-class, neighbour-against-neighbour and even relative-against-relative. Warnings of death in threatening letters, which were very common, raised the stakes. The axiom that those who are going to kill will kill but not threaten beforehand was not always the case in nineteenth-century rural Ireland. Many of those murdered had previously received threatening letters. But then, it must be added, the overwhelming majority who were threatened with death were not subsequently killed. So, receipt of such a letter by no means resulted in imminent death.

Though a poison-pen letter and a threatening letter can be one and the same thing, malicious-poison-pen letters, circulated to various people or exhibited publicly with the aim of humiliating someone or discrediting them, were not very common in Victorian Ireland. Anonymous letters containing live bullets, so beloved of Victorian and Edwardian novelists, were virtually unknown in Victorian Ireland. Also unknown, but occurring occasionally in Britain, was receipt through the parcel post of 'model coffins, tiny skeletons, explosive bullets, bottles labelled "Poison", and vitriol'. Scotland Yard and the Criminal Investigation Department had a collection of threatening letters, 'addressed to all classes of persons, from Royalty and statesmen to shopkeepers', but their numbers were few in comparison to those assembled by the Royal Irish Constabulary (RIC).[2]

Letters of blackmail and extortion are certainly threatening and criminal, but they are of a different genre to the letters dealt with in this volume. The blackmailer's purpose is usually the simple device of achieving unearned gain through threat of exposure. The emotions which can be found swirling around the classic threatening letter are invariably absent in such missives. And while Victorian Ireland shows all the signs of being the threatening letter 'capital of the world', there is no evidence that classic blackmail was a serious problem on the island.

The nineteenth-century Irish threatening letter came in the form of either a letter or notice. These were usually hand-written, although the handwriting was often disguised or capital letters were used throughout. Occasionally threatening notices were machine printed. The phenomenon is inextricably tied up with the fight for land but once the habit had caught on there was no stopping its morphing along more mundane lines. As Judge Curran observed, 'Boycotting, incendiary fires, and other injuries were the result frequently of private animosity, and not of agrarian agitation'.[3] As will be seen, there were two types of threatening letter and notice. One type related to the general campaign to destroy landlordism. The other involved letters and notices which revolved around local, family and neighbourly disputes. These invariably centred on land occupation, grazing rights and the employment of labourers, with occasional country-market town disputes. While a tenant might threaten a landlord and agent, then he could as easily threaten the large farmer or indeed a fellow tenant. Sometimes a labourer threatened a tenant. The emphasis shifts depending on the period, locality and circumstance and is complicated by frequent disputes between tenants and middle-men or farmers who sub-let to tenants. The campaigns of the Land League, and subsequently the National League in the 1880s, focused on simplifying the divisions in Irish rural society and emphasising the notion that society was a binary class system. There was nothing new in this falsehood apart from the successful impact it had on the popular mind, both at home and abroad.

It might, of course, be argued that the landlord's eviction notice to a tenant was in itself a threatening notice, which, in one sense, it certainly was. There was, however, nothing anonymous about these. It is also clear that while there is a relationship between evictions and threatening letters, it was frequently a friend, neighbour or descendant of the evictee who penned any subsequent threatening letter rather than the unfortunate who was being evicted. Leaving the eviction notice sophistry aside, anonymous threatening correspondence was invariably a one-way street. How could it be otherwise? Even the following sent by an anonymous 'Landlord & Loyal Subject' to Chief Secretary Forster in May 1881 cannot qualify, being more in the way of irritated advice:

> If you wish to put an end to murder – intimidation and disorder –
> at once – proclaim the Land League illegal: And arrest this 'Father'
> Garragan of Mullingar and some other prominent Land Leaguing
> Wexford Priests.

The attitude of the authorities to threatening letters varied greatly, as will be seen from the extraordinary divergence in sentences handed down by magistrates and judges, that is, on the rare occasion there was a conviction. In 1863, the inspector-general of the Irish Constabulary asserted:

> No less than 18 such cases [of threatening letters] have also been reported [in Roscommon] since last assizes, and as yet no one has been made amenable for these offences. That offence is about one of the worst known to the law, next to murder. It does not actually inflict death, but it threatens death, and operates to keep the wives and families of the persons threatened in a constant state of terror.[4]

Despite his concern, in fact, the station and barracks-based police tended to place threatening letters and notices behind other agrarian crimes such as murder, shootings, arson and maiming of cattle.

Did threatening letters work? The evidence would suggest that only sometimes and here again, locality and period were determinants. A parliamentary commission into outrages in 1852 heard evidence about a man named Eastwood, who had a gentleman's property at Creggan near Crossmaglen in south Armagh. The local magistrate, on being asked what compelled Eastwood to leave Creggan, answered, 'He received a number of letters, as I have heard and believe, and as his family and others say ... the last notice he got was, that he had but three days to live; and his wife was threatened also'.[5] So, he retreated to Dublin. Many landlords who threw in the towel, especially in the 1880s, left Ireland, moving to London and becoming, by force of circumstance and not wish, absentee landlords.

Memory was long in Ireland when it came to land ownership. In 1900, Tim Healy, while railing in the house of commons over the iniquities of the Anglo-Boer war, observed:

> Those proclamations [of Lord Roberts, as commander in chief of British forces in South Africa] which were to drop like the gentle dew from heaven, result in the destruction of land, the taking away of all cattle and the destroying of the homes of these wretched men. Yet history shows that when a country is invaded, although people may forgive death and wounds, they will never forgive the destruction and confiscation of their property. If a man is hanged he is dead, and there is no more to be said, but when you take away a man's property, his children, his grandchildren and his great-grandchildren will remember it as long as they live.[6]

There was some truth in all this, even, or perhaps especially, when the loss of a farm was no one else's fault but that of the evacuee. Summary RIC outrage reports from 1920 well illustrate this point. One from Larchill, Mountrath in Queen's County [Laois] dated 26 May 1920 ran:

> Letter received from Mrs Hogan and her son warning them to surrender the evicted farm. Three families were evicted from this land in 1873 [47 years previous] and their representatives are now trying to get reinstated.[7]

And another, dated 12 May 1920, from Grandora, Bailieborough in County Cavan, referred back 68 years:

> John Reilly received a letter telling him to give up the grabbed land. The land in question consists of 4 acres rented from a man named Tully in 1852. An eviction later took place and Tully's lost all right to the land but now claim it.[8]

This study makes no attempt to track the origins of the Irish peasant threatening letter. It appears to have emerged as a phenomenon in the eighteenth century. That is hardly surprising, though, as so does the growth of literacy. The penal code may have produced the psychosis within besieged Celtic society to lead to such behaviour but it is more likely that the threatening letter was merely a development from pre-literate times; an odd hybrid of denunciation and what, in South Africa, is called ubuntu or neighbourliness. The threatening letter had a great advantage. It inserted an additional stage between spreading malicious rumour and taking action. It escalated the rumour without the need to take potentially risky physical action.

Dr Robert Saudek (1880–1935), the Bohemian pioneer of work on character and personality, begins his not very exciting book *Anonymous letters: A study in crime and handwriting*, with an alleged quotation from Cardinal Richelieu, 'Give me two lines of a man's handwriting and I will hang him'.[9] It is well for Richelieu that he was not in the RIC, for conviction rates for sending threatening letters were very low, perhaps unsurprising given that, as the inspector-general of the force observed in 1864, 'both officers and men are honestly and zealously discharging their several duties; and, after all, a threatening letter in this country is now considered very much as a thing of course, and excites very little apprehension'.[10]

People react very differently to threatening letters and notices. Among the many threatening letters received by Captain Boycott, who to his credit saw the matter out until winning a rather pyrrhic victory, was the following:

> The tenants request an answer to the following before they pay you the rent: – 1st. Don't you wish you may get it? 2nd. When do you expect the Orangemen, and how are they to come? 3rd. When are you going to hook it? Let us know, so that we may see you off. 4th. Are you any way comfortable? Dont be uneasy in your mind: we'll take care of you. Down with landlords and agents. God save Ireland.

In an observant comment on this threatening letter, the *Daily News* journalist Bernard Becker remarked, 'Such comments as this are agreeable and amusing enough when addressed to a distant friend, but are hardly so diverting when directed to one's self'.[11]

The consequences of threatening letters may or may not have worked for the letter writer but, in some cases, the community suffered. As will be seen, the departure of a landlord from an area meant that the number of servants was reduced, as were the grooms and gardeners. The small shopkeepers and the artisans also suffered with the departure of the carriage trade. And there were unforeseen consequences of threatening letters even if the landlord was not intimidated into evacuation. The lord lieutenant, Lord Clarendon, in a letter to the earl of Erne, dated 26 December 1847, commented:

> Lord Clonmel received a threatening notice and as he had reason to believe that his own people know who the writer was and are concealing his name Lord and Lady Clonmel have stopped all their charities until he is given up.[12]

Threatening letters are ephemeral objects. Those from the Victorian heyday of the phenomenon are not as common a find as the known numbers would suggest. There are a goodly number scattered among police files, court papers and other official archives. Then there are some within the papers of the great landed estates. Solicitors' offices also have a scattering. The psychology of the threatening letter usually means that the letter – or in the case of the high-profile person, letters – is either kept by the recipient or handed into the police. Equally likely, however, is that at the time of death, usually from natural causes, such letters are destroyed by the family, unless they are retained as an amusing curiosity. One such, a rather ragged threatening letter sent to Chief Secretary Arthur Balfour in November 1888, was sold at Whyte and Sons Auctioneers in Dublin in March 2016 for € 360 and another, relating to Carrickmacross sent in 1846, had a pre-commission hammer-price in September 2016 of € 480.[13]

The number of threatening letters recorded by the police as having been handed into them between 1837 and 1901 was in the region of 36,000 but the actual number would have been considerably higher than those reported to the police. Nor does the number include letters sent to or from the Irish diaspora – this book does not deal with Irish threatening letters outside of Ireland. It should be pointed out here, though that during this period, it was not unknown for the phenomenon to exist within or to originate from an Irish community abroad, be it in Britain, the United States and even elsewhere.

In America, the Molly Maguires were certainly frequent users of this form of intimidation. The American writer Ernest W. Lucy recorded in the 1870s:

Persons named Brunnow, John Dunn, Crosby, Brady, Mrs Dalton, who had given evidence against Mollies on trial, were murdered. Many threatening letters were sent, many persons were ill-used and robbed, houses were set on fire ...[14]

Likewise, in South Africa, the colourful Irish journalist Barry Ronan recounted how an Irish gang of about 50 navvies – who called themselves the Irish Brigade – worked on the construction of the railway line from Lourenço Marques [Maputo] to Komatipoort in Portuguese Mozambique. They were led by a former South Lancashire Fusilier called Muldoon, also known as Hutchings. On 1 July 1891, the gang halted two trains making their way inland to the official opening of the new bridge across the Komati River. They removed and consumed a hogshead of beer from the one, and champagne and food from the other, all destined for the event. The gang then hit on the idea of capturing a Portuguese gunboat anchored in Delagoa Bay. In the fair-play tradition of Irish secret societies giving warnings for their misdeeds, the new Portuguese governor-general at Lourenço Marques, Raphael Jácome Lopes de Andrade, was sent the following threatening letter:

The Hirish savages hup the Line will bust your old Fort and your tin-pot gunboat tomorrer Nite. Lock up your greasy reis[15] and keep away from headquarters at berg's Hotell.[16]
    Captain Moonlight

True to their word, with some subterfuge, that is what they did, vandalising the gunboat, sticking clothing down the muzzles of its guns and reversing the Portuguese flag which was attached to the bowsprit stays at the front of the vessel. Muldoon later boasted that 'we could have annexed the whole of the Portuguese territory that night – if it was worth the takin'. Ironically, the Portuguese complained to the British about Captain Moonlight's shenanigans.[17]

Notes on sources:

Most of the surviving Irish threatening letters from the Victorian era are to be found in the National Archives of Ireland, with some in the manuscript section of the National Library of Ireland's collection of family and estate papers. The Public Record Office of Northern Ireland also houses some threatening letters of the period. There are a few Irish-related threatening letters in The National Archives in London.

The majority of the threatening letters and threatening notices in the National Archives of Ireland are contained in RIC and DMP police files, many in the Chief Secretary's Office Registered Letters. The Crime Branch Special Papers and the Fenian Papers also contain threatening letters. Sometimes these letters are without clear referencing, either having no reference number or three or four reference numbers, each number acquired as they moved between government, police or court offices.

It should be noted that thanks to the on-going digitisation project of the Chief Secretary's Office Registered Papers in the National Archives, a significant number of threatening letters for the period 1819–23 are now available online through the archives' website. This will increase as the project progresses chronologically.

Outrage statistics, including figures for general (including agrarian) and specifically for agrarian threatening letters, were printed as parliamentary papers on an annual basis, and later quarterly, usually under the titles 'Outrages (Ireland). Return of outrages reported to the Royal Irish Constabulary for the year 18__ and Return of the number of agrarian outrages which were reported to the Royal Irish Constabulary during the year ____'. Copies of these statistical reports are on the NAI website, reference CSO/ICR/1 (1848–78) and 2 (1879–93). The archives also have loose-boxed copies of outrage reports dating from 1892. These may be found at: NAI, Police Reports, Box 4 (1882–1921), 3/715/4. For a summary report of outrages from the period 1844–80, consult 'Outrages (Ireland). Return of outrages reported to the Royal Irish Constabulary Office from 1st January

1844 to 31st December 1880', c. 2756, London, 1881.

In the National Library of Ireland, there is also a series of Dublin Metropolitan Police statistical tables dating from 1838. See NLI, K.31.

In the National Archives of Ireland of special significance is the following invaluable source:

'Threatening letters (116) from persons mainly in Co. Westmeath (some from Cos. Cork, Kildare, King's, Queen's, Longford, Mayo, Meath and Roscommon), 1868–70. [Also a few letters from 1864–67 and 1880].' There are photographic copies of these letters loose and in a bound volume which has the handwriting of Samuel Lee Anderson. 1 parcel. Chief Secretary's Office, Police and Crime Records, 1848–1920, 3/719/5.

The text of the threatening letters contained in this book is reproduced with the spelling and presentation of the originals. Only the artwork is omitted.

Notes

[1] McCracken, *Inspector Mallon: Buying Irish patriotism for a five-pound note*, 248 pp.
[2] 'Threatening Letters', *The London Journal*, 6 March 1897, p. 218.
[3] Curran, *Reminiscences of John Adye Curran*, p. 248.
[4] NLI, Report on the state of Ireland in the year 1863, Ms 915, f. 39.
[5] *Report from the select committee on outrages (Ireland)*, 1852, p. 538.
[6] *Hansard*, House of Commons, 11 December 1900, col. 560.
[7] TNA, CO 904/121, Précis of agrarian outrages reported this day, 26 May 1920.
[8] *Ibid.*, 12 May 1920.
[9] Saudek, *Anonymous letters*, p. 1.
[10] *Examination of some recent allegations concerning the constabulary force of Ireland*, p. 63.
[11] Becker, *Disturbed Ireland*, p. 127.
[12] PRONI, D 1939/21/9/4, Lord Clarendon to the earl of Erne, 26 December 1847.
[13] *Whyte's history and literature Sunday 13 March 2016* (catalogue), item 112, p. 25.
[14] Ashtown, *The unknown power*, p. 126.
[15] This probably referred to milreis, the Portuguese currency, but possibly to the gunboat's commander.
[16] The Hotel Allemande, then still under construction, was owned by a man named Berg.
[17] For a full account of this episode, see Barry Ronan, *Forty South African years*, chps 11 and 12. For the background to such banditry, McCracken, 'The troublemakers', vol. 2 of *Southern African-Irish Studies*, 1992, pp. 39–53; and Charles van Onselen, *Masked raiders: Irish banditry in southern Africa 1880–1899*, chp 2.

Acknowledgements

I should like to thank the following individuals who have assisted me in the research and writing of this book: Allison Derrett, Supreme Court Judge Mr Justice Adrian Hardiman, Heidi Houlihan, Cal Hyland, Adarsh Maharaj, Patricia McCracken, Sean McCracken, Claire Ní Dhubhcháin, David Traill and Ian Whyte. Special thanks go to William Forgrave and Timothy Smyth, who assisted greatly and who were ever keen to check and find material for me when I was 7,000 miles away from Kildare and Bishop's Streets.

For the reproduction of photographic material, I am grateful for permission granted by the Director of the National Archives of Ireland and the Director of the National Library of Ireland. In particular, a special word of thanks goes to Brian Donnelly of the National Archives of Ireland. Much of the material for this book originated from this archive. The assistance of the staff of both national institutions is appreciated. For background, any historian of this phenomenon is indebted to the pioneering work on nineteenth-century rural Ireland by Dr W.E. Vaughan.

Thanks also must go to my publisher Ronan Colgan with whom I have greatly enjoyed working.

I should also like to thank the staff of the following institutions:

British Library, London
National Archives, Kew, London
National Archives of Ireland
National Folklore Collection, University College Dublin
National Library of Ireland
Public Record Office of Northern Ireland
Royal Archives, Windsor Castle

This work is, in part, based upon research sponsored by the National Research Foundation of South Africa and the University of KwaZulu-Natal. Any opinion, findings and conclusions or recommendations expressed in this material are those of the author and therefore the National Research Foundation does not accept any liability in respect thereto.

Abbreviations

BL	British Library, London
BPP	British Parliamentary Papers
CSORP	Chief Secretary's Office Registered Papers
DMP	Dublin Metropolitan Police
ILPU	Irish Loyalist and Patriotic Union
NAI	National Archives of Ireland
NLI	National Library of Ireland
PRONI	Public Record Office of Northern Ireland
PPP	Protection of Person and Property (Ireland) Act, 1881
RIC	Royal Irish Constabulary
TNA	The National Archives, London

Section I

DELIVERING THE MAIL

1. The phenomenon

Threatening letters and threatening notices were the curse of nineteenth-century rural Ireland. An initial analysis of the statistics reveals the extent of this extraordinary practice as well as revealing who tended to send such threatening communications and to whom.

Part I: Statistical information

During the Victorian era (1837–1901), 36,305 threatening letters were recorded by the Irish Constabulary, later the Royal Irish Constabulary (RIC). That is, on average, 567 a year or about 11 every week handed into police or magistrates and subsequently investigated. This was a vast number in comparison to threatening letters recorded by police forces across the Irish Sea in Great Britain. The RIC classified the threatening letter or notice under the category of outrage.

Tip of the iceberg or flat-bottomed boat?
From 1869, for several years, the method of counting outrages altered slightly, leading to an increase. Arthur Balfour drily observed that:

> It should be noted that while the great increase in the number of these
> crimes is pointed out in Mr. Chichester Fortescue's Return of 1870,
> the fact is there attributed to the condition of the country, and not, as
> it ought to have been, to the method of classifying the statistics.[1]

Balfour then quoted another predecessor of his as chief secretary of Ireland, William 'Buckshot' Forster:

> A different system of enumerating the offences, 'Levying
> Contributions,' 'Administering Unlawful Oaths,' and 'Threatening
> Letters,' was adopted in the years 1869 and 1870, which prevents an
> exact comparison being drawn with other years. This change had the

effect of apparently increasing the number of outrages.

So, there were times when the figures are suspect or at least inflated. In a footnote, Vaughan correctly seeks to put the phenomenon of the threatening letter in context:

> Just over 5,500 threatening letters were recorded by the constabulary between 1850 and 1879; they were outnumbered by evictions ... ; they were vastly outnumbered by notices to quit ... the remarkable restraint of the Irish is shown by the fact that between 1940 and 1944 at least 3 million poison-pen letters were written in France.[2]

The point is well made, but a modification needs to be added, for the official statistics were clearly not the actual number of threatening letters which were despatched to victims in Victorian Ireland. The 36,000 recorded instances of threatening letters and notices in the Victorian era must be considered to be only a proportion of those actually written, if not the tip of the iceberg. The reasons for this vary and need interrogating.

Outrage statistics were broken down into various crimes within two broad sub-categories, general and agrarian. The agrarian figures commenced in 1844 and, although not stated, these were clearly extracted from the general. Threatening letter figures for individual Irish counties and individual provinces began in 1846. Statistics listed by month exist for 1842, 1848–50 and from 1851–1901. So complete sets of general statistics including general, provincial, county and monthly only exist from 1852.

Matters are complicated by the fact that the detailed figures for counties, provinces and months do not always tally with the overall statistics. Between 1846 and 1898, for example, there is a divergence of 26 between the overall general statistics (28,301) and the overall provincial statistics (28,275). Arithmetical problems occur in the figures for 1846, 1887 and 1888, the figures given in the breakdown for county, province or month not exactly tallying with the overall figure given. Added to this, there is ambiguity, at least until 1869, in terms of whether figures for intimidation by threatening letter or notice also included other forms of intimidation. Occasional summaries published of outrage figures over preceding years sometimes differed slightly from those which had appeared originally.

Averaging over the period is, of course, misleading as there were dramatic upturns in such missives, especially during the Famine and the Land War.

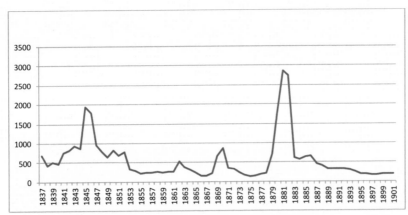

Fig. 1–Threatening letters, 1837–1901: General (including agrarian)

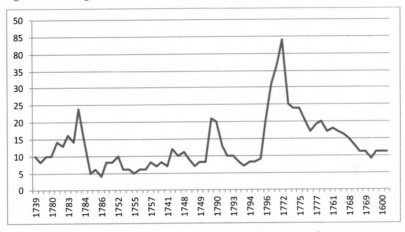

Fig. 2–Threatening letters as a percentage of total outrages reported

Numbers reached nearly 2,000 in one year for the former, and almost 3,000 during the Land-War years. This fluctuation is clearly illustrated in Figure 1. In these generalised terms, the phenomenon of the Irish threatening letter is a barometer of discontent and perhaps even tensions, especially in rural Ireland.

The proportion of outrages recorded as threatening letters followed a similar pattern over the period, as shown in Figure 2. It will be seen that the pattern is similar to the actual numbers of threatening letters recorded.

W.E. Vaughan in his seminal work *Landlords and tenants in mid-Victorian Ireland* states:

Agrarian outrages were the portion of all outrages that the Constabulary [RIC] Office defined as agrarian. Of 197,835 outrages reported by the constabulary in the whole country, outside the Dublin metropolitan area, between 1844 and 1888, 21,423 were agrarian ... The most common agrarian outrages were threatening letters, which accounted for about 45 per cent of agrarian outrages reported between 1845 and 1880. Threatening letters accounted for only 8 per cent of ordinary outrages. Thirdly, they attracted more attention in the press and among officials than ordinary outrages.[3]

If one expands those figures to the entire Victorian era, the total number of outrages reported by the constabulary stands at 290,619. Of these, 36,305 were threatening letters or notices – that is 12.49 per cent of all outrages, the highest percentage of any of the outrage categories. The two sets of statistics are reflected in Figure 3. For separate graphs, see Figures 4 and 5.

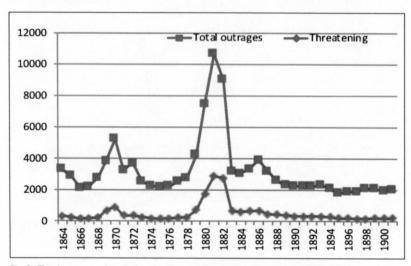

Fig. 3–Total outrages in relation to threatening letters & notices, 1837–1901

The categories of outrages, general and agrarian, included:

Offences against the person (19 categories in 1877), including murder, poisoning, rape, assault, abduction, desertion of children, abortion and 'unnatural crime'.
Offences against property (13), including arson, burglary, highway

robbery, robbery, kidnapping, stealing or maiming domestic animals, sacrilege, levying contributions, demanding money and obtaining money or goods by false pretences.

Offences affecting the public peace (13), including demand or robbery of arms, faction fighting, rioting, administering unlawful oaths, intimidation, attacking houses, rescuing prisoners, resistance to legal process, party demonstrations, injury to property, firing into dwellings, injury to places of worship and having arms or bringing arms into a proclaimed district. There were two categories of intimidation: 'By threatening letters or Notices' or 'Otherwise'.

Other offences (8), including forging coins and notes, prison breaking, injury to railways or highways, injury to telegraph wires, embezzlement, bigamy, and perjury.

The dividing line between the general and the agrarian is hard to determine and one suspects it was of a fluid nature, allocation being made based on whim as much as by rigid categorisation. The agrarian categories tended to be the same as the general, though there were variations over time and especially in summary sections.

Targets of threatening letters

The purpose of a threatening communication was to intimidate and create fear in the mind of the recipient. That sometimes succeeded, as is evident from the people, tenants or landlords who left the district, whether on a temporary basis or, sometimes, for good. We just do not know how many people quietly acquiesced to a murderous threat made against them and steered clear of the authorities. Sometimes there is, like the best lies, a grain of truth in the accusation, which embarrasses the victim into silence. Handing a letter into the police would also have been difficult for those who would have preferred to give the constabulary a wide berth. By the early 1880s, the police were respected, perhaps, but were not held in any great affection by the populace.

Of those threatening letters given to the constabulary, many were kept by the recipients for some time before being handed over. During the Parnell Commission, John Connell, a farmer near Claremorris in County Mayo, recalled:

I remember the rent being paid in April, 1879 or 1880. After it had been paid a shot was fired outside the door of our house, and a threatening letter was pinned on the door. The letter was kept in the house for some time, and was then given to the police. I could not repeat its contents.[4]

Some people destroyed the threatening letter or notice they received. This usually annoyed the constabulary as it hampered their investigations. In 1879, the priest at Brigown near Mitchelstown had a notice outside the chapel, 'at once taken down and destroyed'.[5] One Martha Daly recalled to the Parnell Commission throwing a threatening notice on the floor which demanded that she must explain herself to the Land League.[6] William Delany of the isolated cross-roads that was and is Offerlane in Queen's County [Laois], read half a threatening letter and threw it in the fire. It related to his grazing a horse on a farm at Rossnaclough, where there had been an eviction; for him, the urge to tell someone was too great and Delany spoke to the farmer Henry Cornelius, who, in turn, told the constabulary. They visited the alert Coolrain Post Office, who remembered the envelope and had noted that it bore a Mountreath post-mark. Though it was noted that the 'injured man is in no fear', Delany nonetheless and perhaps wisely removed his horse from Cornelius' land.[7]

William Hayden, the gate keeper at Kilshane House in Tipperary, did not get the opportunity to read his threatening letter because it had no stamp on it, so he refused to pay the two pence owing and the post-boy took it back to the post office, whence it made its way to the Returned Letter Branch, which opened it and forwarded it to the police. It read:

If I ever catch you in town I will take your life away you old liar you damed old rogue your are telling stories of everyone
Parnalite

In turn, the police spoke to Hayden, who gave the rather unconvincing explanation that one night he had locked the estate main gates early and this had annoyed some labourers who had had to climb over them.[8]

There is also a human tendency among many people to hold onto and hide such material as threatening letters. We know that this was especially the case when it came to the gentry, landlords, agents and substantial farmers, who had a habit of keeping threatening letters and notices, whether or not they did anything about them. Papers for landed estates sometimes include such threatening letters among other working papers in the estate office. Personal papers sorted after death sometimes unearthed threatening letters, too, in one case at least that to a deceased magistrate.[9]

Threatening letters were not always kept out of fear but often the reverse, especially when directed at the gentry classes. As one land agent commented, there was hardly a day that passed when he did not receive a threatening letter.[10] In 1863, in Queen's County, the police heard of a threatening notice attached to a gate attacking Samuel Edge, a magistrate, concerning the letting of land. By the time the constabulary eventually heard of the matter, the letter had been destroyed. It was, nonetheless, officially recorded.[11]

The psychological impact of receiving a threatening letter can differ from person to person. An interesting example of one response was Meredith Chambré, a landlord of the Hillthorn estate and a magistrate in south Armagh, who, on 20 January 1852, was violently attacked between Meigh and Killevy.[12] Chambré was not popular in the neighbourhood and was the recipient of 'a very violent' threatening letter. Two months later, a fellow magistrate, Captain Warburton, recorded:

> I asked him [Chambré] for the notice he received, and he told me
> that he had shown it to some friends, and they made him burn it,
> but that he made a copy before he burnt it; he was afraid to let it be
> known that he had kept the original.[13]

At times, magistrates were overwhelmed with the number of threatening letters brought to their attention. In June 1880, J.T. Sheehy, a Mayo magistrate, wrote to the chief secretary of 'threatening letters almost innumerable'.[14]

The question to determine is: what was the multiplier between the police statistics and the actual number of threatening letters sent or threatening notices posted up in Victorian Ireland? It is an impossible question to answer scientifically; perhaps the best we can say is that the hidden or non-recorded threatening letters and notices must have been considerable. Even if the multiplier was only three that would put the total number of threatening letters at 100,000, and would mean that a threatening letter was sent once a week in every one of the 32 counties in Ireland for the whole duration of Queen Victoria's reign.

The agrarian aspect

It must be remembered that the 36,255 threatening letters and notices recorded by the RIC in the Victorian era do not include any for Dublin, though, interestingly, these were negligible. The Dublin Metropolitan Police (DMP) did not record the number of threatening letters handed to them annually. They only kept figures for those taken into custody, those discharged and those convicted. Threatening letters are only rarely separated from statistics for intimidation, conspiracy to intimidate and threats to shoot into or burn a house. All of these combined only averaged around 12 a year in Dublin in the Victorian era. There are a few separate statistics for being arrested because of writing or sending threatening letters. For example, between 1838 and 1841, three threatening letter cases came before the Dublin magistrates; one was dismissed by the magistrate, one was acquitted at trial and only one person was convicted. There were two cases in 1845; six in 1848, though some of these may have been for other forms of intimidation; and there were two cases in 1891 and also in 1893, and one in 1895. These urban threatening letters were sometimes associated with blackmail rather than with the simple rural pastime of intimidating one's neighbour.[15] The great curse of the metropolis, or rather what the DMP concentrated upon, were targets which were easy to detect, drunken behaviour (16,000 arrests in 1865); traffic offences (9,000); and prostitution (4,000). There were usually under a hundred burglaries a year reported in Dublin.

Table 1–Threatening letters recorded for provincial cities

City/town	Date listed	No. of letters/notices	Exceptional years	Average per annum for years recorded
Belfast	1865–98	140	82 in 1872	4
Cork	1846–98	111	None	2
Galway	1873–98	913		35
Limerick	1846–98	1,447	177 in 1846	28
			123 in 1847	
			105 in 1880	
			121 in 1881	
Waterford	1846–98	29	None	0.5
Total		2,640		

An additional consideration is that, at times, certain cities were listed separately by the RIC from the counties of which they were part. There were five of these, Belfast, Cork, Galway, Limerick and Waterford, and as Table 1 shows, only Galway and Limerick show any meaningful numbers.

The big towns and cities were not of great significance regarding either threatening letters or notices. Or perhaps they were different; maybe the letters were more middle-class in nature (relating to blackmail; police informing; and what today would be termed workplace whistle blowing) and thus, such epistles were not reported or were not reported as crime statistics by the authorities.

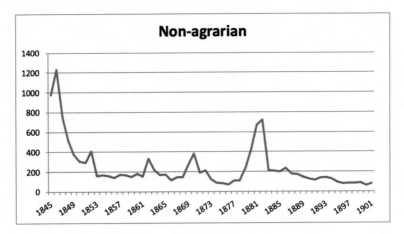

Fig. 4–Non-agrarian threatening letters, 1844–1901

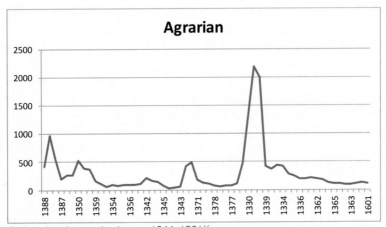

Fig. 5–Agrarian threatening letters, 1844–1901[16]

11

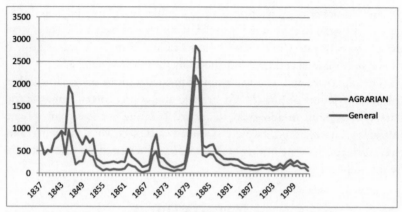

Fig. 6–Agrarian threatening letters within the total number of recorded threatening letters, 1837–1901

Figure 6 illustrates the agrarian figures within the overall general figures, illustrating the divergence between the two.

Placed side by side, two things emerge. Firstly, the agrarian figures closely follow the pattern for the general list, so there are few abnormalities in trend. When general outrages were high or low, so were agrarian outrages. Of the 36,255 threatening letters and notices recorded by the RIC in the period, 28,482 were agrarian and 7,773 or 21 per cent were not. That 7,773 includes the 2,640 (34 per cent) in Table 1 for the provincial cities. What does the divide of about four-fifths agrarian and one-fifth general or non-agrarian mean? The fact that the two sets of statistics mirrored each other suggests a link.

The answer is that many of these general letters and notices were, in fact, agrarian-related. The agrarian unrest spilt over into the clachans, villages and market towns of Ireland. This was inevitable given the interdependency between towns and tenant farmers, in particular in terms of gaining credit from shopkeepers and traders. Problems like a dip in the rural economy would lead to an increase in threatening letters. This was exacerbated during the Land War and ensuing rural unrest of the late 1870s and well into the 1880s, when boycotting and similar political and quasi-political strategies were quickly adopted from the old Irish peasant tradition of trying to terrorise one's opponent with the least possible chance of retribution.

In fact, the vast majority of threatening letters were agrarian-related, testament to the effectiveness of the national school system which emerged from the old hedge school, under government patronage, in the decade

Victoria came to the throne. One cannot write a threatening letter if one cannot write or does not at least have ready access to someone who can. One also has to have access to some paper and a pen and ink, and very often an envelope and a penny postage stamp. Sometimes no stamp was affixed, meaning the recipient had to pay two pence for the privilege of receiving the threat. Occasionally the stamp was affixed to the envelope with the queen's head upside down as an act of defiance, but more often than not, the regulations of the Irish postal service were adhered to by the writer.

Breakdown by province
Threatening letter statistics relating to the provinces for the Victorian period run for 55 years from 1846 to 1901. These amount to 28,272. As will be seen clearly from Figure 7, Ulster had the lowest number with 4,690 and Munster the highest with 10,008. It is interesting to note that Leinster is ahead of Connaught, the figures being 7,316 and 6,258 respectively. This is in spite of the fact that many counties in Leinster, such as Wicklow and Carlow, had very few instances of threatening letters. There was a long tradition of threatening letter writing in the midlands, however, and, in particular, in Counties Westmeath, King's County [Offaly], Longford and, to a lesser degree, County Meath; the tradition also spilled over into the Connaught counties of Tipperary, Roscommon and Leitrim.

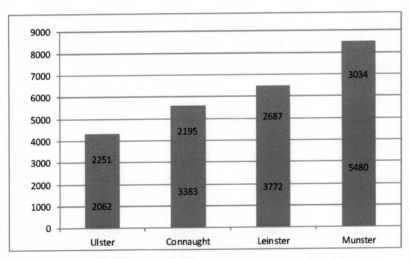

Fig. 7—By province: Agrarian and non-agrarian threatening letters: 1849–98
Agrarian threatening letters shown above and non-agrarian below.

In the period 1849–98, the proportion of agrarian letters swung from 48 per cent in Ulster to 64 per cent in Munster, as shown in Table 2

Province	Agrarian	Non-agrarian
Ulster	48%	52%
Connaught	61%	39%
Leinster	58%	42%
Munster	64%	36%

Table 2–Percentage by province: Agrarian and non-agrarian threatening letters: 1849–98

Figures 8, 9, 10 and 11 give provincial images of the situation regarding general threatening letters in each province.

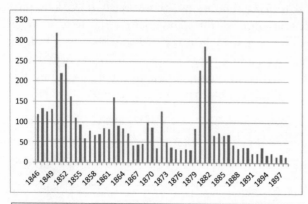

Fig. 8–Threatening letters (general): Ulster, 1846–98

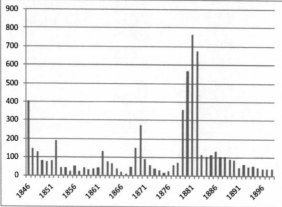

Fig. 9–Threatening letters (general): Connaught, 1846–98

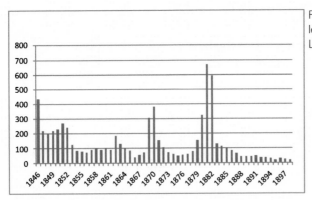

Fig. 10–Threatening letters (general): Leinster, 1846–98

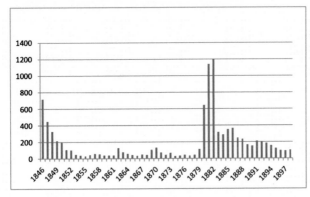

Fig. 11–Threatening letters (general): Munster, 1846–98

The 32 counties of Ireland

The primary areas for the threatening letter phenomenon were in the south, the west and parts of the midlands. The overall numbers of threatening letters reported for each county between 1846 and 1898 is clearly illustrated in Figure 12 and reflected proportionally in Table 3 along with the percentages.

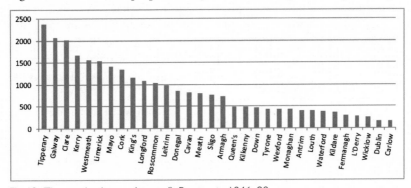

Fig. 12–Threatening letters (general): By county, 1846–98

Table 3–Threatening letters (general): By county and percentage, 1846–98

County	Number	Percentage
Tipperary	2,376	9
Galway	2,072	7.5
Clare	2,011	7
Kerry	1,673	6
Westmeath	1,554	6
Limerick	1,533	6
Mayo	1,416	5
Cork	1,337	5
King's	1,150	4
Longford	1,083	4
Roscommon	1,027	4
Leitrim	969	3.5
Donegal	854	3
Cavan	807	3
Meath	804	3
Sligo	764	3
Armagh	726	3
Queen's	493	2
Kilkenny	484	2
Down	464	1.5
Tyrone	432	1.5
Wexford	431	1.5
Monaghan	429	1.5
Antrim	400	1
Louth	397	1
Waterford	384	1
Kildare	352	1
Fermanagh	288	1
L'Derry	270	1
Wicklow	245	1
Dublin	161	0.5
Carlow	160	0.5
	27,546	100%

Seasonal variants

There was a definite seasonal ebb and flow in threatening letter writing. During the years up to the great epidemic in threatening letter writing during the Land War era, the pattern of threatening letter writing tended to remain constant, as Figure 13 shows. During the harvest time, writers were otherwise occupied but became increasingly busy as winter progressed, with missives peaking around Christmas and again in early spring. The decline then began in late spring. The overall pattern was roughly the same throughout the year except for a slight plateau in high summer.

Even so, there was some variation depending on the weather and levels of political excitement. The two most notable discrepancies occurred in 1879 and 1880 when, as will be seen in Figure 14, the pattern and the volume of letters were different. Figures 15 and 16 show the average statistics for March – the month when most threatening letters were traditionally reported, and for September, which had fewest threatening letters.

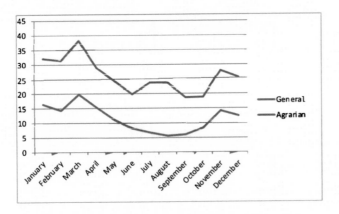

Fig. 13–Average monthly threatening letters recorded, 1848–78

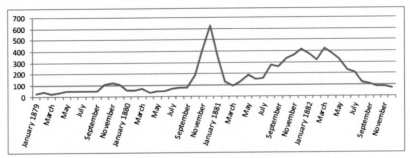

Fig. 14–Monthly threatening letters recorded, 1879–82

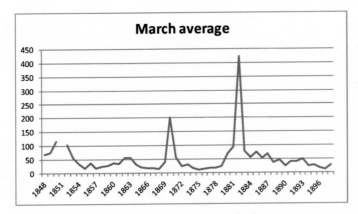

Fig. 15–March: Highest monthly average threatening letters

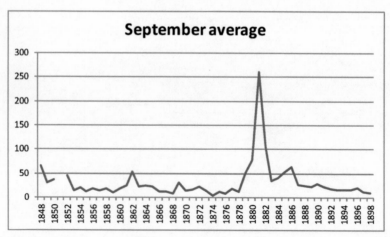

Fig. 16–September: Lowest monthly average threatening letters

Part II: The victims

It is perhaps excusable to believe that the main recipients of threatening letters and threatening notices were tyrannical landlords engaged in evictions. The reality was more complex, however. Threatening letters, invariably, related to the ownership and occupation of land and were aimed not only at landlords and their often-hapless agents but also family members of landlords and land agents. More often, though, threatening letters were sent to a wide range of community members: large farmers; smaller tenant farmers; middlemen; subtenants such as the occupiers of small tenant sublets or conacre plots; tenant occupiers of land vacated because of eviction and sometimes what was, in effect, forced emigration; those in the dying occupation of agricultural labourer; and even those market town-based merchants who offered credit to the agricultural sector. To this list must also be added law enforcers such as magistrates, sheriffs, bailiffs, summons' servers, Emergency men and assize judges. One category of victim of threatening letters died out in the early Victorian era, however. This was the tithe proctor or collector, who was a prime target prior to the reform of the Irish tithe laws.

Sometimes there were threatening letters which, while directed to one person, included the names of others who were disapproved of and, by extension, threatened. The following well-written and rather self-indulgent example came from south Armagh, one of the areas where such letters were regularly produced. It is also interesting because it mentions a policeman. Constabulary members did sometimes receive threatening letters but, until the 1880s, they were generally immune from threatening outrages:

Co. Armagh
Look to this.
Jonesboro', Dec'. 12, 1851. To all this concerns, and beware of Genl. Avenger. I am not Fools. I am giving you timely warning, all Tyrants and oppressors of the Poor. Its like the Thief of the Gallows; its over you particular landlords, particularly in the seed time, if they don't give their tenants Seed Oats to put in their land, and lower their rents, it will be measured with their corpse. And their is Mr. Chambrié [magistrate and landlord], a Beggarman, he had better keep close, for, if he does not, he may have his coffin ready; but we will bury him when he will neither have coffin or shroud around him, for its too Good for an oppressor of the Poor, as an idle-hearted rascal; besides who prides in the downfall of his country men; we need not wonder (he is no Irishman), and there is poor Bumper Squire Jones [magistrate], he would not be bad, was it not for his bad rascal of an agent, Johny Hill, the House Racker; but between Hill and Hell there is but one letter; if Hill was in Hell Jonesboro' would be much better. Mr. Fortescue [magistrate] is a good man, but there is room for improvement; and Crawford [RIC sub-inspector], the desperate Rascal, he had better watch and pray, for if all police in Ireland were watching him, he will go the road, for Hell is yawning for him long since. We will send him to Fiddler's Green. It is long since he should have got it; there is an Establishment in Jonesboro' that will soon be set flames to. It will take Whipper in McDonald [Peter McDonnell? Landlord of Meigh] to never sleep, and to hell with all the Police of Ireland. We will send all who wears the cloth to Blazes. Hell is open for Crawford.
I am, General Vengeance[17]

A lot of the politics surrounding threatening letters and notices may be ascribed to local issues and conditions. Any outsider was fair game. And an outsider was not just a foreigner, but could be someone from the next parish, or in some circumstances, a nearby townland. An interesting example of this is apparent in two threatening letters sent to a fairly well-to-do man called Dwyer who was constructing a road near Ballingarry, County Tipperary. The writer is upset that Dwyer is using labourers brought in from Callan in County Kilkenny, but the two places are only 12 kilometres apart![18]

Involvement of women

Women were not excluded from receiving threatening letters and notices. One of the most hated people in Mayo in the early 1880s was Harriet Gardiner (1821–1892), who lived with a companion woman, Susanna Pringle, in a fortified house called Farmhill outside Killala.[19] She gained a reputation for large-scale evictions, as well as being eccentric and not pandering to Irish rural conventions. Apart from her fortified house and the guns she carried when out and about, she showed no fear of the Land League and its 'secret messengers'. Whatever her sins, it is difficult not to see an element of misogyny in contemporary attacks against her.

In Clare, equally vivified was Mrs Mary O'Callaghan, the daughter of John Westropp of Attyflin, Limerick, who himself, in one communication, had been threatened with the fate of 'Sodom and Gomorrow'.[20] The O'Callaghans lived at Maryfort, Lismeehan, near Tulla. Mary's equally strong-minded sister Alice was married to Richard Stacpoole of Edenvale in County Clare. Both sisters were blamed for making 'their husbands the tyrants that they are'. Colonel O'Callaghan, formerly of the 62nd Regiment, owned nearly 5,000 acres of Clare. His was an old Cork family which had moved to Clare in Cromwellian times.[21]

O'Callaghan was responsible for the famous Bodyke evictions in the late 1880s, but even before that, he had been boycotted during the Land War. The extent to which the treatment of the womenfolk in his family later influenced his hard-line attitude to evictions is worthy of investigation. Perhaps also what the RIC described as the 'revoltingly obscene' language used by girls and women at the evictions had been replicated in previous threatening letters received by the old Crimean War veteran.

In the early 1880s, Mary O'Callaghan, though regarded as 'an Irish version of Lady Macbeth', was described as a 'graceful, well-dressed, thoroughbred Irish gentlewoman'. As the post-boy refused to deliver letters to her home in Maryfort, Mary O'Callaghan would walk to the post office herself, armed with a rifle and a revolver. She had a reputation for never missing a shot at a rabbit at 300 metres, so she was not molested. A widowed relation called Westropp, who owned a small property, was not treated with such circumspection, however. Not only were her cattle attacked but Mrs Westropp received a threatening letter described by one London journalist as 'savagely coarse and brutal in its wording'.[22]

Given the involvement of women in late nineteenth-century Irish politics and their position within many households, it is hardly surprising that women sometimes received threatening letters. Often these letters to women were aimed not at the recipient, however, but at her male relative or relatives. Sometimes they were addressed to both husband and wife. Two examples of letters addressed to women from the late 1860s may be given to illustrate the point:

Headquarters Dublin

Mrs Murry   Dysert
It has been laid before us about 10 days ago here that you husband was the cause of a law suit in youre neighbourhood that he was the promoter and encouraged that law I don't know the parties at all but we understand that there was robbery and treachery through your husband in the case I must now apprise you that mr Murry must return the cost of the law to the person that gave it to him whatever that sum may be I do not know at present he must dismiss one man out of his employment he will allowd to have any Dealings with that man or any of his family or no other person will be allowd to give or take with them

He must give up Nallys field he has more land than he requires we wont allow such person to take fields of Grass our rules are entirely opposed to such in Cease he don't obey our orders don't blame annybody but youre self I empress on you Madam the nesesity of having our Orders Carried out without Delay

I remain madam perhaps youre best friend[23]

A second and even more bizarre letter was found in a house raid by the constabulary in April 1869, in the trouser pocket of a man called James Naughton, who was a member of the secret, oath-bound agrarian fraternity, the Ribbon movement. Naughton was a 'friend' of a man named Fox, who featured in the letter and to whom the recipient, a Mrs Bridget Carroll, had given it. Bridget Carroll lived at Lisnagree near Streamstown in Westmeath. It would appear that this was an instance, not at all uncommon, of threatening letters being sent within feuding secret organisations, in this case over a land issue:

Mises Carroll,
We were on the road gone to you but we were stoped on a Count of
you being a widow it was good luck for you that we did not go if we
did all of youse that we would find in the house would never help
John Fox till another man's land. You are full as good arogue as Fox.
You gave him all the report you could to take another man's land don't
think that you or Fox will be let to carry out your point as yours taken
if ever you or any of your family gives any further assistance to Fox,
we will pay you a visit that will bring death and desolation on you and
your family. You are getting this chance. We have made a very close
search for Fox. It was good luck for him that he wasn't found. Have
this between Fox & his enemy. When we go to that country again we
will not spare man woman or child we will take then (out) of a face

William Reade, the famous Westmeath resident magistrate, was of the opinion
that the letter was in the pocket of an associate of Fox's, 'with the view of getting
up a counter party of Ribbonism to protect Fox'.[24] It is important to note that
this threatening letter was not voluntarily handed into the authorities.

Women might also be collateral victims of threatening letters directed at
their husbands. So frightened was the wife of a Kells landlord on seeing a letter
threatening her husband with death if he did not reinstate a gardener he had
dismissed that she had to leave Meath and go to Dublin.[25]

The copy of the following threatening letter posted on the gate post of Athy
Catholic church in the 1880s was obtained by the ever-vigilant Irish Loyal and
Patriot Union:

Notice to the Kavanaghs of Chapel Lane, Athy. Drive no more
Presenters or Police As I am Captain Moonlight I will visit you by a
nearly Date and leave youse a neaxample to all mankind.
Captain Moonlight

Below were two coffins 'carefully and tastefully drawn'. But more interesting
was the Parnell Commission's comment: 'The notice was written in a female
hand'.[26]

In Boyle, County Roscommon, in 1884, a Winifred Killelia, having been
evicted from a farm, was suspected of writing a threatening letter (also complete
with illustrations of two coffins) and a threatening notice. A handwriting
witness led to her receiving a year's imprisonment.[27]

Threatening letters were also sent with the aim of defending women, especially those who were threatened with eviction. One such was reported in Limerick in 1863, when land agent John Harte was cautioned from removing an unnamed widow from her house and land which she held under the Count de Salis. Interestingly, it turned out that the letter was written by a woman servant of the widow.[28]

The land-grabber

One victim of the threatening-letter phenomenon was also regarded in society as a villain. This was the person who knowingly or not took over farming land from which someone had been evicted. These individuals were frequently the recipients of vicious threatening letters.

The issue of land-grabbers raised particular ire among activists during the 1880s and gave the authorities a particular problem. As with much else, the matter of occupation of land which had been vacated because of eviction or 'forced' migration was by no means simple. Land-grabbers were more often than not local men. Being small tenant farmers, they had little of the protection that the state afforded to threatened landlord. The courts were also not always particularly sympathetic or helpful to such small farmers. An instance, quoted by Pat Finnegan in his book *Loughrea, 'that den of infamy'* is of the following anti-land-grabber notice posted up in the Craughwell area:

> Despite the many appeals made to our brother farmers, those of them as are still deaf to the voice of reason and justice still wish to continue the evil work of land jobbing. The Irish National Land League warns farmers against such work – which is daily bringing unknown evils on the tenant farmer's cause. Still, regardless of those warnings, two wretches are to be found in our midst who have taken land contrary to the rules of the Land League. Let all honest and upright farmers in the locality shun such men's company. Let those souless wretches be excluded from society as some unclean things! Let no tenants be found in the locality to assist or work for them. In a word, let traitors who are in the camp be held up to scorn and contempt of the civilised world. If this is done, Ireland will shortly be able to make a clean sweep of Irish landlords and Irishmen will ere long be able to live on the land that God and nature intended as theirs. Tenant farmers of Craughwell and surrounding districts be up and doing. Now or never is the time to show our heartless 'rulers' that we want our rights or else. – Down with all land grabbers. The land for its lawful owners – the people. God save Ireland from her enemies.

The police gathered up, as was their way in city, town and country, such polemical notices. No doubt to their irritation, the magistrate at the upcoming Loughrea petty sessions asserted that these notices were not treasonable.[29]

Notes

1 *Agrarian outrages (Ireland), Memorandum as to the principle upon which outrages are recorded as Agrarian, and included as such in the returns laid before parliament*, p. 2.
2 Vaughan, *Landlords and tenants in mid-Victorian Ireland*, p. 150, n34.
3 *Ibid.*, p. 141.
4 *Special Commission Act*, p. 113.
5 NAI, CSORP 1879, 20441, 23 November 1879, 3/636/21.
6 *Special Commission Act*, p. 113.
7 NAI, CSORP 1884, c21286, 3/644/27.
8 NAI, CSORP 1884, 21336, 3/644/27.
9 *Report from the select committee on outrages (Ireland)*, 1852, pp. 250 and 542.
10 Reilly, *The Irish land agent*, p. 57.
11 Report on the state of Ireland in 1863, NLI, ms915, f. 155.
12 McKeown and McMahon, 'Agrarian disturbances around Crossmaglen. Part x: The Shooting of Meredith Chambre', *Seanchas Ardmhacha: Journal of the Armagh Diocesan Historical Society*, 19, no. 2 (2003), p. 206.
13 *Report from the select committee on outrages (Ireland)*, 1852, p. 6.
14 Townshend, *Political violence in Ireland*, p. 115.
15 See, for example, *Statistical tables of the Dublin Metropolitan Police, for the year 1865*, Alexander Thom, Dublin, 1862, pp. 6–9. DMP crime statistics for the Victorian era can be found in the NLI, Ir 3522 d 6, 4 vols: 1838–1870, 1871–1879, 1881–1894 and 1895–1906. Statistics for 1851 and 1880 are missing.
16 Agrarian statistics for 1842 and 1843 have not been located.
17 *Report from the select committee on outrages (Ireland)*, 1852, pp. 184–5.
18 NLI, Ms 15 349, 21 February 1836.
19 See http://www.ouririshheritage.org/page/harriet_gardiner_b1821_d1892 (accessed 14 January 2017); O'Connor and O'Connor, *When crowbar and bayonet ruled*.
20 Gibbons, *Captain Rock, night errant*, p. 211.
21 http://www.clarelibrary.ie/eolas/coclare/history/bodyke_evictions/ maryfort_house.htm (accessed 24 March 2021).
22 Becker, *Disturbed Ireland*, pp. 335–7.
23 NAI, Anderson Ledger, p. 68, 26 April 1869.
24 NAI CSO RP 14363, 24 September 1869.
25 Gregg, 'The Irish cauldron', p. 255n.
26 *A verbatim copy of the Parnell Commission report with complete index and notes*, Irish Loyal and Patriotic Union, London and Dublin, 1890, p. 78.
27 NAI, CSO RP, 3/644/27, file 1973/7010, 1 September 1884.
28 NLI, Report on the state of Ireland in 1863, ms915, f. 180.
29 *Western News*, 10 July 1880, quoted in Finnegan, *Loughrea*, p. 34.

2. Behind the threatening letter

Several questions need to be asked at the outset concerning the motivation behind the writing of threatening letters. Who wrote these letters, why did they write them, who were the victims and what impact did threatening letters have on those victims? The issue of evictions and threatening notices and letters will be dealt with when the Famine is examined in a later chapter.

The writers

By the very nature of the occurrence, mystery hangs over the authorship of many Victorian Irish threatening letters. The few convictions that occurred, however, would suggest that the bulk of them were written either by labourers or more often, by tenant farmers or the sons of farmers, ironically, as Clifford Lloyd pointed out, the same source as supplied the Royal Irish Constabulary (RIC) with recruits.[1] There is nothing surprising, though, in the fact that the sort who got involved in the Moonlighting and the Molly Maguires would turn a hand to dishing out threats by notice and post.

Of course, just how anonymous many of these threatening letters really were to the people who received them is a moot point. One letter in the 1830s was reported as follows: '20 March. – Sunday night a threatening notice was posted on the house of Mr. James Barns, of Whigsborough parish, and barony of Eglish [King's County], ordering several persons to give up potato ground to him, or mark the consequences; offenders unknown'.[2] But the recipients of such notices must have had some idea who was behind the campaign. Quite a few threatening letters were aimed at preventing the recipient going to court against someone, for example.[3] Here again, the person behind the letter must have been known to the recipient.

Threatening oneself

In his book on the infamous Parnell letter forger Richard Pigott, James O'Connor asserted:

One of Pigott's odd fancies was writing anonymous letters to himself, or to others, as his purpose needed ... If Pigott suspected any of his boon companions of harbouring similar impressions regarding his course of life, the anonymous letter trick was sure to be played on him also.[4]

The Irish police were well used to a situation where the recipient of a threatening letter had also been its author. In such cases, the motivation was invariably to extricate oneself from some obligation, sometimes contractual. There was such a case with a shopkeeper and refreshment room owner, Patrick Murphy, of Rathdowney near of Abbeyleix in Queen's County [Laios]. He had contracted to sell coal to Sir E. Burrows for an Emergency protection party at Bushfield and now, as secretary of the Rathdowney Land League, was in an embarrassing situation from which he needed to extract himself.[5]

Another example related to two labourers in County Limerick called Daniel McKnight and David FitzGerald, whom the authorities believed had written threatening letters to themselves warning them not to work for a new employer. A Mrs O'Brien, for whom they had worked, had sold the use of some land to a Mrs Whelan. O'Brien had ordered the men, on threat of dismissal, to work for Whelan. For whatever reason, they did not want to do so.[6]

Similarly, in Tubbercurry in County Sligo in April 1897, three threatening notices were discovered relating to a farm at Doocastle where there had been an eviction and where a man named Matthew Kellegher now farmed in a caretaker capacity. His son, Matthew junior, was also involved in the saga. The police, who stated that the Kelleghers had a bad reputation, were cynical about the threats and believed the drama had been concocted by father and son 'with the object of convincing their employers that their post of caretakers was a dangerous one, and thereby of obtaining better pay'.[7]

In the world of threatening letters, all is not always as it seems. Given the high moral justification against the tyrant landlord, the heartless land agent, the landgrabber and the rent-payer – besides the fact that such villains were often anything but villains – attacking such individuals was frequently a cloak for less worthy motives. Leaving aside the 'outing of the other', greed, revenge and jealousy were never far from the surface in most threatening letters. The police were quick to pick up other motivations too. W.E. Vaughan cites an instance where the authorities suspected that a wife had written what appeared outwardly to be an agrarian threatening letter against her husband and in Claremorris, in County Mayo, the following drew a raised eyebrow from the RIC:

moonlight office 1884

Mr Anthony Regan, Sir, take notice that you must give up that land
you took of late from Mr Burk
you old ruffian how dare you Keep any honest mans land.
I believe you thought Captain moonlight dead but you will soon
know he is still alive ...

The authorities could find no trace in their records of an earlier alleged
threatening letter to Regan, nor did they think he was afraid. Another
threatening notice from nearby to Catherine Holster contained the following:

Captain Moonlight and his gang has made up their mind to come at
the rising of the moon and to pull down the rafters and every bit of
timber of the roof of this house And when you will see the roof
falling down they will see you running away to your own parish and
dont come back to this house again

Both Regan and Holster had been in possession of their land for some
time and the police found it suspicious that these threatening letters suddenly
appeared when it was proposed to remove the nearby police hut. In the Regan
case, the magistrate observed:

I have a strong opinion that the letter in this case was written for the
purpose of preventing the Police being withdrawing from Coolaght
[RIC] Hut.

Several theories were put forward to support this suggestion. The police
hut had been erected to protect a woman called Bridget Connell, who had
been shot at and wounded some time before. As she had now received
compensation, the hut was to be removed. The police felt she was in no
danger but the magistrate said both she and the servant at the police barracks
had a pecuniary interest in the hut remaining where it was. It was also stated
that people who had taken evicted farms:

... feel less timid while the police are so near. The foregoing would
constitute motive for this outrage [of posting up a threatening
notice], for a like purpose, were committed last July and August.[8]

Suspicion fell on Bridget Connell's son, Patrick, who was brought before the assizes. However, as the police were to find out, he was intelligent and read newspapers and knew all about comparing handwriting, so all the authorities could obtain was a signature, which the handwriting expert in court said was insufficient to make a judgement. The case was therefore dismissed.

So, threatening letters could be sent to oneself to maintain a victim status and possibly for obtaining some financial gain, or, more honourably, because one was insecure and felt safer with the police near at hand.

Delivery of threatening letters and posting up of threatening notices

The question of who actually wrote threatening letters will be discussed elsewhere. However, having written or induced someone else to write the letter for one, the letter then had to be delivered to the intended recipient. Frequently a third party was used for this, probably as an additional security measure to avoid detection or as an indication of hierarchy within a family or community. The ubiquitous Irish corner boy was, not surprisingly, in on the game. One of the very few examples of someone being apprehended red-handed in the act of pasting up a threatening notice occurred in Bruff, south of Limerick city, later a key area in the Irish Civil War and now celebrated as the ancestral town of President John F. Kennedy.

At midnight on 4 September 1881, three RIC men were standing on one of the two bridges over the Morningstar River in Bruff when Constable Henderson observed a boy about 20 metres off 'put his hand up' to the village water pump. The constable gave chase down a lane and managed to catch the lad, whom he brought back to the pump where a threatening notice had been attached. The victim was a shopkeeper called Berkery, who was being boycotted. The case was interesting, not least because it involved the celebrated Father Eugene Sheehy who, apart from being one of Éamon De Valera's teachers, was a prominent Land Leaguer who was with Parnell in Kilmainham until September 1881, and who, years later, was in the GPO in Dublin during the 1916 Easter Rising.

The Bruff pump threatening notice read:

On with the cause Down with landlordism
Confusion to landgrabbers.
Shopkeepers of Bruff if you sell any article to Berkery Bobbies we
swear we will visit you with Dynamite or lead
Paddy Moonlight
Darby Dynamite
Tipperary

A second threatening notice was found by the same police patrol on a nearby house, this one signed Rory of the Hills. A face and a rifle were drawn on both.[9]

Another case of either the author or the delivery boy being caught delivering a threatening letter was in June 1847 in Tipperary. A 'rockite' threatening notice was found in the pocket of a man who had been arrested by the constabulary. Although not posted up or sent to anyone, it referred to another notice which had been delivered to a Mr Doolan and Captain Shepherd in August 1846. The resident magistrate was unsure what to do in such an instance and consulted legal opinion, who advised, 'I think that Collins may be committed to trial for sending a threatening letter – ascertain if he wrote it'.[10]

Distance from a police barracks

Sir Francis Head commented that if one took a sixpenny map of Ireland, nailed it to a tree and at 25 yards discharged at it a load of snipeshot from a gun, the result would look something like the distribution of police stations and barracks across the island.[11] It could be argued that there is at least a slight correlation between the number of threatening letters and notices reported depending on the frequency or scarcity of police barracks in an area. The phenomenon was more prevalent where constabulary barracks were scarce, though this cannot be argued in the cases of Counties Tipperary or Westmeath, which were well endowed with such barracks. However, in the west and Kerry and Cork, where agrarian trouble was frequent, police stations and barracks were more scattered. The Rev. Hoare of Achonary in Sligo made the point in 1847, when discussing police protection after receiving a threatening letter:

> It is not attended with any addition of expense to the public, I having two of the police here at night, as I provide them with lodgings fuel & candles – nor is it any inconvenience, but rather the contrary, as it affords a protection in a very remote neighbourhood. My house is situated as respects Police Stations, about 2 miles from Chuffpool – about 4 miles from Tobercurry, & about the same distance from Temple House.[12]

But this proposition, of course, applied to all outrages, not just threatening letters and it is a pertinent point that the police were a restraining influence. There are very few cases where a landlord or land agent was attacked when guarded by RIC men.

Motivation

It was the case that some threatening letters were written 'on commission'. It is a *sine qua non* that to write a threatening letter, one had to be literate or semi-literate and one had to own a pen or pencil and a piece of paper. That is important. The 'starving masses yearning to breathe free' had no inclination for such games as threatening letters. Nor did they have the means of production had they wished to engage in such behaviour. It is impossible to be certain, and there are cases to contradict any generalisation, but an analysis of many hundreds of these letters draws one to several stark conclusions, the first being that those in grinding poverty did not tend to send anonymous letters to their perceived enemies. The impoverished labourer with his conacre potato patch was less likely to write a threatening letter to the 30-acre tenant farmer from whom he sub-rented than that tenant farmer was to write to the larger farmer who had a field which the tenant regarded as rightfully his own. Correctly, much has been made by modern historians of the young unmarried men, sons of farmers, who had attended the national school and who were the backbone of the agrarian groups who, under various names, terrorised sections of the local community, not least by writing threatening letters.

Matters are complicated by the fact that it was often not the particular person who had been wronged who wrote the offending letter – it was as likely to be a relative or a neighbour. Captain Moonlight, Captain Rook, Captain Tenant, Captain Thunderbolt, Mary Maguire or the like could well have been a lone individual. Equally, it is very probable that many letters were written by an individual who felt that they were acting on behalf of a community. The vile threat, invariably of death, was mixed with a righteous indignation that a principle against the individual in a community had been violated. Those who wrote these letters invariably did so out of indignation, spite or righteousness – three emotions which did not caution restraint. It is very rare that a letter was written to an individual as if it was sent by the person supposedly wronged. It was not a case of 'I want my land back' but rather, 'The Widow O'Rorke must have her land back'.

A corollary to this was that the person receiving the letter was being targeted not only because of an incident or development, but also because of what he or she represented. It was as if the sending of these letters was some form of primeval ritual, asserting the rights of one society over another, or of a collective over an outcast.

As mentioned elsewhere, some landlords believed that a specific individual in a community was responsible for writing threatening letters. This is an interesting idea and on occasion, as will be seen, it was true. It is equally possible, as in any secret association, that there may have been more than one specialist in the craft. This would, in part, explain the sameness and consistency of content, be it the stilted near-comical tone of the pseudo-legalese or the narrow range of objects included in the threatening art. That the threatening letter was only rarely written by the person demanding justice adds to the proposition of outsider involvement. For reasons of protection, a letter opposing the eviction of the Widow Maguire was written in the third person. It could not be otherwise. The tone and approach, though, invariably suggest that, in fact, it was not the Widow Maguire who penned the threat but a relative, a neighbour or whatever secret young male fraternity, calling itself Captain Moonlight, Captain Rock, Molly Maguire, Ribbon or Whiteboy, terrorised the townlands after dark. Such was the quasi-mafioso nature of rural Irish society.

There were, of course, plenty of opportunities in such situations to revisit old scores and extract revenge under a cloak of upstanding piety. This opens up another problematic issue, though. Threatening letters were sometimes targeted at the man in the Big House and, of course, the much-maligned Irish land agent was, in the parlance of modern terrorists, a 'legitimate target', but letters were more likely to be tenant-on-tenant or at least tenant-on-larger tenant farmer. Threatening letter writing cannot be dismissed simply as an example of class warfare. Sometimes, despite a moral land justification, things boiled down to a simple enough matter.

As an example of this, one 'drunken' farmer called Thomas Feehan of Tybroughney in County Kilkenny received in one day a threatening letter, a random shot fired at his house and an ineffective attempt at arson of his house. This may have had to do with gaining permission to build labourers' cottages. Equally, though, and noted by the constabulary, it may have been because Feehan 'refused to allow farmers sons named Conway & Power in the locality to join in dances held at his [Feehan's] house'. The constabulary believed that this had created bad feeling and 'some notices of a threatening nature were found about Feehan's house recently, but he thought they were only "tricks" & took no notice of them'.[13]

Also targeted were the lesser employees of the landlord, such as the bailiff and the process server; the drivers, who herded up and impounded the stock of those tenants who owed rent; the gripper, who arrested those tenants against whom a court order had been obtained for non-payment of rent; the keepers who watched the tenant's crops; and the hapless assistant agent, who did not have the authority or respect afforded the land agent himself. All were fair game in the enterprise of threatening letters.

Then there was the matter of tenant-to-tenant threatening letters, or labourer-to-tenant, or tenant-to-middling farmer. If anything, such missives exceeded those which transcended class. In 1880, William Bence Jones wrote:

> The interest of the labourers is not all identical with that of the farmers. Their treatment by the farmers is of the very closest and hardest kind ... If the farmer were treated by the landlords with one-half the hardness they show the labourers, there would be plenty heard about it ... May heaven forgive those who represent the Irish tenant as an innocent, simple being, unable to take care of his own interests or make a bargain for himself. A more barefaced fiction was never put forward ... Of course, as in every class everywhere, some are sharper and some softer; but as a body Irish tenants are as sharp and shrewd and as well able to hold their own as any class in the country.[14]

Within this category must be included letters sent to those men who 'occupied' the farms of evicted tenants, the infamous landgrabbers. Even the renting of a single field was enough to have one pilloried by one's erstwhile friendly neighbour and later, of course, by the Land League. This follows the timeless principle of prison life, namely that extreme and disproportionate resentment is caused if one prisoner gets three potatoes on the dinner plate and another only gets two. The right to the land is a tricky one in Ireland and it is best, in many instances, not to enquire too deeply into the lineage of a farmer's tenure. For example, how many families involved in such moral outing during the 1880s had worked the same farms they now occupied before the Famine? However, if it was someone else's land and a political cloud could descend over it, then it was open season for some grabber-baiting.

Kyla Madden observes that, 'the sheer volume of cases brought before the Forkhill petty sessions court (many of a trifling nature) suggests that the people were exceedingly litigious'.[15] The legalistic tone, as discussed elsewhere, of so many threatening letters was an extension of this. And yet, a few men and women could cause a lot of trouble, and indeed, give a false impression as to the actual state of a district. The problem was bringing the core agitators to book.

An interesting example of how one man could keep the pot boiling related to 34-year James Bowe. He farmed 50 acres at Huntstown, near Tullaroan, west of Kilkenny city. The farm was described as tolerable, though Bowe claimed it was poor wet land. As well as his elderly parents, Bowe had a wife and two children, all of whom he supported from the farm. He was well known to the local constabulary and magistrate having been part of a 'disorderly assembly' on 6 May 1881 at Kilmanagh. For this he was confined in Kilmainham Jail in Dublin, along with others, tried but found not guilty by the jury after an hour's deliberation.[16]

Bowe's activities, however, went beyond participation in rowdy demonstrations and he was regarded by the authorities as a threatening-letter writer, who, in particular, had a grudge against the local constabulary. On several occasions, threatening notices were found near the chapel calling for boycotting of the police and, in particular, calling on people to stop supplying them with milk, butter or fuel, and to cease to provide transport cars for police and bailiff. There was, in addition, a notice denouncing a farmer named William Dillon for having paid his rent. It was also alleged, and with some evidence, that people were directly intimidated by Bowe when he saw them talking to the constables, denouncing these folk as informers. A further complication was that, not so far away from Tullaroan, were nearly 200 constabulary and military, employed to protect about 50 Property Defence Association men who had been brought in to assist boycotted landlords. However, Bowe's campaign seems to have been specifically aimed at the small local police station.

He was remarkably successful, and several rather sad notes to the police have survived from those who were intimidated into ceasing to provide milk to the couple of constables, one of which ran:

Dear Mr Morrissy,
We are sorry that circumstances would not allow us to give milk any longer.
We are sorry for it to refuse people we received so much kindness from always.
But we trust you will not blame us that you will understand about it.
Will you kindly excuse us to Mrs Doyle.
Hoping you dont mind and that you will not be inconvenienced or Mrs Doyle.
Dear Mr Morrissy
Yours sincerely
Lilie Walshe

Constable Thomas Doyle (35547) was one of the two constabulary members so deprived of milk for their tea. Another letter to the police station from

M.Y. Walsh commented, 'with the help of God these times will soon change'.

Targeting the constabulary head on was perhaps rather foolish and was certainly not widespread during the Land War. Naturally, the eye of the authorities rested on Bowe and, not surprisingly, attempts were made to prove his guilt. But the fear or reluctance of witnesses played in Bowe's favour, as did the fact that the only example of his handwriting ran:

Dated this 6th day
of July 1881
James Bowe

Nevertheless, it seems fairly obvious that Bowe or an associate was guilty. Several of the threatening notes were written on the inside of envelopes originally addressed to members of Bowe's relatives. It is interesting that even with this apparently clear evidence of guilt, the authorities doubted that they could get a conviction. Even the celebrated handwriting expert John Shaw Peake, who was frequently used in such cases, said he could not form an opinion on such a scanty sample. Meanwhile, the inconvenience of the RIC station's two men was receiving the attention of the government of Ireland and it was decided to support the constabulary's request that Bowe be arrested and imprisoned under the provisions of the Protection of Persons and Property (Ireland) Act, usually referred to simply as the PPP, and which had been passed at Westminster in March 1881. Bowe was arrested on 13 June 1881 and conveyed initially to Naas Prison. The imprisonment clearly had a negative effect on his family and a petition in July was made for his release. However, the constabulary opposed this on the grounds that such a release 'would endanger the peace of the neighbourhood of Tullaroan and surrounding districts'. It was only three months later, on 10 September 1881, that James Bowe was allowed to return home.

What is particularly interesting about the James Bowe matter is that he seems to have had no personal cause for his actions, as was almost invariably the case. He had not been evicted nor did he appear to seek any additional land. His motivation appears to have been genuine advanced patriotism, although the farmer boycott notices may have had a thread leading back to some perceived injustice done to James Bowe.

Tullaroan had a reputation for being a Land League stronghold. Even after Bowe's detention without trial, a threatening notice appeared on 17 July 1881 which clearly highlights 'the cause' as at least one motivating force:

Bycot Office Mayo

Men of Tullaroan, let it not be said of you that you will be traitors to the cause for which poor Davit, Dillon, and Father Sheehy now wear their prison chains by working or holding any communication with the exterminating and rack renting Billy Scully or with any of his bailiffs or inderstrappers, – the men who said they would put down the Land League by evicting widows and ophans and now boast that they can save their hay with Land Leaguers. The men who shall remain working or go work to him after this notice being posted, their names shall be made known at a future date from this office. I will also give an account of the brave men who will have the work for the sake of Dear old Ireland

Signed Rory

Clearly, threatening letters and notices were usually documents of intent or supposed intent. But there was another category which needs to be recorded. These were letters and notices informing the recipient or the authorities why certain acts had been committed. An 1832 report by magistrate colonel Ralph Johnson of Queen's County [Laois] recorded:

On the night of the first day of the commission a party of Whitefeet assailed the house of Oldglass, the residence of Robert White, Esq., and having nailed a threatening notice to the hall-door, they fired several shots into the house; the bullets were found lodged in the walls and wood-work inside.[17]

Politics

Political threatening letters did exist in Victorian Ireland but they did not constitute the vast numbers disseminated in the rural setting and which mainly related to the occupation of land. Politicians and the politically ambitious did not tend to sit down and write anonymous threatening letters to voters telling them to vote for them. Their tactics were different.

Between 1864 and 1866, Lord John Wodehouse, later the earl of Kimberley, was lord lieutenant of Ireland.[18] This was in the period in the run-up to the 1867 insurrection. According to Samuel Hussey, who may well have just been passing on stoic Dublin bar humour, 'the Fenians used to issue mock proclamations, in ridicule of Wodehouse', signed 'Woodlouse'.[19] Humour in such activity was very rare.

What did exist and was very common were threatening letters which made reference to political activity, events or organisations like the Land League. Sensational events such as the Phoenix Park murders led, in the 1880s, to the use of 'Invincibles' as a sign-off for many threatening letters, which, of course, had nothing to do with the 'murder society'. And for some time after the Phoenix Park murder informer, James Carey, was shot, in 1883, by Patrick O'Donnell on the S.S. *Melrose* 20 kilometres off Port Elizabeth (Gqeberha) in the Cape Colony,[20] Carey's name was mentioned in the text of the more effusive of the threatening letters. An example was the threatening notice signed 'God save Ireland', which was pasted on a side window of the Munster bank in the town of Tipperary in January 1884. Part of this read, 'For so sure as there is a God of justice above, the same fate which befell Carey is yours'.

The next month an attack on a land agent called Bell was posted up in the same town, part of which ran:

> Will you allow this tyrant Bell to trample on your rights – to evict you from your homes and to place in your stead the scum of society [the Emergency men] no-swear a thousand times by all that's dear to you that he must need the death of James Carey unless he ceases at once to act as Agent to Mansergh. God save the people.

Similarly, in May 1884, 65 kilometres north at Nenagh, still in County Tipperary, a boycott notice commenced, 'Notice public opinion will be brought to bear upon any Carey for holding any communication with Hourish Bailiff ...'[21]

Six months after James Carey was killed, the following threatening letter was received by a man named Patrick Doherty at Shanballymore, just north of Tipperary town:

> You are hereby cautioned not to take any land in Greenane this year for grazing or other purposes as Agent Bell is after putting Manserghs tenants to costs. If you take it be prepared for Careys Death.
> An Invincible[22]

Elections
It is hardly surprising that the near-universal practice of writing threatening letters should spill over into political elections. There is, however, a paucity of such letters in official files, an indication perhaps that in this instance, recipients decided not to hand them into the authorities. Of course, evidence of

intimidation was frequently led when appeals against election results went to court. Sometimes the outcome was that election results were overturned and the person polling second best, even with a fraction of the original victor's votes, surprisingly (and for one term only) found himself a member of parliament.

Stephen Gibbons in his *Captain Rock, night errant* quotes the following threatening notice from the 1841 election campaign in troublesome Carlow, where the two conservative candidates defeated the opposition, including the repealer Daniel O'Connell junior, for the two county seats by fewer than ten votes:

> Anyone who votes for [Colonel Henry] Bruen may prepare for eternity. It is better a villain should die, than a nation should be enslaved. The Kilkenny boys and Wexford will do THEIR DUTY, and visit every man's person and property with their dreadful vengeance, who votes against God and the holy Catholic church. We are sober, know our duty, and are organised. It is not now as in 1798. Beware, Catholic traitors. This is the last awful warning you will get from the people.[23]

There is a collection of 10 threatening letters for the 1852 general election in Ireland. These were obtained by the eccentric travel writer Sir Francis Bond Head (1793–1875) and reproduced in his extraordinary book *A fortnight in Ireland*, which was published in London by John Murray in 1852. 'Galloping Head' had been a soldier and then a mining supervisor in South America. Then, in 1835, he had secured the position of lieutenant-governor of the very troublesome colony of Upper Canada. Unfortunately for Head, a rebellion broke out in 1837, which Head subdued, though he received criticism for not taking pre-emptive action. Recalled to London in 1838, when he defended his actions in Canada, the prime minister Lord Melbourne replied, 'But Head, you're such a damn odd fellow'. Head did not hold public office again, though belatedly, he was made a privy councillor in 1867 when the dominion of Canada was established.

After Canada, Francis Head devoted himself to being a country gentleman near Croydon. Here he spent his time horse riding, being an essayist and writing travel books relating to the Pampas and Andes, the West Indies, Canada and, in 1852, Ireland. The last of these is a strange hotchpotch, the first part being an excellent and most useful commentary on mid-century Dublin and the west of Ireland. The second part, however, is mostly devoted to an argument that the 'priesthood of Ireland [is the] cause of the moral degradation of Ireland'. One hundred and forty pages, or a third of the book, are devoted to this dubious discourse. However, within this, there is interesting material, including a section on election threatening letters. These are summarised in Table 4.[24]

Francis Head's argument was that Irish priests had by their 'spiritual and temporal intimidation and coarse language' advocated their views through such letters. There are three matters here. The first is that in some regions, priests were undoubtedly mixed up in electioneering and advocacy. That is not disputed and lasted into the 1880s and 1890s and beyond. This, in turn, was used by the threatening-letter writers as a weapon to intimidate certain voters whom they considered politically unsound. Utilising what certain priests said, however, was very different from concluding that priests were behind the writing of these threatening letters and Francis Head provides no evidence that they were. The third point is the more general one that while it is recognised that landlords sometimes tried to interfere with how tenants voted,[25] it would seem that, at times, tenants were also not averse to intimidating fellow tenants to vote in a particular way.

We do not know how Francis Head got hold of these 10 threatening letters but there is no reason to doubt their being genuine. In tone and style, down to the art work, they ring true.

Table 4–1852 general election threatening letters

Constituency and place	Threatening art work	Message
Leitrim, Manorhamilton	Vertical coffin blacked in with ink; written on either side is: here lies the body of John Cunningham a traitor to his country	John Cunningham, take notice if you dont give your vote to the man whom it was asked for on Sunday last, you may have your coffin to Manorhamilton with you. So take warning in time, do as the rest of your neighbours do, – if you dont you will be shot like a dog. A civil Caution
Queen's [Laois], Durrow	Two flintlock muskets, a cutlass and an oval peppered with eight small holes of shot	Notice. Etan Durrow town – Please Mr Poter i sit down For to trouble you with those few lines for to let you know that we wont take you short. Prepare yourself as soon as possibly can, you went against your Clergy, and what can you expect – Peter gunnonde the Crippled Dog

Unidentified	None	Notice. Take notice John Lang that you will not receive from the sooper John Coleman any milk or if you do it is not a notice you will get but dedly wounds Sign buy me CAPTAIN THUNDERBOLT
Unidentified	None	To Mr Turner*** Sir Take notice that if you go to give your vote against – you may quit both your mills: besides your life is in danger also your son – in like manner. You may please yourself, but mark what will follow.
Unidentified	None	To Mr *** I herfore warn you if you go against us leave this place or lose your life. You do not know the instant you or your wife and child will be killed. Tom and Short without shame or fear
Waterford	Horizontal coffin containing sketch of human figure Waterford	Never shew your face in Waterford again if you do mark the consequences – We will send you home dead you turn coat –You will pay for this you blackguard –Your enemy till death – The Clergy
Waterford	Horizontal coffin with 'Ok for Shame' written inside	Mind yourself or you will soon get a bullet from us the piple of Waterford
Unidentified	Horizontal coffin blacked in with ink; underneath the coffin was written: This	Connor Mic Grab, Take notice that you must give up the Medo you taks from that bastely & drunken vagabond Mic Muldoon he sould his country & his holy religion to the enimy so give up the Medo or mark what will be done to you – there is sut of the poor mans house on his hand – he is gettin Castle money, to sell you, we will make

this drunkin upstart as por as his fader was
who made money by robbin the poor –
He must get no Gras in, or House no
dealin wid him now is the time to stand
together if not America is our dom, we
must put this upstard out of the country,
let his medo rot & his land to feed Crows
– If you do not give up the Medo remember you will be sorry so take warnin or
make your will at once –
A friend.

Underneath the coffin was written:
This is your end if you hold the Medo.
No one would take the traitors Mic
Cormics Medo in Dimor. No one would
take the traitors Muldoons but you.

Probably Dublin county, possibly Tyrone[26]	Vertical coffin blacked in with ink	On the dwelling house door of James McKenna: If you vote for Hamilton, here is your coffin.
Unidentified	Horizonal (with uneven side lines) coffin blacked in with ink	Take notice of this *Below the coffin image was written:* Dear Sir I have to inform you that I have to pay you a visit on the night of the 16 inst. with regard to your vote which I hope you will give for the good of your country. But do not attempt giving it to —, or any other Devil like him – so I hope you will prepare and go with your vote for and save me the trouble of going to visit you the second time. If you do, remark what follows for I swair by the piper that played before Moses or the water that flowed from the Rock I will send your soul jumping to the lower pit of perdition and then let come to pay you the compliment to inhume your mortal remains which I think that your neighbours would not disgrace themselves by doing. So I will deliver the next verbily.

Six incidents are also cited of groups of people coming to someone's house at night and intimidating them and mentioning the wishes of the clergy in terms of how they should vote. These were at:

Carrickateaur (person intimidated: Michael Ledwith)
Cloonsherin, near Killashee, County Longford (John Geraghty)
Carrickatrave (Thomas Devine)
Unspecified (Denis Evers)
Unspecified (Bernard Burns)
Longford (John Mallow)[27]

Sectarian letters

It is perhaps an extraordinary observation in relation to the threatening letters which have survived that there are comparatively few outright sectarian threatening letters from Victorian Ireland. The reason for this is most likely because few were ever written and those that were, tended to be such as the following one from County Tyrone, grounded in the somewhat different politics of the northern counties:

> Take notice William Coalman [a Catholic] if you take the house of William Delworth [a Protestant] that the hammer and the sledge will be your fate Remember things will not be as they are in times past we want neither Papist nor Repealer in our land and you I will see you, I will take this friendly advice in time, but if you will persevere in this matter, you may have your coffin ready and the mass said for the dead – for remember death will be your fate. You may see by this time we don't want to do you any harm but there are enough instances for you in Ballynakelly and other places but if you come there your will be death beyond doubt and flames will be your bed for your house will be on fire and you will be Hammered to death I think I have said plenty on this subject but remember if you will all this happen for we are loyal Protestants of Killyman   No surrender   God save the Queen[28]

The scarcity of surviving blatantly sectarian letters is not to deny the underpinning religious divide in society or to question the underlying role that religion played in many of the contentious issues of the day. The two-way street of sectarianism certainly existed and flared up now and then, but as a generation of scholars has now established, the fissures in Irish society were far more complex than a simplistic religious division. That complexity equally applies when looking at the phenomenon of the threatening letter.

Inspector-General Sir Henry Brownrigg of the Irish Constabulary was asked by the 1852 parliamentary select committee on Irish outrages if 'combinations are against persons of different religious persuasion as much as against another?' His reply was, 'I do not think there is the least distinction in agrarian outrages'.[29] A decade later, in an annual constabulary report, Brownrigg recorded that a parish priest called Rev. Close received through the post a letter 'informing him that the Orangemen would have their month (July) in spite of Pope or Police'.[30] Equally common were threatening letters against clergy of the Church of Ireland. However, these were invariably related to the cleric's ownership and renting of land rather than any obvious attack against Protestantism. The *Tuam News*, never a paper to stand back on a controversial matter, raised the issue of Dean West of Roveagh, just east of Clarinbridge in Galway:

> I soon found myself in the midst of Dean Wests evicted tenants. The Revd evictor has the audacity to stand in a pulpit while he has flung 80 souls on the worlds highway who cry to Heaven for vengeance.

In 1870, in Meath, the following threatening letter was received by a landlord:

> John, – If you do not quit your contrariness before this day week I will blow out your brains – if you had all the Plece [police] in Virginia [town]. So I give you this to take notice to keep your tongue quite.

A sketch of a coffin appeared at the end of the note. The magistrate, who claimed to know the public house in which 'these crimes are hatched', believed this to centre around a Protestant landowner who would not allow a Catholic farmer to pass over his land. But there was no evidence that sectarianism was a key factor in this rather traditional dispute.[31]

It must also be said that there were occasions when a priest was the recipient of a threatening letter and, as the following example illustrates, from Clerky in County Mayo dated 1843, sometimes from a member of his own flock:

The right for clergy

Just	10s	for marriage
	1s	for baptism
	1s	for mass for the dead
	1s	for certificate
	2s	for usage

No legacies – confess at the chapel – no oats for the curates – no potatoes for the clerks.
If they employ servants, let them pay them –
Any man refusing to join this paper, let his name be mentioned on the back, and posted on the crane, and he will be punished.
And don't ye delay until ye serve the parish, and ye must meet James Egan's Crossroads, on Sunday next, to go into the tower, and serve the priest, let them confess at the chapel – No more.[32]

It is true that more often than not the landlord and land agent were Protestant and the tenant farmer and labourer Catholic, and that there was a belief held by some landlords in certain parts of the country that the outrages were sectarian.[33] But, as will be seen, Catholic landlords, even Valantine Browne, 4th earl of Kenmare, received threatening letters. Kyla Madden in her book *Forkhill Protestants and Forkhill Catholics* quotes from a threatening notice, posted up in the parish of Creggan in south Armagh warning landlords 'of every creed and persuasion':

Whoever pays that impost called tythe shall be in a short time freed from all worldly cares by him who has slumbered these many days but has now recovered from his drowsiness – therefore we beseech you have not a hand in your own deaths. We are nameless bit not without authority.[34]

There are letters which certainly have religious undertones. In the 1830s, there were such undertones when a farmer called John Legate of Fossey in Queen's County received a notice to dismiss two servants who 'were trustworthy, and Protestants'. Fearing assault, Fossey complied with the demand.[35]

Practical joke
Given the very large number of threatening letters circulating in Ireland it is hardly surprising that the phenomenon was well known by contemporaries.

Occasionally, this led to threatening letters being sent as a practical joke to someone perceived as being gullible. An example is given by Sub-Inspector Samuel Waters of the RIC in his manuscript memoir written in 1924. In the mid-1870s he was stationed at Castletown Bearhaven in County Cork. While posted here, and unbeknown to him, Water's wife Margaret and a Mrs Ogilvy, the wife of the commanding officer of the coast guards, took a dislike to a 'wretched curate' who had come from England. To chase him away the two women composed a 'blood thirsty' letter, complete with 'a huge sketch of a skull and cross bones'. Unfortunately, the threatening letter was sent by the curate to Dublin Castle and Waters was instructed to investigate. The inspector soon discovered the truth and then had to persuade the curate and the inspector general that the matter was a 'silly joke', without revealing the names of the writers. This he managed to achieve, though the two women were not repentant and indeed, followed up their campaign by giving the curate a box of sweets laced with a 'powerful physic'.[36]

Impact

The image of the gruff old Irish squireen reading a semi-literate threatening note addressed to him, with the postage stamp stuck on with the queen's head upside down, screwing the paper up into a ball and throwing it into the wastepaper basket or into the grate of the roaring wood fire with a curse, is a myth. Most people who receive threatening letters cannot resist the temptation to keep them. The hapless Captain Boycott, on one occasion, noted that he had a bureau full of threatening letters. Samuel Hussey also said as much for himself.

For most folks, a threatening letter was a sinister and worrying thing, an act of terrorism in itself. In July 1881, at the height of the Land War, a Limerick magistrate observed:

> The terror exercised over the Tenantry throughout the country by these notices is incalculable. The main reason farmers do not settle with there landlord is the fear [of] being made marked men by the promoters of such notices

In the case the magistrate was considering, the culprits appear to have been a 28-year-old single blacksmith and two 37-year-old single men who were the sons of two local farmers – all suitable profiles for such activity and moonlighting.[37]

At the small farmer and tenant level, a threatening letter was frequently received with great fear and treated nearly as a dreaded mystical phenomenon. Like Captain Flint's black spot, a threatening letter was interpreted by some with great trepidation. In the 1860s, there was a case at Ballybeg near Kilbeggan in Westmeath, then a key county for threatening letters, where a threatening notice was posted on an outhouse door of a farmer called James Murray, who was too afraid even to take it down.[38] The 1887 royal commission into the land acts was not incorrect when it stated that tenants would rather not pay their rent than face boycotting, 'which depended for its success on the probability of outrage'.[39] And it was the whole family that was affected, not just the boycotted farmer. The harshness of the system comes out in a notice found in Kerry on 20 February 1886 which threatened to boycott a girl who had been seen walking with the daughter of a boycotted farmer.[40] But the matter went further. The *Limerick Leader* of 22 January 1887 reported the proceedings of the National League meeting held at Rathdowney in Queen's County [Laois] on 9 January, at which it was said that the names of those who had joined the league would be posted up. It then added the sinister rider, 'Those who, in the meantime, will abstain from joining, cannot but be looked upon as unfriendly to the cause'. As is the way in such circumstances, no neutrals were allowed.

In his neglected last novel, *The Land Leaguers*, Anthony Trollope has the Catholic butler to the Jones household near Headford in County Galway receive a threatening notice during the Land War period. The old retainer approaches Edith Jones, one of the daughters of the big house:

Then he [Peter McGrew] took out from a dirty envelope a dirty sheet of paper, and exposed it to her eyes. On top of it was a rude coffin. 'Don't it make yer hair stand on end, and yer very flesh creep, Miss Edith, to look at the likes o' that?' And below the coffin there was a ruder skull and two crossbones. 'Them's intended for what I'm to be. I understand their language well enough. Look here,' and he turned the envelope round and showed that it was addressed to Peter McGrew, butler, Morony Castle. 'They know me well enough all the country round.' The letter was as follows:

'Mr Peter McGrew,
'If you're not out of that before the end of the month, but stay there doing things for them infernal blackguards, your goose is cooked. So now you know all about it.
        'From yours, "MOONLIGH"'

Edith attempted to laugh at this letter, but Peter made her
understand that it was no laughing matter.
'I've a married darter in Dublin who won't see her father shot down
that way if she knows it.'
'You had better take it to papa, then, and give him warning,' said
Edith. But this Peter declined to do on the spur of the moment,
seeming to be equally afraid of his master and of Captain
Moonlight.

In the end, the old retainer remained loyal to the family and was indeed
present when the young son of the house was murdered. As an interesting
reflection on the impact of threatening letters, at least on some people in
certain circumstances, Trollope has Captain Yorke Clayton, a resident
magistrate, drily and perhaps not inaccurately comment on the butler and
the threatening letter he had received:

Of course he [Peter McGrew] finds it to be a great compliment. To
have a special letter addressed to him by some special Captain
Moonlight is to bring him into the history of his country.[41]

Trollope had worked for the Post Office in Ireland in the early
1840s, so was acquainted with the country, and he returned to Ireland twice
in the summer of 1882 to research material for *The Land Laeguers*. This was
at the height of the agrarian troubles so the novel is full of accurate
information, though he mistakes the timing of the Phoenix Park murders for
April instead of early May. The passage above strongly suggests that Trollope
had seen a threatening letter during his mission, for the tone of letter and
description of the accompanying artwork have an authenticity about them.
William Bence Jones, writing in July 1880, asserted:

In fact, in Ireland, in any difficulty, the first resource of many is
intimidation. The frequent threatening letters we read of in the
papers are a proof of this, though ninety-nine out of a hundred are
rubbish – only attempts to frighten. The threats are by no means
always threats of outrage, but of all kinds of indefinite wrath, loss of
favour and of help, which the unhappy offender will or shall
encounter. Many will threaten and try to intimidate, who never
really intend to commit an outrage.[42]

The content of threatening letters was designed to frighten the recipient and was usually based on controversy over a factual matter, frequently the circumstances surrounding the occupation of a piece of land. Whatever the rights or wrongs of the matter, the recipient was placed on the defensive. This, coupled with the element of the unknown, at the very least, concentrated the recipient's mind and, at worst, led to the setting-in of a degree of paranoia. Either way, there was a reluctance to destroy the hateful document which, for the insecure and the hesitant, quickly took on the foreboding of a nemesis. And nemesis it was in some instances. While most threatening letters did not lead to violence against the recipient's person, very few of the agrarian murders or attacks on property were not preceded by the sending of threatening letters. On occasion, burning hay ricks, maiming and torture of domestic livestock or shooting through windows at night were accompanied by a threatening notice posted nearby.

What is interesting about Irish threatening letters and notices was that such a large number were handed into the local RIC police barracks. That was, in fact, a more defiant act than throwing the message into the wastepaper basket or turf fire. By handing them in, previously private matters were exposed to an audience beyond the family. Lord Oxmantown was not far off the mark when he commented that 'as large as the number [of outrages] appears to have been from the official returns it falls far short of the reality'.[43]

Flight and the consequences

There were recipients who packed up and left the area or even Ireland – as William Trench drily put it, 'The timid fled from the country altogether, whilst the bolder residents never stirred out of their houses unless armed to the teeth and prepared for an attack'.[44] Threatening letters did indeed frighten people and some landlords did leave either the district or the island. Viscount Lismore left, having endured as much harassment as he could stand.

This, in turn, had other impacts that were often not intended by the sender. When such local potentates ceased residing on their estates, employment for many vanished overnight. In the Lord Kenmare instance, when due to the impact of the Land War, he shut up Kenmare House and moved to live in London, 'All the labourers employed on the estate are discharged, as well as some of the gamekeepers'.[45] One journalist estimated that the departure of Lord Kenmare resulted in about £200 a week in wages being lost in the neighbourhood.[46] Similarly, when the Inchiquins closed up Dromoland Castle in County Clare for a period, one shopkeeper, presumably from Newmarket-on-Fergus in County Clare, complained bitterly that, 'we used regularly to make a bill of a hundred pounds at Christmas, for blanks and other things given away. Now the house is shut up and we make nothing!' So also, a modern stable complex at Edenvale was shut up by Richard Stacpoole, 'and so another centre of local industry and activity is made sterile'.[47]

Carrying out of threats

An ever-present question is whether the writers of threatening letters carried out their threats. From the number of murders in Ireland, the answer is sometimes, but clearly these were exceptions. What does, however, appear to have been true almost invariably is that when rural murder was attempted or successfully carried out, the victim had previously been given 'fair notice' by way of a threatening letter. It seems to have been a 'point of honour' to warn the intended victim. As one conspirator was reported as saying, 'I will never consent to his death until he be fairly warned first; it is the rule and the law, and notice I say he must get'. In this instance, the Ribbonmen duly posted the following notice on every Catholic chapel in the area:

> To the Landlords, Agrents, Bailiffs, Grippers, process-servers, and usurpers or underminers who wish to step into the evicted tenants' property, and to all others concerned in Tyranny and Oppression of the poor on the Bath Estate.
> TAKE NOTICE
> That you are hereby (under the pain of a certain punishment which will inevitably occur) prohibited from evicting tenants, executing decrees, serving process, distraining for rent, or going into another's land, or to assist any tyrant, Landlord, or Agent in his insatiable desire for depopulation. Recollect the fate of Mauleverer,[48] on this his anniversary. Dated May 23, 1851.

More often than not, the letter was to an individual. Of course, the sending of a threatening letter was an effort to psychologically attack the victim. Killing a man was one thing, making him suffer before he was killed was more satisfactory for those seeking crude revenge. As William Trench commented after the murder of Thomas Bateson, land agent to the Templeton estate near Castleblayney:

> Ribbonmen in a disturbed district do not generally threaten idly.
> They had abided by their wild rule of fair play in giving their victim

warning, and they were now steadily and stealthily plotting his sure destruction ...[49]

Notes

[1] Clifford Lloyd, *Ireland under the Land League*, p. 137.

[2] BBP: *Papers relating to the state of Ireland. House of Commons, 7 July 1834*, Command paper 459, p. 27.

[3] *Ibid.*

[4] O'Connor, *Recollections of Richard Pigott*, pp. 21–2.

[5] NAI, CSORP 1881, 3/638/4.

[6] TNA, CO904, 6217.

[7] TNA, CO903/6, 7982.

[8] NAI, CSORP, 1884, file 15205, 3/644/28.

[9] NAI, CSORP 1881, 3/638/19.

[10] NAI, CSORP, Outrage papers for Tipperary and Sligo, 1847, file 27/1450.

[11] Head, *A fortnight in Ireland*, p. 42.

[12] NAI, CSORP, Outrage papers, Tipperary, Sligo and Roscommon, c37 715, December 1847.

[13] NAI, CSORP 1884, Boycotting notice, 21191, 1 May 1884, 3/644/27.

[14] Bence Jones, *A life's work in Ireland*, pp. 36–7.

[15] Madden, *Forkhill Protestants and Forkhill Catholics*, p. 117.

[16] *Kilkenny Journal*, 13 July 1881.

[17] Ashtown, *The unknown power*, p. 86.

[18] Moody, Martin and Byrne, *A new history of Ireland: IX, Maps, genealogies, lists*, p. 499.

[19] Hussey, *Reminiscences of an Irish land agent*, p. 164.

[20] J.L. McCracken, 'The death of the informer: James Carey: A Fenian revenge killing?', *Southern African-Irish Studies*, vol. 3, 1996, pp. 190–9.

[21] NAI, CSORP 1884, Threatening notice 21358, 10 January 1884; 21357, 7 February 1884; 21196, 14 May 1884, 3/644/27.

[22] NAI, CSO RP, 1884, 3/644/27.

[23] Gibbons, *Captain Rock, night errant*, p. 256; Walker, *Parliamentary election results in Ireland*, p. 69.

[24] Head, *A fortnight in Ireland*, pp. 374–80.

[25] Comerford, 'Churchmen, tenants, and independent opposition, 1850–56', p. 403.

[26] Walker, *Parliamentary elections results in Ireland*, pp. 81–6.

[27] The Longford moonlighters need not have concerned themselves as the conservative candidate they opposed, Laurence King-Harman, received no votes at all.

[28] *Evidence taken before Her Majesty's commission of inquiry ... 1845*, p. 907. Quoted in Gibbons, *Captain Rok, night errant*, p. 260.

[29] *Report from the select committee on outrages (Ireland)*, 1852, p. 195.

[30] NLI, Report on the state of Ireland in the year 1863, ms 915, f. 139.

[31] Gregg, 'The Irish cauldron', p. 255.

[32] Gibbons, *Captain Rok, night errant*, p. 259 (from BL, Peel papers, Add Mss 40524, f. 129).

[33] See, for example, Madden, *Forkhill Protestants and Forkhill Catholics*, p. 83.

[34] *Ibid.*, p. 99.

35 Ashtown, *The unknown power*, p. 91.
36 Ball (ed.), *A policeman's Ireland: Recollections of Samuel Waters, RIC*, pp. 46–7.
37 NAI, CSORP 1881, 3/638/19.
38 NAI, CSORP, 1870, 3/630/17, 26 October 1869.
39 Quoted in *Ireland in 1887*, p. 218.
40 *Statement submitted to the prime minister by the Irish Loyal and Patriotic Union*, p. 40.
41 Trollope, *The Land Leaguers*, p. 204.
42 Bence Jones, *A life's work in Ireland*, p. 157.
43 Reilly, *The Irish land agent*, p. 69.
44 Trent, *Realities of Irish life*, p. 229.
45 Hussey, *Reminiscences of an Irish land agent*, p. 224.
46 Becker, *Disturbed Ireland*, p. 243.
47 Hurlbert, *Ireland under coercion*, pp. 214 and 221.
48 Lindsay Mauleverer was a land agent on the Hamilton, Tipping and Jones estates, who was murdered at Crossmaglen in May 1850. See Madden, *Forkill Protestants Forkhill Catholics*, p. 110.
49 Trench, *Realities of Irish life*, pp. 196–7 and 208.

3. The sign of death:
Delivery, language and image

Delivering threatening letters

There are very few instances, though beloved of novelists, of letters or notices being tied to stones and thrown through windows.

The author of the threatening letter, no doubt for fear of detection or because the person was semi-literate, was not always the writer. As already mentioned, the deliverer of threatening notices was frequently a friend or relative of the aggrieved, although getting someone to deliver the missive could be a challenge. One interesting case was in Queen's County in the 1830s when it was recorded:

> On the night of Sunday the 26th of last month, and during the sitting of the commission, a party of Whitefeet, all well armed, broke into the house of a man named Walshe, a tenant of Mr. William Sevan, at Capponellan, near Durrow, and swore him to deliver a threatening notice of a very atrocious character to Mr. Harrison of Dairy Hill, a gentleman with whom he has no connection whatever.[1]

Captain Fitzmaurce, giving evidence before the 1852 parliamentary select committee on outrages, was asked if threatening letters 'travel by post generally'. He replied, "yes; and often posted at night on doors and other places"'.[2] On the whole, personal threatening letters went through the ritual of going through Her Majesty's Irish penny postal system. This clearly implied the sender was acquainted with the system and had access to envelopes as well as paper and ink. That in itself is an interesting reflection on the type of person who was involved in such pastimes, perhaps denoting a degree of education, wealth and sophistication. As suggested previously, threatening letters were rarely written by the destitute.

The use of the postal services was an interesting reflection of the great success of the penny post in rural Ireland. It must be remembered that the service was only introduced in the early Victorian era, although Dublin had its own penny postal service much earlier. Of course, the Irish threatening letter long precedes the official penny post of the 1840s and the opening of a network of village post offices throughout Ireland, but there is no doubt that the penny post greatly facilitated the sending of intimidating messages and by so doing greatly increased the number of threatening communications sent to neighbours, land agents, landlords or the constabulary.[3]

There was a tendency not to post the threatening letter in the town or village where or near where the antagonists lived, but to go much further afield. The obvious explanation for this is that it was to ensure the security of the sender. Post Office staff, who tended to be keen to assist the police, knew everyone and generally remembered anyone who bought a stamp, especially those who did not normally buy stamps. But the practice of travelling some distance to post a threatening letter also had a ritual component attached, a cross-county border communication giving additional gravitas and importance.

Occasionally threatening notices were sent through the mail but as they were, more often than not, for the attention of the public as much as for the victim, they were invariably nailed to gateposts, barn or front doors, stumps of trees or the like. They were sometimes pasted up on walls, gateposts or windows, in villages and towns, often in alleyways. Probably the most regularly chosen site for such notices was near the entrance to the local Catholic church. As well as catching a crowd, this would have added to the righteousness and seriousness of the accusation, a matter discussed elsewhere. Be that as it may, the local parish priest was as likely to have the notice removed as to leave it be. Interestingly, the vicinity of public houses, another place where people regularly congregated, was rarely used as a place to lay down the rite of Rory of the Hills (the traditional custodian of the rights of the rural poor), although notices and letters were, on occasion, drafted in a public house.

Structure and language
Most Irish threatening letters were short. Generally, one sheet of paper was used, more often than not approximating the normal letter size of 4½ by 7 inches (114 x 178 mm) or sometimes slightly bigger, approaching a modern A5 size. From that small size, they ranged up to quarto (254 x 203 mm) but the larger size was more common for threatening notices, as distinct from threatening letters. The number of words on a threatening letter varied, of course, but there was a tendency for the page to be filled, even if some of the space was taken up with art works. Indeed, one sometimes gets the impression that the latter half of a threatening letter has drifted off the key issue as the

writer endeavours to fill the whole page. That said, most agrarian threatening letters were about 100 words long, only occasionally extending to two sides of a sheet. Missives exceeding 250 words may have indicated something different, perhaps the use of a letter writer other than the complainant, or a more educated letter writer. The threatening letters written by or connected with organisations, such as the Molly Maguires, moonlighting groups, the Land League or the National League, had a tendency to be more long-winded. In the Lee Anderson hoard of threatening letters from the late 1860s and early 1870s, which are very traditional and firmly land-based in origin, the usual length of a letter is about 115 words. In this collection, there is a great variation in length, however, ranging from 30 to 440 words.

Ink was the usual medium used for threatening letters and those threatening notices which were not printed. Despite what novelists supposed, blood was very rarely used. Occasionally pencil was employed. An interesting case of this in 1884 was a drawing of a coffin and a man with a gun with the message 'Hawthorne is no more'. This was drawn on the inside wall of a vacant house at Bough, south-east of Cootehill in County Cavan, in itself an interesting deviation from the medium of paper. The drawing was 'scarely perceptible when visited by the police' and almost completely obliterated by the time the district inspector arrived. Several other threatening letters had been received by others previously associated with the farm. James Hawthorne was not unduly perturbed and refused police protection when it was offered, stating that frequent police patrols were quite enough.[4] The paper used was frequently of poor, cheap quality and came from a variety of sources – sometimes a page from a notebook, an envelope, and scraps of paper or a regular, if grubby, sheet of stationary.

Legalese

Leaving aside the bad English and crudeness, there is a sameness about many Irish threatening letters. Many of them are written in what the writer obviously considers to be a legal format. George Cornewall Lewis, writing in 1836 in his *Local disturbances in Ireland*, asserts:

> In their threatening letters they affect the form and phraseology of
> legal notices, thereby intimating that they administer a law
> subsidiary to, or rather substituted for, the law of the state.[5]

This, no doubt, was with the intention of overawing the recipient as well as giving an indication of legal legitimacy, fair-mindedness and attention to due process, none of which was actually the case. Vaughan cites one Monaghan case, in 1852, where the writer ended, 'signed by order of the Irish parliment'.[6] This thinking applied to the vigilante groups which raided homes to steal weapons and sometimes cash or, as was common, to drag out some hapless individual who had offended and who was then severely beaten, sometimes to death, on the dusty road. The mock trial, a kangaroo hearing, at which the victim was tried in his or her absence and then delivered a warning letter, were all part of this belief that due process was being followed.[7]

Some letters were brisk and warrant like:

Hereby
Give up this land at once
If you dont your life will pay penalty
Signed by order of the Irish
Invincible[8]

Among this pseudo-legalese, there might appear the occasional element of sarcasm and, if not actual, certainly twisted logic. After the infamous murder of Major Mahon of Strokestown, a number of similar threatening letters were sent to the victim's family members and to the estate's agent. These were obviously written by the same person and demanded a full remittance of rent arrears. With some word variation, they ran as follows:

As a Token of Gratitute for a former kindnefs bestowed on me &
my family I write you those few lines Apriseing you your
Approaching Fate unlefs you Become a better man that what you ar
present to your tenants you will Share in the same Fate as yr
Kindsman the Demon Major Mahon did ... If you do not comply to
this Fly to England ... if it was known that I wrote you this I would
Share in the same Fate as is intended for you so hold it yourself as to
Rofs Mahon any part of Europe he goes he will fall if known he is
there is a fund at present formed in this Country for shooting
Oprefsors. the subscribers chiefly American Emigrants from this
Country there is 2 men Appointed for going to the northern
Country to you & a Mr Dodvilla Co Cavan they are to begin their
Journey 11th Instant umlefs you change your way from Oprefssion
take heed to the Contents of this if you make any Effort to
Goodnefs you will often hear from me
    I remn for your Welfare

In the earlier period, though less so in late Victorian Ireland, the concept of early warning of attack existed in certain parts of the country. This was, in part, to accentuate the intimidation, but also to give the veneer of 'fair process'. A County Wicklow gentleman received the following in the early 1850s: 'This is your second warning; you will get a third, and as sure as you receive the third so sure your doom is sealed, and you may prepare your coffin.'

Captain Fitzmaurice, a magistrate, believed that generally, most people who were physically assaulted in what was considered to be an outrage case had received threatening notices beforehand. This was also the view of Sir Henry Brownrigg, inspector-general of the Irish Constabulary, 'in a large majority of cases'.[9]

The threatening letter could, therefore, be a document of formulaic content. The problem with this – whether the threat was ever carried out or not – was that the majority of Irish threatening letters have an artificial ring or tone about them. Fights over the possession of land, or over the rent paid or not paid for land, were essentially matters of monetary self-interest. Only rarely does one encounter a threatening letter which, while threatening death or violence, has an individual ring about it.

One such was sent to a magistrate J.A. Nixon who held land near the ancient village of Freshford in County Kilkenny, and who, in December 1880, had been serving legal notices on some of his tenants. This threatening letter ran to a hefty 298 words in length. It demanded a reduction in rent or 'your family will have a most unhappy new year of it the black night will come on you when you least expect it ...'. The letter also ends in traditional fashion, 'if you dont look to your tenants we now promise you will get the death Lord Mountmorris [Lord Mountmorres murdered at Rusheen 12 days before] got and many other lords we expect such wont be the case hoping to be in good friends usual J.A. Nixon your respective tennantry'.

The interesting part of the letter is the middle section which read:

you wont ask a poor man when he will with [hold] rent has he a cow has he a pig or goat to supply his poor family with milk how can [you] look on your fellow creatures in such a manner why we cant afford a pound of meat for Christmas.

Such personal touches are very rare in threatening letters.

Metaphor

There were occasions in some threatening letters, though it was not the norm, when a metaphor was used. A nice example came as a postscript in an 1886 threatening letter written in an attempt to get a labourer to give up his job. After the 33-word note, claiming to be the second sent, there was a poor drawing of a coffin in which was written 'Free will go or die'. Then was written, 'For the great O'Reilly the time is short. the fish is near the bait he has need to watch his cork'.[10]

Schoolmasters

It is an intriguing concept that there were, within a community, specialist threatening letter writers, like a medieval guild. Bence Jones certainly believed one man, an artisan in his nearest town, wrote threatening letters. The 1852 parliamentary select committee into Irish outrages also contains interesting references to national schoolmasters performing this task. The crown solicitor for the north-east circuit, M. Hamilton, told the parliamentary committee that he had prosecuted schoolmasters for writing threatening letters under the Whiteboy Act.[11] The role of the schoolmaster as a direct or indirect agent in promoting the threatening letter phenomenon and the connected and wider Whiteboy agrarian movement undoubtedly predates the establishment of the national schools and dates back to the hedge schools.[12] An interesting example of a schoolmaster's art of threatening letter writing came from County Cavan in 1869 and ran:

> 85 Regiment Finian Centre
> To Messrs Rowntree and Sons
> I hereby state that this is to command you to leave the foot walk leading to the town of Mullagh in the same position as it was when you purchased that farm ... I command not to bring death to your own door
>> Searching Station
>> Bebeuket Patrol
>> Dum Spiro spiro
> NB I don't want to make a ballad of it – but – if you don't do what I say mark the consequence

A good example of a threatening letter, most likely written by a schoolmaster, was directed against a bank manager in 1884. It ran to 270 words:

Men of Tipperary

Once more we have to bring before the mind of the Public the cowardly conduct of one of our Tipperary Capitalists Samuel Hewston whose well known character as J.P. and manger of the Munster Bank must I am sure be today so fresh in the memory of many of you to need no explanation of mine.

This genius who is under the impression that he can exercise some of his tyrannical power over some families who in consequence of the depressed state of the country for the past few years had the misfortune to come in contact with this living serpent. In the trying circumstances under which this country is at present struggling. I as a friend would advise him to stay his power until some future period and not to be the first who would disturb the peace and happiness which now and always did exist in and around Tipperary.

The day that you will be the cause of sending any poor family homeless on the road side from thenceforward your days are numbered. For so sure as there is a God of justice above, the same fate which befell Carey is yours. as your former peaceful paths will from that moment be pursed with a vengeance – the hand of the slayer will fall upon you and death may come when least expected. Notwithstanding all the innocent blood which for the past twelve months has been spilt upon that accursed tree of the gallows yet there are true hearts in Ireland whose courage cannot be cowed down by either the Prison or the Scaffold.

God save Ireland[13]

The involvement of schoolmasters would explain why some of these threatening letters were 'in a very good and well-spelt handwriting'. One also has to take into account that there may have been deliberate attempts to disguise authorship by resorting to poor and sloppy English. There appear to have been those who were happy enough, for payment, to take a shot with rifle, shotgun or blunderbuss at the local landlord or agent, so there is no reason why money could not be made in a moral cause in a semi-literate society, and, as will be seen in a later chapter, with no fear of execution if caught, to write a few lines of blood-curdling prose.

Shop-boys were also sometimes suspected of having written threatening letters, on request, for rural consumption. The authorities were well aware that there were serial writers of threatening letters, whatever their primary trade. Inspector-General Brownrigg recorded:

> There is much reason to believe, not only from similarity of style, but for other reasons, that many of these threatening letters are got up by one and the same party – a remark which applies also to incendiary fires. I may mention, that some years ago, the inhabitants of the county of Down became alarmed at the increase of both of these descriptions of offences, and I was sent down by the Government to investigate the matter; when I was enabled to discover, not only that many threatening letters had been written by one and the same person, but also that he was the incendiary in nearly all cases. This man was arrested, convicted, and transported.[14]

As mentioned above, the paper used for threatening letters varied and many were written on 'mere careless scraps of paper'. But the widespread use of the postage system to disseminate threatening letters indicated the use of envelopes and an understanding of the postal system, all of which would have been familiar to a schoolmaster.

The minutes of the 1852 parliamentary select committee on outrages in Ireland reproduced six examples of threatening letters. Most are short but one is of considerable length and may be considered a good example of something which might well have been penned by a schoolmaster or certainly by another educated person. It was addressed to Stewart Maxwell, a landlord in south Armagh, and ran as follows:

> Sir,–Receive an advice from a well-wisher, and also a tenant on that once thriviog and industrious estate, but also its Wealth and prosperity are no more, it is now bruught to beggary. Like all others the question is, how Is this brought upon it, the reply is by an oppressive agent and his unworthy master, A man unworthy of the position of life which he has obtained, While other landlords have given their tenants a Reduction of their rents, he Refuse to give them any acknowledgement Whatever, and is Backed up to it By you his agent; For when any person asks any request of him he sends them to you, and says he has left the whole management tu you, and you then, the working tool, sets to work all manner of cruelty upon your vassal tenantry, pulling Down their cabina, teuring them from their farms, and Driving through the world, either Death in

the Workhouse, or their chance of death in the emigrant ships, swearing by the holy Book of Moses that you will be a terror to them all.

Can such talk prosper; it has done so for a while, But ere long there will he and to such cruelty; the whole cry amongst the tenants is away such men; the all rejoice in the Death of the oppressor; you are in a perilous situation at present; your life is in Danger; there are meu now a days Who come down from Carrickmacross, and that upper country, who hire to shoot Landlords and Agents; and there was a man Come Down through this estate, he being sent here by the tenants of the portnorris estate, and he made Agreement with the Writers of this advice to shoot you and your master for 50l., the first opportunity; you are in Danger every Day you pass out of never Comen home With your Life and We thought it our Bounden Duty to give you some warning that you might either make some arrangement that might satisfy your enraged vassals, or prepare a sheet and coffin, and some means of conveying your body Back to Derry, for if you Were Dead, the would not let your remains rist in this Country, the Would exhume your body, and Buru it as Warning to all tenants who shall from henceforth Come for your Country. And We also Warn you that the Blood Money is now half Collected, and Lying in our houses to Deliver over the contractor for shooting you, and if you were shot in the midst of Deliver over the contractor for shooting you, and if you were shot in the midst of Daylight you need not have Any hope of the perpetrator ever Comeing to Justice, if thousands saw him committing the Deed, for instance see how Malavery Was Killed amongst the eyes of the Whole Country, and not one ever enterferd. No not even the Jury When it came to a trial the would not suffer one hair of his head to fall, they said that that Ageut Was taking the Lives of thousands By a long and lingering Death, take warniog in time Lest you Wish you had Done so when to Late.[15]

Several things strike one about this out-pouring. The first is the length – 540 words. This is far in excess of the norm and suggests a self-indulgence which might well be exercised by a schoolmaster. Then there is the spelling. The person who can spell well-wisher, industrious, oppressive, oppressor, Carrickmacross, lingering and exhume is not going to write meu, teur, comeing and enterferd, nor is he or she going to make grammatical errors, particularly in relation to tense usage. Reference to the 'holy Book of Moses' and to 'vassal tenantry' might also suggest a learned person rather than an outraged and bitter toiler of the soil. The letter is obviously written with great intent, covering the main threatening bases including the *de rigueur* reference to a recent murder (Malavery). Finally, the drawing of the regulation coffin, the outline of which is partially filled in with ink, includes a three-dimensional aspect, usually lacking, which also smacks of the schoolmaster.

Signed threatening letter

An interesting saga surrounding a threatening letter being written by an outside third party occurred in March/April 1846 and involved land owned by Jenico Preston, the celebrated 12th Viscount Gormanston (1775–1860). It is unusual not least in that it carries a signature, though as later discovered, this was of the wife of the man who initiated the writing of the letter.

On 26 March, Viscount Gormanston received a lengthy letter signed by Mary Morgan, who claimed to be the daughter of Dinis Carolan. Twenty years earlier, Carolan had, according to the threatening letter, been promised tenure of his farm as long as he paid his rent to Lord Gormanston. However, the intervention of a land agent and two bailiffs meant that instead, Carolan had been turned out 'and left … to the mercy of the waves'. He had petitioned to be reinstated and Gormanston had apparently agreed and offered Carolan a 'good breakfast'. But again, his lordship's retainers had intervened and denied him even 'bit and sup'.

The letter should have ended at this point, but it did not; instead, it took a very sinister and foolish turn, which inevitably would lead to trial and conviction:

> I give your Lordship notice, that I will put an end to the three
> families, also I will put a end to your lordship and all the heirs that
> will come after you, unless you consider us. I have found out a
> remedy that will soon put an end to the whole of yours. Please send
> an answer to Mary Corralon. She is married to Thomas Morgan,
> Boggin Parish of Kilmainham Wood

A postscript did not help the Morgans' situation:

> Your estates was before without heir and will be in short again
> without one, unless you consider and restore back the land to us and

60

that shortly – we will give you time to consider, but the sooner you do the better as this is a Bad year and us in a state of Starvation.

Lord Gormanston passed the letter on to the authorities who were quick to act as it contained key names. Indeed, it was not long before Constable Robert Crags, stationed at Kilmainhamwood, south-east of Kells, had the name of the person who wrote the threatening letter for Thomas Morgan, whose father-in-law had left the farm in 1826. Morgan appears not to have been literate, later signing a statement with his mark. The writer of the threatening letter had been John McCabe of Cormeen, who later wrote an unsworn confession. This statement is of more interest than the actual letter which McCabe wrote as it gives the only known narrative of the surrogate letter writer at work:

On the last fair day of Calanstown I was in my own home at Cormeen when Thomas Morgan of Boggan came to me and asked me would I write a letter for him. I said I would and we went upstairs to a room over the kitchen. There was not then any one in the room. Morgan brought the papers, I asked him what letter he wanted me to write, he said his brother in law held some land from Lord Gormanstown about twenty years ago that the agent and bailiff had knocked him out of it by treachery, that he made several applications to his lordships help for it, That His Lordship made his an offer of it, and that then between times Mr Cruise put him off it, and that he would send him a letter that he had found on it on way to put an end to him and that he all as one had the curse of the widows before, and that his estates were without heir before this, and that they would again, I said I would not write any such letter, He was going away and said he would get someone else to write it. I then thought to myself and called him back and wrote it, and while I was writing it John Malachy of Mayo pig jobber came up and sat on a bed in the room and when Morgan left the house I told him what I wrote, and he said I was wrong in writing it. I said it was better I should write it, as if anything was done I would know who did it. I put Thomas Morgans name in part of the letter near the end of it, and I also put his wifes name 'Mary' or 'Peg' to it. I think Morgan came to me because he worked a long time as blacksmith for Counsellor White, & Hume to pay his men for him. The letter produced is the letter I wrote for Thomas Morgan. it was not so

alive when I wrote it. I think Malachy was in the room which I was
writing half the letter there is not the word in the letter but that
Thomas Morgan told me to put in, the bed on which Malachy was,
was about as far from the table I was writing at as the cross of this
room from the window to the chair (a few feet) There was nothing
to prevent Malachy hearing what Morgan said to me to put in the
letter, he didn't not tell me whether he heard it or not. Malachy was
sober. I cannot say if he drank any this was about 12 of clock on the
day[16]

Later that day, Morgan appears to have had an even more compromising
version of the letter written into an old account book by someone called
Thomas Lurgan. Morgan then sat on the McCabe letter for 12 days before
posting it in Drogheda on 26 March 1846.

In none of these examples of surrogate letter writing, including the
Morgan epistle, is a fee mentioned. It is, however, unlikely that such a service
did not warrant at least a token of appreciation let alone a service charge.

Patriotic language

There was a tendency for the simplest of land disputes or calls to boycott to
be expanded into the battle for a patriotic cause. A Tipperary threatening
letter over a call to boycott in May 1884 commenced with, 'Irishmen your
country calls upon you to shun and avoid the Dwyers (Oughries) of Foilduff
...' after describing how the recipient had turned out onto the roadside a poor
man, his delicate wife and children, as well as 20 years previously using
bribery and fraud to cheat the same man's father out of part of his farm. The
notice concluded, 'Irishmen your country calls upon you to boycott, Boycott,
Boycott, and save poor Ireland from such crawling wretches. God Save
Ireland'.[17] As noted in another chapter, when the prince of Wales was due to
be married in 1863, a mill manager in Limerick was sent a threatening letter
warning him not to display 'party flags', presumably of a loyalist variety.

Gaelic

Captain Warburton, when asked by the 1852 parliamentary select committee
on Irish outrages if all threatening notices were written in English, or
sometimes in Irish, replied 'I never saw an Irish one; all English'.[18] No
threatening letter in Irish has been unearthed in a 15-year search, so if they
did exist they certainly were not common. It is true that Clare, Mayo and
Galway, where the Irish language was strong, were key spots for the

phenomenon of threatening letters and as such, one might expect Gaelic to be used sometimes tenant on tenant. If a letter was directed to someone of a superior social status, such as a larger farmer, a shopkeeper, a land agent or a landlord, then English would have to be employed or the exercise would have been futile. And this might explain, in some cases, the poor English usage over and above what one might expect from someone with even a limited education. It might, of course, be argued that our principal reservoir of source material – government and police files – meant that only letters in English were handed in and thus, only these survive. Similarly, landed estate papers, a lesser source, would have only received letters in English for reason of the reader's comprehension.

There are two other factors which come into play, the first being the decline of Irish, especially after the Famine years, and especially the rapid decline in the numbers who spoke only Irish, less than 10 per cent in the last half of the nineteenth century. Even those who were bilingual numbered fewer than 20 per cent.[19] In addition, if the number of peasant farmers or landless labourers who spoke only Irish by 1880 was small, the number of them who were literate in the Irish language must have been even smaller.

Pidgin English

In his book *Recollections of an Irish police magistrate*, Harry Addison included a chapter entitled 'The Threatening Letter'. This tells the tale of his father, a magistrate, receiving a threatening letter and the way he dealt with the matter resulting in the apprehension of two men for the crime. Leaving aside the father's somewhat gung-ho attitude, several things strike one about the episode. The first is the scientific manner in which the father examines the letter: looking carefully for a watermark, feeling the paper and studying it against the light of the window. The second interesting point is that the son gives the reader a copy of the threatening letter, but in a translated form, stating:

> I have turned the words into good English, as few of my readers, I
> fear, could understand the strange terms used in the original. I have
> also suppressed the real name of the victim, though every Limerick
> man of a certain age will recognise it.[20]

The language of the threatening letter was frequently semi-educated. Grammatical mistakes were common. Capital letters were only used in a haphazard manner. Full stops were frequently missing, leading to great confusion when trying to determine what was being said. Comprehension is often dependant on a knowledge of circumstance. What is the writer trying to say in the following?

> I take the opportunity of leting you know that there is Parties gone to use the revolver With you if you doo not keep your Self quite your last imployer Has got one already and it will be the last the reason whitch is very Well nower to yours and to others whict your Sent to imegreate. I am afraid that yours Will be Served as bradly was _____ been this

The reader might be able to translate given the references to his previous employer, to emigration and to someone called Brady. County Court Judge Curran remarked that, 'The unlimited supply of whisky at wakes is a constant cause of much of the crime in Ireland'.[21] As Mr Littleboy, the recipient of this rather incomprehensible threatening letter, was still at Barberstown Castle in 1881, he clearly did not subsequently become a victim of the letter writers' threats.[22]

An unusual outrage case, which included a threatening notice, came before the authorities in County Armagh in 1851. A very rare account of a gathering of four men central to events, and involving a National School teacher, was given by a witness in an account of a visit to the house of a publican and grocer called Kelly. The first drink ordered was half a pint of whiskey followed by a naggin, or about 200 millilitres; after this there was another naggin, and so it went on.[23] It is difficult not to surmise in many such cases of threatening letter writing that the writer was, as must frequently have been the case, drunk or at very least had drink taken when the missive was penned. In 1884, there was a case of a boycott notice found on a mill wall in Borrisokane in north Tipperary under the title banner 'Stand and read'. It related to turf-cutting banks owned by Colonel Saunders. The former cutter, and therefore prime suspect, was a 70-year-old man named Thomas Cleary. The local RIC district inspector, however, described Cleary as a 'most respectable farmer', and suggested that, 'as the night before the notice was posted was a fair night here, it [the posting up of the boycott notice] may have been done by some half drunken fellows more out of a spirit of mischief than for the purpose of doing any real harm'.[24]

Sentences in threatening letters were often staccato, or whole paragraphs had no capital, comma or full stop. Language was usually stiff and rather pompous. Occasionally the style was an attempt at being formal, or what the writer imagined to be formal. Capitals were, in such instances, frequently used, sometime imitating a flourished style, as in a printed poster for a circus or a fair.

Invariably, the tone of these threatening letters was a mixture of pomposity, sweet reason and moral rectitude, laced as a counter-point with a concluding stylised viciousness. Occasionally there was a nice turn of phrase. In 1863, one Limerick threatening letter relating to an eviction notice criticised William Lynch, a land bailiff, for 'giving bad advice to his employer'.[25] In August 1881, the following notice was found on the chapel gate at Carras in County Mayo:

> Notice. – Any man who pays more than 2l. 10s per acre for the
> Davros Meadow will get a clear receipt to the other world.
>
> Rory of the Hills

The judgement – for the note frequently stated what action would be taken for non-compliance – was invariably death. To emphasise the point, as will be seen elsewhere, a variety of ill-drawn and unimaginative art works commonly illustrated the conclusion.

Religious symbols were, however, excluded from threatening letter iconography. That is not to say that religion did not feature, even in phraseology and everyday parlance. Take a Pay-No-Rent notice found down the road from Carras at Millcross in 1882:

> Any person coming to pay rent to that son of a hoor, Perry, or
> coming to settle with him in any way, I am still thirsty for their
> blood; so by the God of Heaven do not be the cause of my coming
> from Templemore, or if you do i will pay the rent for you to the last
> farthing; and ye land-jobbers that are in the habit of buying the
> grass in the lands of Newgrove clear out on the 1st day of March
> instant, or by the Immaculate jesus I will clear ye out. Clear out,
> clear out.
> Captain Moonlight[26]

Nom de guerre

Although the sender of threatening letters or notices was usually disguised, they were rarely unsigned. Indeed, it appears to have been a point both of honour and of tradition to complete the intimidating missive with a pseudonym, or more appropriately *nom de guerre*. At the start of the Victorian era 'Captain Rock' was the most regular contributor to the genre. By the mid-Victorian period, while there were still occasional occurrences of 'Captain Rock', 'Rory of the Hills' became the dominant signatory followed by 'Captain Moonlight', though there are examples of other names employed. Rory had various misspelling and representations, such as 'Red Rorry of the Mountain'. The allusion to the hill country is interesting, harking back as it did to the wild men of old who came down from the untamed hill lands and forests and harassed the new English settlers. 'Captain Moonlight' declined somewhat in usage as the decades passed, which is also interesting as the verb 'to moonlight' still retained common currency.

In 1842, several threatening letters aimed at trying to bully the recipient into sacking an employee were variously signed off as 'Captain Rook Rockbrook' and 'Captain Rook Rock Hall', perhaps a taste of gentle threatening humour.[27] Bullying and bullying language were the dominant order of the day, of course, and it was not simply the letter's recipient who was subjected to such behaviour. Anyone who interfered in the process was likely to be subjected to threats. The act of removing a threatening notice in itself merited self-righteous condemnation. Increasingly in the 1880s, such notices carried a rider in strong terms. One such near Carrick-on-Suir read, 'Let no hand take down this but a traitor to the cause'.[28] Another example, this time in County Kilkenny in 1882, was a used envelope with a threatening notice written on it. On the side flap of the envelope was written, 'do not take down'.[29] The priest, policeman or concerned person generally, however, did remove such notices. But, of course, matters could become complicated, as near Letterkenny in County Donegal when the police 'told the people that no man had a right to touch the [threatening] notices but the magistrate'.[30]

Colourful turns of phrase and stark imagery

In line with the speech patterns of rural Ireland, there was no shortage of colourful phases and images appearing in many threatening letters. These usually relate to suspects in letters which were written by the sender personally rather than on the sender's behalf. From Abbeyleix in Queen's County we have the following:

> You bloody wretch we are on your track you cannot escape this time you may get it before 5 May which think you will your sentence it is to be Shot and Quartered in Pieces If you knew your Grammar you would give up Kelly's Farm long a go – PS you think Lord Devesy

[DeVesci] can save you we are watching him a long time and missed him in London and at you may think it a hoax but twice will tell if we catch him at Carlton terrace or in Kingstown [Dun Laoghaire] he will get the Dagger or Pistol it is a toss up between you and him now.

A similar short notice emerged from the same county in the same year, but from Mountrath: 'Any person found communicating with Thomas Tynan or working for him will be Boycotted. Mind this is genuine'. Down in Tipperary, a man who foolishly bid for a farm demanded by a local was told he would be killed 'as sure as there is a devil in hell'.

Further north in Crossmaglen, a threatening notice sent to Robert McGeough was just as strident and dragged in Parnell and Davitt for good measure:

By God Take notice you bloody tyrant that you may order your
coffin anytime for your life will be taken by day or night By Jesus we
will get rid of all such cattle like you before very long so the sooner
you prepare for the other world the better. The balls are ready for
you. You bloody whore
down with landlordism & tyrants Parnell for ever the land for the
people God save Davitt for the Irish[31]

Perhaps no threatening letter was, however, as colourful as that received a generation before in Rich Hill, also in south Armagh, and addressed to Nancy McCanney:

This is to let you know, Nancy McCanney, that your Brother, Hary
McCanney was pleas'd to say that he had warrents and orders For
Such & Such orrange men in the Low Contry & if he Come & will
Give them Wilingly To Mr. McConnell or Mr Sturgen In Keady he
will Get leave to mind your work or otherwise Be all the Secruts of
hell your house Shall Be Burned to the Ground. Both his Soul &
your Shall Be Blwed To the Blue flames of hell. Now Teak this for
warnig, For if you Bee in this Contry Wednesday Night I will Blow
your Soul to the low hils of hell And Burn the House you are in.[32]

Name calling or insults

While threatening letters are, by definition, meant to intimidate, it is remarkable how few contain either foul language or even insults. Certainly some did, but it was not the norm. The reason for this is that the threatening letter had a purpose. It was a demand to do something and a warning of what would happen if that requirement was not fulfilled. However, there were exceptions. The following has survived from Cork, where matters were rather bitter by late 1880:

> Dear Richardeen,
> I am going to pay you a small compliment that is only too well due to you, you pimping, soup-capping, bastard. Take my word, as sure as God is in Heaven I will stain my hands in your blood, and yellow George, and father one eye Robert.
> Yours truly
> Captain Moonlight & Co.[33]

Four years later the following was written in red ink to James Foley of Cahir in Tipperary:

> This is to give notice that if you dont give up the farm you got lately so that honest people may come by their own I will riddle your old rotten carcase with lead or I will give you the dagger whenever i can find you late or early.
> Rory of the Hills
> Look at the colour of your blood and remember death.
> Rory & c

And again in 1884 and not so far away in Clonmel:

> Look out
> For the Traitor. Ned Tobin has been appointed hea Emergency
> Bum. Boycott Him. Dont enter his house or hire his cars. [34]

W.E. Vaughan cited overtly offensive threatening letters of the earlier Westmeath bubble period which threaten post-mortem castration; tell a recipient that he had an 'unnaturally semi-masculine daughter'; and, unusual for Ireland of the period, dragging racism into matters, another which asserted 'I will leave you a dead nigger for your wife'.[35] Whether the following threatening letter from Swanlinbar in County Cavan in 1884 also has racial undertones is not quite clear. The letter begins, 'Now you little low & coloured brat take notice that if you have anything to do with that evicted farm ...' A second note was changed somewhat to, 'Note you little undermindng little brat Take note that if you have anything to do with that farm of McCaffreys ...'[36]

Of course, anti-English sentiment was *de rigueur*. This, however, falls into a unique category of its own. It is superficial to dismiss this as racism, its cultural undertones of denouncing the Sassenach going far beyond the crudities of vulgar hatred. In fact, very few of the quarter of a million outrages committed in Victorian Ireland were against English people. Scots came second and English third, with the Irish being the overwhelming recipients of outrages including threatening letters and notices.

Threatening art iconography

Though it could not be termed literature, one book dealing with Irish outrages of the period had a distinctive and blood-curdling cover, reminiscent of the Victorian penny-dreadful. This was entitled *The unknown power behind the Irish nationalist party: Its present work and criminal history*. It was written by Frederick Oliver Trench, Lord Ashtown of Woodlawn, near Ballinasloe in County Galway, who owned extensive stretches of land also in other counties. He was an ardent and volatile unionist who, not surprisingly, was, at times, boycotted.[37]

The artwork in Irish threatening letters is interesting, raising the question of a link with a longer tradition of illustrations and illuminations in Irish written texts. The fact that artwork was used seems simultaneously to hanker back to a mythical and better past. The threatening letter, being not just a demand, was also a ritual which involved certain language usage, mode of delivery and presentation. That presentation was enhanced by ritual drawings, usually executed in a primitive ritualistic form.

The art work covered three principal categories of horror art: blades, firearms and coffins. Knives and cutlasses are to be found in quite a few threatening letters. Invariably, these have an eighteenth-century feel about them. They are not the cavalry officer's sword or the sword-stick but resemble images from children's books about pirates. The same is also the case with the antiquated firearm represented. One will look with difficulty for the Winchester rifle or the Colt revolver, and the early breach-loading Enfield. Firearms are usually flintlocks, be they a blunderbuss or a muzzle-loading pistol. There was rarely a revolver or pistol, or even the carbines carried by the constabulary. It is as if, in the art work, a statement is being made about a lost past before the Famine, though it may equally just be an example of traditional practice.

It might be argued that the weapons represented were those of the countryside, as in parts of Victorian Africa where the tower-musket dominated long after it was regarded as obsolete among European settler society.[38] But is that correct? Why is the pike not a frequent image on the threatening letter? Or was that symbolic of something else and as such considered inappropriate for dealing with the man whose field the sender was determined to acquire by foul means? There were certainly more modern arms being smuggled into Ireland from the late 1860s, particularly in the towns and cities, though they were rarely if ever used in the cause of Irish freedom in the Victorian era.[39]

Coffins were the most commonly depicted motif on Irish threatening letters in the Victorian era. They were easy to draw and they were a clear symbol of death, the overwhelming outcome if the recipient refused to comply with whatever the writer demanded. The sketches of coffins are invariably placed at the bottom of the page, unlike the skull and cross-bones which are as likely to be at the head of the letter as at its conclusion. Most coffins are portrayed in outline, in part, no doubt, to economise on ink. Some are partially shaded with varying crosshatchings, although some are completely blacked in.

Motifs of coffins with handwriting inside the art work were fairly common, and the message is usually short. Sometimes, to hammer home the point, the victim's name is inscribed in the coffin outline. Only two examples have been found of a sketch of a coffin with a body in it, and only one discovered which is an attempt at a three-dimensional representation. A rare example of coffin art appeared in an 1836 threatening letter sent to a man who was constructing a road in Tipperary and who had made the fatal error of using 'foreign' labour brought in from a good 10 kilometres away. The threat of death and a contemptuous comment about 'priests and peelers' was followed in the letter by a drawing of a coffin, which contained a body wrapped in a shroud.[40] Equally unusual was a threatening letter artefact in the guise of a small wooden model of a coffin with a threatening letter inscribed on it. This work of craftsmanship was produced in County Meath in 1863 with the aim of preventing an eviction.[41]

It should be noted that, in the 1880s, the more political threatening notices tended not to carry any threatening art, that generally being reserved for the traditional threatening correspondence. An exception was the Bruff village pump threatening notice in September 1881, and quoted elsewhere. This and a companion notice also found in the village had a rifle and a spider face in the bottom left corner of the short notice.[42]

There are several instances where threatening art became theatrical, threatening performance art, so to speak. Bence Jones, in his eccentric memoir *The life's work in Ireland of a landlord who tried to do his duty*, penned the following:

> On the morning of Friday, December 3, market-day, a threatening notice was found stuck on my hall door, and a hole dug in the grass near, three inches deep, as an emblematical grave, in which, the notice said, I and my son were to be buried.[43]

John Lambert of Aggard House in County Galway was in the forefront of the boycott campaign. Among other acts perpetrated against him was a mock grave dug in front of his house, with a note nearby stating that if he 'did not cease persecuting his tenants' he would end up in the grave.[44] Similarly, Viscount de Vesci, whose wife had done so much to encourage the local lace industry, was rewarded by finding 'images of coffins and guns scratched in the soil, with portraits indicating his agent or himself'.[45]

Notes

[1] Ashtown, *The unknown power*, p. 87.

[2] *Report from the select committee on outrages (Ireland)*, 1852, p. 42.

[3] Ferguson, *The Post Office in Ireland*; Johnson, 'The Dublin Penny Post – 1773–1840', *Dublin Historical Review*, vol. iv, no. 3, March–May 1942, pp. 81–95.

[4] NAI, CSORP 1884, 21459, 3/644/27.

[5] Lewis, *On local disturbances in Ireland*, p. 102, quoted in Madden, *Forkhill Protestants and Forkhill Catholics*, p. 94.

[6] Vaughan, *Landlords and tenants in mid-Victorian Ireland*, p. 153.

[7] On the matter of perceived legitimacy, see Madden, *Forkhill Protestants and Forkhill Catholics*, Chapter 6. See also Gibbons, *Captain Rock, night errant*, p. 25.

[8] NAI, CSORP 1884, 3/644/27, Threatening notice Agrarian, Kilmucklin, County Tipperary, 14 May 1884, addressed to John Scully.

[9] *Report from the select committee on outrages (Ireland)*, 1852, pp. 8, 42 and 128.

[10] CSORP 1886, 3/646/35.

[11] *Report from the select committee on outrages (Ireland)*, 1852, pp. 14, 25 and 148. See also, Gibbons, *Captain Rock, night errant*, p. 40.

[12] Beames, *Peasants and power*, p. 97.

[13] NAI, CSORP 1884, Threatening notice 21358, 10 January 1884, 3/644/27.

[14] *Examination of some recent allegations concerning the constabulary force of Ireland*, p. 71.

[15] *Report from the select committee on outrages (Ireland)*, 1852, p. 186.

[16] NAI, CSORP, Meath outrage reports 1846, 3/704/29.

[17] NAI, CSORP, 1884, 3/644/27, file 21578.

[18] *Report from the select committee on outrages (Ireland)*, 1852, p. 16.

[19] Akenson, *Small differences: Irish Catholics and Irish Protestants*, p. 137.

[20] Addison, *Recollections of an Irish police magistrate*, pp. 187–93.

[21] Curran, *Reminiscences of John Adye Curran*, p. 215.

[22] NAI, Anderson Ledger, p.24. Threatening letter to C. Littleboy of Barberstown Castle, Staffan, County Kildare. Posted 10 February 1870. Barberstown Castle, dating from the thirteenth century, is now a hotel.

[23] NAI, CSORP, Outrage papers, 1851, Armagh, 3/705/20.

[24] NAI, CSORP 1884, 21191, 1 May 1884, 3/644/27.

[25] NLI, Report on the state of Ireland in 1863, ms 915, f. 181.

[26] *Special Commission Act, 1888*, pp. 433 and 455.

[27] NLI, Larcom papers, ms 7519, 1842.

[28] CSORP, 1886, 4123, 3/646/35.

[29] CSORP 1881, 17968, 3/638/31.

[30] NAI, CSORP 1881, 44693, 3/638/31.

[31] PRONI, Crossmaglen conspiracy trial 1883, February 1881, T3194/1.

[32] Miller (ed.), *Peep O' Day Boys and Defenders*, p. 129. Original in the NAI, Rebellion Papers, 620/23/207.

[33] *Special Commission Act, 1888*, p. 112.

[34] NAI, CSORP 1884, 3/644/27, Report of outrage, 25 May 1884 and Boycott Notice, 15 June 1884. This probably refers to an Emergency man.

[35] Vaughan, *Landlords and tenants in mid-Victorian Ireland*, pp. 151–2. NAI, CSO RP, Tipperary outrage papers: 1869/16344; 1869/11937 and 1870/14290.

[36] NAI, CSO RP, 1884, 3/644/35, file 25131.

[37] Patrick Maume, 'Frederick Oliver Trench', *Dictionary of Irish Biography*, vol. 9, pp. 462–3.

[38] McCracken, *Saving the Zululand wilderness*, pp. 79–84.

[39] Police reports sometimes monitored the importation of arms. See, for example, NAI, Fenian papers 'R', box 12, 'Seizure of arms', DMP, G Division, memoranda signed by Daniel Ryan (in the handwriting of John Mallon), 31 April and 17 April 1870.

[40] NLI, Ms 15 349, 21 February 1836.

[41] MLI Report on the state of Ireland, ms 915, f. 154.

[42] NAI, CSORP 1881, 3/638/19.

[43] Bence Jones, *A life's work in Ireland*, pp. viii–ix.

[44] *Irish Times*, 13 October 1880, quoted in Finnegan, *Loughrea*, p. 40.

[45] Hurlbert, *Ireland under coercion*, I. pp. 168–9. See also Gibbons, *Captain Rock, night errant*, p. 20.

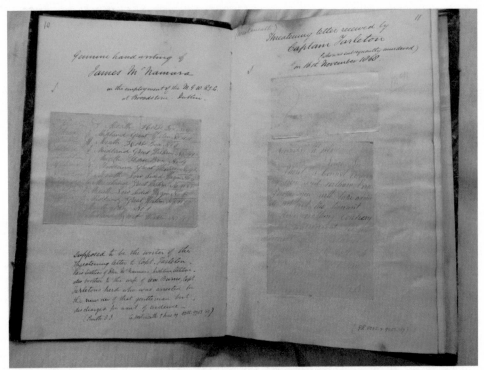

Threatening letter ledger from 1867–71 in the National Archives of Ireland, compiled by Dublin Castle's Samuel Lee Anderson, who used photography to compare handwriting and try to identify letters' authors. This is part of a hoard of more than 100 threatening letters from Westmeath and adjoining counties, collected from magistrates and collated in Dublin Castle to ascertain if there was a pattern or whether serial letters had been written. (Courtesy of the National Archives of Ireland: CSOPR 3/719/5)

Letter and envelope dated 1869, from 'Captain Rock', posted from Athlone and addressed to Peter Rush of Corr in Westmeath, containing a death threat and examples of threatening art.
(Courtesy of the National Archives of Ireland: CSOPR 3/719/5)

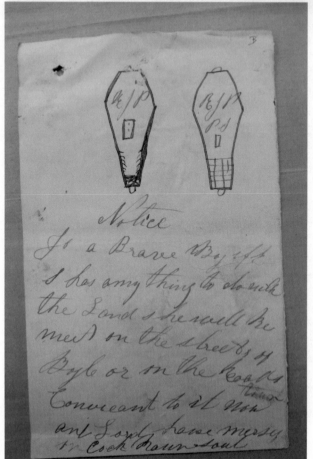

Above—Paper was sometimes in short supply in rural Ireland. In 1881, at Tullaroan, west of Kilkenny city, envelopes were used to write threatening notices. The name on the used envelope pointed the police towards their suspect's family, though a handwriting expert was hesitant and no conviction was secured.
(Courtesy of the National Archives of Ireland: CSOPR 3/638/31)

Left—'A woman's hand'. The authorities believed that this threat, aimed at Patrick Sheerin of Doon, Roscommon, had been written by Winifred Killilea in July 1884. She had been evicted from a farm that Sheerin intended to take over. She was convicted, after handwriting samples were compared, and sent to Sligo jail for two months.
(Courtesy of the National Archives of Ireland, CSORP 18103, 1884)

Above–'Slaves of the soil'. A threatening notice in a disguised hand against the 'two headed landlord' Scully from 'Red Rory the mountain. War Captain', Westmeath, 1869.
(Courtesy of the National Archives of Ireland: CSOPR 3/919/5)

Right–Letter to accused land-grabber Thomas Moran of Streamstown near Mullingar from Rory of the Hill, with greetings of God Save Ireland and Erin-go-Braugh.
(Courtesy of the National Archives of Ireland: CSOPR 3/919/5)

Left–1881 threatening notice, complete with shamrocks, boycotting the local south Armagh dispensary and warning against informers.
(Courtesy of the National Archives of Ireland: CSO Letter Book 15, 1881)

Below–Threatening art at its technical best, which is not surprising as it stemmed from office politics in the Ordnance Survey of Ireland office in the Phoenix Park, Dublin, in 1842 and was sent to its head, Captain Thomas Larcom, in an attempt to get him to sack a fellow employee, 'a blody orangeman'.
(Courtesy of the National Library of Ireland: Larcom papers, ms 7519)

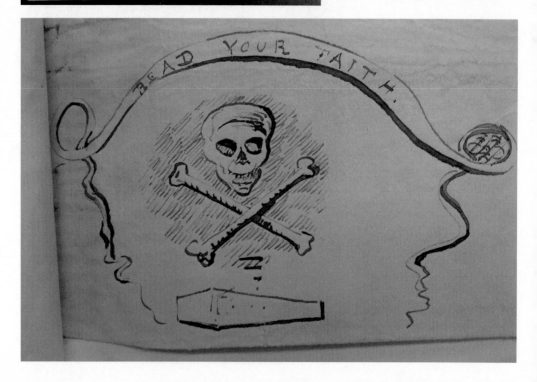

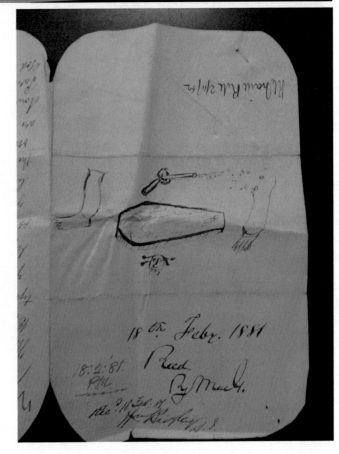

Take warning that if you go in behalf of that prodestant pup of a policeman you may first of all make your coffin. and if you prove to one of the B section men that you serged you will not prove to anny more you are spaired a little to long and take nothing more to doo with orange Brooks let him do his own bisvos while he gets lave that will not be very long Death is your Doom if you disobay and Death to Brooks without any delay

Above–An attempt to intimidate a witness in an Armagh court case in 1882, in support of 'that protestant pup of a policeman', with a brave effort to draw a stamp on the cover.
(Courtesy of the National Archives of Ireland: CSO Letter book 15, January 1882)

Right–A rare example in a threatening letter of two severed limbs, an equally rare three-dimensional coffin, an antiquated flintlock being discharged and an unusual skull and cross bones.
(Courtesy of the National Archives of Ireland: CSO Letter book, 15, February 1881)

Rare example of a grave in threatening art. This letter also includes dry powder, a musket and human image.
(Courtesy of the National Archives of Ireland: CSOPR 3/719/5)

Coffins were the most popular images in threatening letter art, no doubt because they were easy to draw with a nib and Indian ink. Frequently, there was a separate written message within the coffin.
(Courtesy of the National Archives of Ireland: CSOPR 3/719/5)

 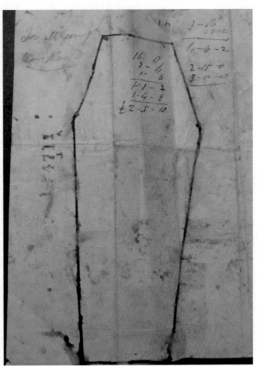

Above left–In this example of threatening art, directed at Patrick McManus of Galmoylestown, County Westmeath, greater attention was given than usual to a human figure. Although drawn in 1869, the assassin is in regency clothing, a generational throwback common in such representations where antiquated swords, muskets and pistols are drawn.
(Courtesy of the National Archives of Ireland: CSOPR 3/719/5)

Above right–If not handed into the local police barracks, frequently some time after they had arrived, threatening letters were kept by the recipients – but not always out of fear or superstition. Here the recipient has used the paper to jot up some costings.
(Courtesy of the National Archives of Ireland: CSOPR 3/719/5)

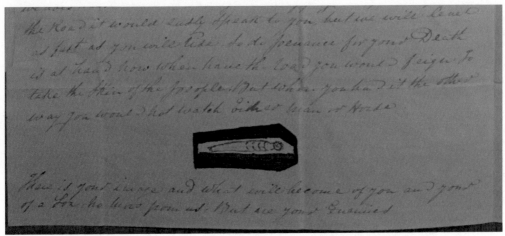

The only known example of Irish threatening art containing a body wrapped in a shroud in the coffin. Dating from the 1830s, it comes from Ballintaggart parish in Ballingarry, north-east of Cashel in County Tipperary, where John Dwyer made the mistake of employing 'foreign' labour from 10 kilometres away to repair a road.
(Courtesy of the National Library of Ireland, Poe papers, Ms 15,349)

Left—When the mafia came to Sligo. The three circles of an Italian secret society and exotic princely names surrounded this threatening letter received in Sligo in 1852 by an Italian exile, who foolishly lectured against a cardinal back in Rome and who was then censured from the pulpit in Sligo.
(Courtesy of the National archives of Ireland, 3/705/27)

Below—Boycotting was often accompanied by a wider campaign of threatening notices. They were mostly hand written and this example includes a flintlock pistol from an earlier period.
(Courtesy of the National Archives of Ireland: CSORP 3/719/5)

4. The peaks and plains

Threatening-letter activity in Ireland surged in two very distinct peaks during the Victorian era. The first related to the Famine years when the annual reported was almost 2,000, and the second occurred during the Land War with almost 3,000 or between 40 and 50 threatening letters and notices reported per week. Threatening letters could also have relatively short-lived surges, as in 1869/1870 when nearly 900 were reported.

The Famine years
The Famine dominated the second half of the 1840s and is generally accepted by historians to have brought with it a new era in Irish history. 'The ubiquitous threatening letters – [were] the preferred method of intimidation in Famine Ireland', comments Ciarán Reilly.[1] As can be seen from Figure 17, threatening letters tallied by the authorities rose in these years, peaking in 1845 and remaining high in 1846, before declining. Surveying the figures reveals several interesting points. The first is that the number of threatening letters, even before the Famine, was quite high. These are the years after the Tithe War and during the height of O'Connell's campaign to repeal the act of union.

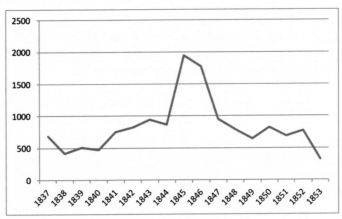

Fig. 17–Threatening letters reported, 1837–53

What is interesting about threatening letters and notices during the Famine years is their sheer number, which shows that the peasant farmers refused to accept the grim situation emerging in rural Ireland and were hostile to the, at times, dilatory efforts made to assist the impoverished and, in places, starving population.

A particular theme, generally confined to the Famine years, was the threatening letter which related to the distribution of Famine relief, be it the distribution of food or the allocation of Famine public works relief. One such received by the relief committee of Coolaney in Sligo in March 1847 demanded that certain persons were to be turned off public works in favour of placing 'on a greater number of each family'.[2] A document written in October 1845 from the Achill area in the relief commission stated:

> The Potato crops in part of these Districts are a complete failure, some will not have any after the 1st March while others have not suffered. I am happy to say that I have not suffered. The people of the districts where the rot is greatest are *threatening to turn out on the first scarcity of food appearing* they posted notices last night warning the people against paying any Rent, but I believe there is not any system Established amongst them and I think they could not have any meeting last night without my knowledge.[3]

Printed notices also appeared in these Famine years. One entitled 'Address of "Molly Maguire," to her children' was found at Cloone in County Leitrim in July 1845. In its demands for no rent until the harvest and then only if fair, it was not unlike such notices circulating 36 years later in the Land War. It differs from that period, though, in the multitude of clauses or rules set down. The 1845 document mentions religious tolerance; assisting the good landlord to get his rent; tolerating eviction after two years of no rent being paid; not travelling by night; not taking arms from anyone; and avoiding the military and police – 'they are only doing what they cannot help'. The notice's final rule runs, 'Let bygones be bygones, unless in a very glaring case; but watch for the time to come'. However, the notice concludes by warning heartless landlords who break the rules. To her children, 'Molly Maguire' asserts:

> take no life, or limb, without first giving your victim their written warnings, should they be not regarded let him that loves the danger perish in it, but I hope none will be found so obstinate for all the

Military or Police under Her Majesty will not save the tip of the wretch, that will have no feeling for my Starving Children.[4]

It would be false to think that the only target of threatening letters and notices during the Famine, or indeed afterwards, was landlords and their land agents. Other associates in the rural and small-town economy were perceived as being a legitimate target. A letter posted in Tullamore in King's County in 1846 asserted: 'Landlords use no tyranny, keep your trumpeters at home, tenants gather all your corn into your farmyards; also threaten agents, land jobbers, moneylenders and millers.'[5]

In November 1845, a threatening notice was posted on a farm gate in Coolinhila, County Limerick, 'cautioning the people of the townland not to sell corn until provision should be made for the poor'.[6] In Islandeady, halfway between Westport and Castlebar, a work-relief scheme came to a halt on various issues relating to the granting of relief tickets and wage rates paid to workers. Two threatening notices were found and there were scenes of violence when workforce gangs were attacked by large numbers of people with sticks and stones. The threatening notices made their way into official hands. The first read:

We the lower part of the parishioners of Islandeady Call on ye who are at work in the Upper District contrary to our wish and against our interest to at once withdraws from said work, or else ye will mark the consequence with loss of life

The second went as follows:

Take notice. That any man seen filling this channel across this road shall forfeit his life, and otherwise any man working at this Hill without regular wages, he may as well work for nothing.

Gentlemen take notice that we want nothing but some earning to support us for this year, and if we dont get it, we cant see ourselves starving

Demanding employment was a common enough theme of a threatening notice during these difficult years. In Roscommon, in December 1846, two Molly Maguire threatening notices were discovered along a line of public work between Drimmin and Ballintubber. Addressed to the clerk of works and two overseers, they demanded that more labourers be employed by the following Monday or 'they might mark the consequences'. Statements were taken by the magistrate under oath. The men stated that they were afraid to continue with the Board of Works if not protected by the authorities. Subsequently, the office of the constabulary was instructed by the magistrate to provide 'the most ample' protection to the individuals concerned and to liaise with the resident engineer concerning this. The new and first Catholic under-secretary at Dublin Castle, Thomas Reddington, was informed.[7]

Demanding work as a threatening letter theme would re-emerge again in the early 1880s. One 1881 Sligo letter commenced, 'It has come to my turn to write to you if you do not go forth with some work in the Country and dont have the people starving you will be shot like a dog in a bog. The poor in Corran are starving for want of work'.[8]

As seen elsewhere, Carrickmacross was never a district to hold back when it came to the deployment of intimidating tactics, including threatening letters and notices. The following notice, dated 30 September 1846, was found on the chapel gate by a constabulary patrol on the night of 3/4 October 1846:

Notice

The tenants of the
Marquis of Bath and E.J Shirley Esq
Will assemble in
Carrickmacross
On Monday, the 5th inst
At one o'clock PM
To make a
Temperate and Peaceable
Appeal
To the
Landlords and Agents

For permission of the Present Years rent, and a reduction for the Future proportionate to the peoples ability to pay

Society is in a distempered state, when the industrious millions have not food to sustain their toil

September 30th 1846

Arthur French, the magistrate, was quick to react and police were drafted in from Ballytrain, Broomfield and Castleblayney to supplement the 26 policemen already stationed in Carrickmacross. A similar rally was held in Ballina that same week. The dragoons arrived too late to witness the event but it was reported that a parade had been led by men carrying poles, on one of which was a loaf of bread and on the other a placard proclaiming that no rent would be paid. [9]

Meanwhile, the balladeers were actively voicing concern and denunciation at the situation in the countryside. Several of the verses of one ballad-sheet entitled 'A new song called The Advice', which came into the possession of Dublin Castle in 1846, ran as follows:

If with our requests they [landlords] will not comply,
We'll tell them on the spot that we would sooner die,
That our families are starving and we never will fail,
But fight till we die for both corn and meal.

But see how the landlords has played us new pranks,
By sending the poor for to draw on the Banks,
Where they have them like foxes, caught by the tail,
And then they must sell off their corn and meal.

And don't let your children be going to the bogs
Instead of potatoes a-looking for frogs.
Nor either like Highlanders, eating green kale,
And cursing their fathers for parting their meal.

We'll all long remember the year Forty-six,
And we fear that the landlords will play us new tricks,
Except we take courage and never to fail,
But to die on the fields or keep corn and meal. [10]

Evictions

A direct correlation between an increase in the number of threatening letters reported to the authorities and the rise in tenant evictions is not surprising. However, eviction-related threatening letters were less likely to be sent by the victims of such evictions. Instead, letter writing was undertaken by neighbours or relatives (or both) protesting at the tyranny of such action and swearing vengeance. Comments on how little resistance there was to evictions during the Famine are accurate if threatening letters are excluded. [11]

As common as eviction-related threatening letters were those sent when the land agent or landlord attempted to rent an evicted tenant's farm to what became to be known as a 'land cantor' or later as a 'land grabber'. Even here, though, nothing was simple. Sometimes the hostility was the product of greed and resentment that the farm had not been awarded to the writer. Great excitement often surrounded the run-up to allocation of a vacant farm, too. A threatening letter from the Lough Iron area in Westmeath dated 16 February 1869 ran as follows:

> Mr Christopher Cunningham beware don't interfere with Andrew mcknallys land leave it between the friends to bid for it are you aware that no land cantors are alloude in this country seme last year if you bring me to give you a call you will fall with powder and ball. Let no farmer show his nose dare to oppose again danger[12]

It might be argued that the eviction notice itself was a threatening notice and the tenantry were simply reciprocating. There was certainly a great deal of sympathy, in England as well as in Ireland, for the fate of evicted tenants. William Gladstone, when prime minister, stated in the House of Commons in 1870: 'We have made ejectments cheap and easy, and notices to quit have descended on the people like snow flakes. All these things have been done by Parliament, and no compensation has been made to the Irish tenant.'[13]

Eviction and threatening letters went hand in glove, affecting not only the landlord and the agent but also frequently, indeed more so, the subsequent occupier of the farm. So, as with disputes between tenants and between the gradations of farmers and the landless labouring population, on the ground the threatening letter tended to be similarly directed against the landgrabber.

Notwithstanding, the correlation between evictions and threatening letters is not straightforward; however, Figures 18 and 19 reflect the trend of evictions from the Famine until the Land War of the early 1880s alongside rates of threatening letters reported over a similar period.[14]

There appears to be a correlation between the number of threatening letters in the Famine years and evictions at that time. After the Famine, however, there is an undulating low plain in eviction numbers until 1879 when the figures for evictions rise again, but not to the levels of the Famine years. However, when looking at the statistics for threatening letters for the Land War years, there is a marked reversal of the pattern shown during the Famine years, with numbers far outstripping those of the Famine upsurge. In fact, nearly twice as many threatening letters were reported to the authorities in the Land War

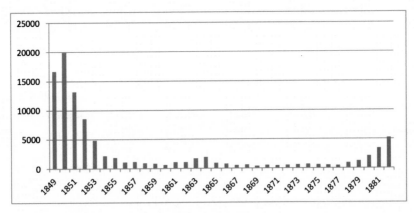

Fig. 18–Approximate numbers of evictions, 1849–82

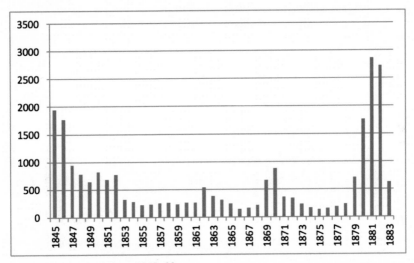

Fig. 19–Threatening letters, 1845–83

era as in the Famine era. This might be because of earlier reluctance to hand in such letters to the police. During both the Famine years and the Land War, one can be sure that the actual number of letters written was considerably higher than reported. But the trend is there and it is likely that this was because, by the early 1880s, the threatening letter and notice were as much a quasi-political tool as a weapon in the tenant's hand.

Another factor needs to be pointed out as well. Evicted tenants were regularly readmitted to their old property on certain terms and conditions. This practice varied from decade to decade but the figures provided by Vaughan

79

suggest that this reinstatement was from 28 per cent in the 1850s, 17 per cent in both the 1860s and 1870s and 5 per cent between 1880 and 1887.[15] Overall, Michael Davitt gives the RIC eviction figures for 1849–82 as 482,000. Of these, 119,000 (25 per cent) were readmitted as caretakers. There was also the 'redemption' practice in some parts, whereby a landlord let the vacant farm subject to the risk that the evicted tenant paid his outstanding rent within six months and regained the property.[16] Nonetheless, whether reinstated or not, the evictions happened and exacerbated ill-will and bitterness, which may have resulted in threatening-letter writing.

Finally, the quantity of threatening letters and notices circulated during the Famine should be treated with caution. These were extraordinary times. As a proportion of reported outrages before, during and after, threatening letters did not dominate as they did during the Land War 30 years later, as illustrated by Figure 20.

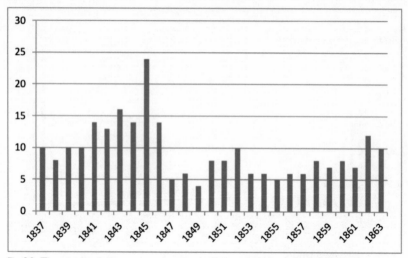

Fig. 20–Threatening letters as a percentage of all reported outrages, 1837–62

This figure clearly shows the proportional increase and climax during the first year of the Famine. However, this then declined sharply and such missives only represented 5 per cent of all outrages by 1847, a level lower than it had been in the pre-Famine era.

Secret oath-bound organisations

In 1848, at the height of the Famine, a series of tenant farmers in the townland of Drumilly in County Armagh had been evicted for owing large arrears of rent. Consequently, the area was in a 'unsettled and turbulent' state.

The vacated houses were left untenanted and were either burnt down maliciously or 'thrown down at night'. By December 1849, notices were appearing in the district, including at the Catholic church, threatening anyone who occupied the farms at Drumilly. A police report as late as 12 June 1851 recorded that the properties remained untenanted and:

> the lands have been waste ever since, except that the people of the neighbourhood including some tenants on the property who drive their cattle on the lands to graze, but while they do so, they keep watch so that no person on the part of the landlord dare venture to drive the cattle off or seize them for either rent or trespass – nor will any person tell the landlord [Mr Turner] whose cattle they are.[17]

At the time, the Ribbon system was blamed by the authorities for this state of affairs. Certainly Ribbonism, in whatever nebulous guise, was also considered by the locals to be a powerful influence in the area.[18] It is sometimes difficult to disentangle the differences between secret agrarian societies such as the Whiteboys, the Molly Maguires and the Moonlighters. One tended, chronologically and regionally, to blend into another. A particular feature of this semi-organised outrage crime, however, was that the sphere of influence of such activity could be wider than simply the townland or the parish. The Anderson hoard, discussed elsewhere, had letters posted in Athlone and Dublin which related to alleged injustices many miles away. For the earlier pre-Famine era, Michael Beames has pointed out how the secret society oaths might well bind the oath-taker to travel some distance on society activity. He also notes that this effort was sometimes spelt out to the recipients of a threatening letter: 'you will put me to the trouble of coming a long way to execute the desine according to the custom of the contry'.[19]

If many modern professional historians see the Irish land question as anything but the simple formula of the Irish nationalist traditional narrative – a struggle between suppressed peasantry and an alien, exploitative land-owning usurper – then they have shied away from the concept of Whiteboyism and Ribbonism as well-organised and cohesive entities.

The landlord vision of Ribbonism was not so distant from that of their enemies in that many also believed that a network of formalised secret societies indeed existed. Their attitude may be summarised as follows:

> There are few who have not heard of the Ribbon Societies of
> Ireland; those dark and mysterious confederacies, which, springing

up from time to time in different localities, have spread terror and dismay into the hearts of both rich and poor, which have done so much to discourage the influx of capital into Ireland, and to proprietors, who would be only too glad to be allowed to reside upon their Irish estates, and in the midst of their Irish tenantry, could they do so in peace and safety.[20]

This attitude was quite similar to that of the authorities, although one suspects that the spectre of Ribbonism was a convenient vehicle that allowed them to justify the introduction or renewal of coercion measures. It cannot be denied that secret societies existed in nineteenth-century Ireland. It is also clear that these were malevolent toward the ascendancy class, and their apparatus is also clear. Fenianism later became a more organised urban equivalent. It, too, though having more of a structure and unity of purpose, was also a hotpotch of disparate types of individuals with differing agendas. The label of Ribbonism was widely used in certain parts of rural Ireland, with the threatening letters undoubtedly emanating from Ribbon lodges and associations. However, these productions often as not carried the signature of 'Rory of the Hills', and were essentially a local phenomenon, spawned by local circumstances and with narrow local aims. It is pushing the evidence even to claim that they were Irish nationalist, though occasionally there might be a link with national politics for a while, but rarely for any extended period of time. The famous Irish detective John Mallon recounted to his biographer a conversation that he had as a boy with his father, a small tenant farmer in south Armagh in the 1840s:

'Father, secret societies are bad, are they not?' The older man rested with his foot on his spade and thought for a minute or so. There came into his eyes a curious glint that the son had not often noticed before, as he waved his arm in the direction of the hamlets and irregular homesteads that dotted the countryside and said: 'Those houses you see beyond would not be there to-day if it were not for the Ribbon Society'. That was not quite what the youngster had expected. He was disappointed and replied; 'Ah! father, you cannot get away from the recollection that the O'Neill massacred the Protestants away over there because he was afraid that the Protestants might one day become powerful enough to put the Catholics to death; but surely that was no justification?' 'Very well, let it remain there', was all the old fellow answered, and he went on digging, and the subject was for ever afterwards a closed book for father and son.[21]

Some 35 years later, when head of the detective division in the Dublin Metropolitan Police (DMP), Superintendant Mallon penned the following in a G-division report:

> The Ribbonmen or Hibernians are chiefly the sons of small farmers, or respectable farm servants and labourers from the Northern part of Leinster and the adjoining Counties in Ulster and Connaught, and their presence in Liverpool, Wigan, Newcastle-on-Tyne and so on may be accounted for by the fact that they cross the Channel in large numbers in pursuit of employment from Newry, Dundalk and Drogheda.[22]

The threatening letter and notice were tools especially used within Ribbonism when a court had been constituted by the lodge and sentence of death decreed in the absence of their victim. The letter of warning was then part of the 'rules', a matter for the society's code of honour. In theory, this gave the condemned man or women a brief window of opportunity to escape the county – or preferably the island.

The Molly Maguires differed little, if at all, from the Ribbon lodges. These ad hoc collectives were partial to sending threatening letters. During the Famine, merchants at Newry were warned by them through such letters not to export any meal out of the harbour.[23] In a great many instances, however, the name of a secret society was used as a cover for an individual out for his own purpose and personal gain.

Post-Famine period

The journalist Bernard Becker, writing of County Mayo in 1880, an important location for threatening letters, observed, 'All over this part of the country people complain bitterly of loneliness'.[24] Whether the reported increase in mental-health problems in post-Famine Ireland can be equated with the steady outpourings of threatening letters is doubtful. In police reports, occasionally there is a reference to insanity connected with threatening letters. In Kilkenny in the mid-1860s, there was a case reported where 'it appeared after the case had been tried, that the man was insane, and they would probably be called on to have now a second inquiry as to the state of his mind since that period'.[25]

As the graphs have illustrated, reported threatening notices and letters fall off significantly in the post-Famine period. It should be noted that unlike the later Land League and National League, the Tenant Right League of the 1850s was not closely associated with threatening letters. But the phenomenon was not extinguished. By the late 1850s and early 1860s, between 6 and 12 per cent of all outrages were threatening letters. However, within the specified band of crime designated by the constabulary – 'Against the Peace' – the proportion of threatening notices ranged from 45 to 64 per cent.

Reports of the inspector-general of constabulary, Sir Henry Brownrigg, assist in studying the phenomenon. His manuscript report for 1863, housed now in the National Library of Ireland, is particularly helpful. Vaughan categorises 38 per cent of threatening letters cited in this report as the result of landlord-tenant disputes; 26 per cent as relating to the taking of evicted land; 20 per cent as disputes with neighbours; 2 per cent as disputes within families; 9 per cent as disputes between tenants and sub-tenants. The remaining 5 per cent were due to other causes. Moreover, significantly, Vaughan has calculated that 51 per cent of recipients of threatening letters contained in this 1862 Brownrigg report were tenants; 33 per cent landlords and agents; 7 per cent bailiffs and 9 per cent others.[26]

Brownrigg concentrated on agrarian threatening letters and tended to brush aside or make no comment on non-agrarian threatening notices or letters. That in itself illustrates the official attitude to the phenomenon. Recipients included not only landlords, agents and tenants but also a carpenter, medical doctors, hotel keeper, justices of the peace (who were frequently also farmers), a militiaman, parish priest, national schoolmaster, shoemaker, tin plate workers and town merchants.

Brownrigg listed agrarian crime for each county, frequently naming the victims. As might be expected, when it came to threatening letters and notices, most of these entries relate to the ownership of land; occupation of land; renting out of land; as well as eviction from land. However, there were some exceptions and less usual subjects of letters and notices which are worthy of noting. These include the following (victim's name in brackets):

Armagh: (Edward O'Hanlon, poor farmer) Demanding he give up some grass land.
(John McCoy, farmer) Demanding he surrender some bog land.
(Andrew Shepherd, draper and merchant) Demanding he

increase his weavers' wages and also for him to reduce the rents of his houses and gardens.

Carlow: (Peter Maher, comfortable farmer) Demanding he discharge a workman.

Cavan: (J. Sproule, meal factor) Relating to him giving evidence in a legal
case.
(Mr McClenaghan, land agent) Cautioning him against interfering with the farmers as to their mode of cropping their farms, rules having been issued by him for their guidance. This is an interesting example of a conservative reaction to an attempt at reforming agricultural practices.

Cork: (John and William Hassell, tin-plate workers) Threatened for having given evidence against two leaders of 'the so called "Nationalist" party in Cork, for inciting a riotous mob on the night of 10th of March', the date of the marriage of the prince of Wales. Their father also received a threatening letter concerning this matter. The constabulary thought it expedient to place two of their men in the family home as a guard at night.

Donegal: (McColgan, undertaker, and Grannery, farmer) Demanding that they do not build on a certain piece of land.

Down: (Thomas McClure, J.P.) Demanding that he withdraw from an agreement to purchase a farm from a tenant who had subsequently regretted the sale.
(Mr Knox, farmer) Demanding a vacant house should not be let to a certain person – 'The labourers did not like this'.
(Revd Mr Close, parish priest) Informing him that the Orangemen would 'have their month (July) in spite of Pope or Police'.

Fermanagh: (James McCartney, farmer) Demanding if he did not sack a certain herd [herdsman] his cattle would be shot. A man was sentenced to six months' hard labour for sending this letter.

Kerry: (Christian Goodman, hotel keeper) Demanding he 'give employment to painters'.

King's: (No name given) Threatening letter related to the taking of a dog.

Leitrim: (J.J. Byrne, J.P.) Threatening letter received by this magistrate who was very active 'in putting down crime'.

Limerick: (Alexander Roger, manager of Russell's Mills) Threatened not to display any 'party flags' to mark the marriage of the prince of Wales on 10 March 1863.

Longford: (A. Cusack, agent) Letter threatening parties from taking a meadow.

Louth: Brownrigg notes at the end of this section, 'The other threatening letters were of a ribbon character but not related to land'. Sadly, no details were given.

Tipperary: (Pat Ryan, farmer) Warned against interfering with his brother's land.

Westmeath: (W.G. Marshall) Ordered to give up lands of Huntingdon because 'he had not given so much employment as the previous occupier'.

Wexford: A threatening letter was addressed to certain members of the Constabulary to deter them from prosecuting any more of the inhabitants of Enniscorthy. Threatening letters to the police were rare, or perhaps rarely reported.

The Brownrigg document also highlights three cases of fraud or a hoax in the writing and sending of threatening letters. One case in King's County involved a man named Charles Daly who received through the post a letter threatening him with the same fate as 'the Shepherds', who had been murdered, if he took a piece of land. Brownrigg notes, 'In this case there were reasons for thinking the letter originated with Daly himself'. No further explanation was given but, as illustrated elsewhere, cases where the victim and perpetrator were the same person were by no means unusual. Brownrigg also mentions a letter found hanging on a gate relating to Michael Brien in Wexford concerning his taking land which had been formerly occupied by a man who had been evicted. This was regarded with suspicion by the constabulary, who wondered if it were not a hoax.

More intriguing was an incident of a woman, the wife of a land agent, who, when alone in the family home, was robbed of cash on a table set there to pay the labourers, as well as of a loaf of bread and some whiskey. A description of the thief was widely circulated. Subsequently, a threatening letter was left at the house, purporting to come from the thief who claimed to be 'the natural son of a Gentleman whose agent had been robbed'. The letter demanded a further £10 be left with the woman previously robbed 'as the price of his desisting from more serious outrages'. This juicy saga, of an illegitimate son of the landlord forced into a life of crime, spread throughout the neighbourhood. However, when the constabulary investigated, they extracted a confession from the hapless woman that the entire story was a fabrication. Brownrigg drily concluded, 'The motives were obvious. Nevertheless the story gets currency in quarters where the sequel is never heard of'.[27]

Occasionally Brownrigg expresses frustration at the lack of action in a threatening-letter case. Of the spring assizes in Westmeath, he states, 'I am aware that it is the fashion to throw the fault of undetected crime upon the Constabulary ... However, in the threatening letter cases, I am at a loss to know why some persons are not made amenable, especially as in one instance, four or five of the letters are in the same hand-writing, though of course great difficulty arises, in identifying handwriting in those cases'.

Tenants at war with each other

A substantial number of threatening letters were a consequence of internecine unease and conflict within Irish peasant society. By the nineteenth century, the phenomenon had acquired a veneer of modernism and, at times, even a political respectability. In essence, though, it had not changed in at least a hundred years. There was an innate conservatism in much of tenant society, which often expressed itself in reluctance to change or to accept change, the battleground being control and possession of land. In the 1880s, many landlords who strove to improve their estates, their output and the lot of the tenants were faced with passivity bordering on passive aggression or outright hostility.

At the level of inter-tenant relationships, which were often hopelessly mixed up with family, clan and neighbourhood dynamics, the tension was frequently greater than in a simple tenant versus landlord situation. What on the surface might seem a small enough issue could be blown out of all proportion. In June 1845, at Charles Keary's dairy farm in the townland of Rathurles in County Tipperary, a shot was fired through the door of his dairy. A threatening notice left in the farm yard demanded that he discharge his dairy maid and act in a kinder manner to his neighbours. The police supposed that the cause of the outrage centred on a dairy maid who was a stranger to the area and, 'contrary to a former practice, sends quantities of milk for sale to the town of Nenagh, instead of selling it at home'.[28]

The quantity of threatening letters and notices reached such a level that in 1881, one finds an RIC district inspector writing of Brittas, west of Kilkenny city, that, 'the people are so unreasonable as to think no person has a right to take ground from another on any pretext'.[29] A good example of this was at Crickstown near Ashbourne in 1883. A farmer named William

Bobbett took grazing land from a magistrate called Richard Bourne. Villagers had been in the practice of grazing cows on this land, paying a sum per cow. As soon as Bobbett gave notice for the villagers to withdraw the cattle, the trouble began. On 9 September, he received a threatening letter, posted in Dublin, some 30 kilometres away. This warned Bobbett 'On the Company Command', not to make a 'Fitzharris of yourself', a strange allusion to the Phoenix Park murders. As a postscript, the letter also alluded to another person called Gull Clarke, though it is unclear whether this individual was connected with Bobbett or not. Presumably Bobbett was to pass the message on: 'cutting men down and talking bad of them to you I must tak to him on the head of it and not tak to him but meet him and give him a taste shillaleu'.

Moonlighting was frequently a class-on-class affair. It involved secret, after-dark gatherings, sometimes of a large number of people, aimed at intimidation, raiding homes, firing shots into homes, assault and destroying property and livestock. These activities, it has to be said, were, more often than not, against fellow tenants and farmers. Large-scale landlords were more usually the victims of boycotting and murder, as were their agents and servants, although boycotting was also applied within the tenant class.

The Westmeath bubble

Anyone interested in the phenomenon of the Irish Victorian threatening letter will sooner or later come across the Anderson hoard. This is a carton of threatening letters dating mainly from 1869–70 in the Fenian papers in the National Archives in Dublin. They were assembled by Samuel Lee Anderson (1837–1886), the crown-solicitor for Kilkenny and Waterford, whose main task was as investigator of Fenian and political crime. This was a consequence of the direct intervention of the head of the Irish government, Lord Lieutenant Earl Spencer.[30] In September 1869, the following instruction went out from the under-secretary's office to William Morris Reade, resident magistrate for Westmeath, who was based in Kilbeggan, a village famous for its whiskey and, at the time, also infamous for its threatening letters:

> His Excellency having given directions that all the threatening letters
> which have been submitted during the last twelve months should be
> photographed, you are requested to send up any originals which
> may be now in your possession and not required for any prosecution
> or enquiry still pending.[31]

It is characteristic of Spencer that he was ahead of the pack when it came to such investigative tools. Photography was already being used by the Irish police who, by the late 1860s, had a collection of mug shots of suspects, some imprisoned, some not.

The reason for the Irish government's interest in Westmeath and its adjoining regions was straightforward enough. On-going trouble there had been blamed on the catch-all of Ribbonism. The aftermath of the 1867 Fenian rising, coupled with a turndown in the agricultural economy, resulted in rising numbers of outrages in 1869 and 1870 in parts of the country, partly in Connaught but mostly in Leinster. Within Leinster, the trouble was centred on Westmeath and the adjoining areas of Meath and King's County. In 1868 and 1869, 15 outrage-related murders occurred and 14 people were shot at.[32]

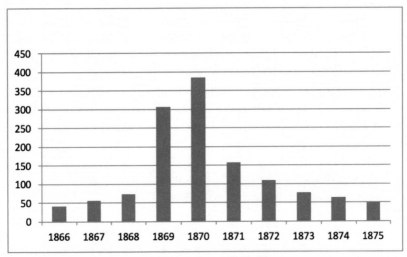

Fig. 21–Threatening letters recorded in Leinster, 1866–75

Threatening letters were an important part of this unrest. Figure 21 clearly shows the rise in the instances of threatening letters which were recorded by the authorities in Leinster, with Figure 22 narrowing this down to the Westmeath and Meath bubble.

The only other county to rival Westmeath was Mayo. However, Mayo was the standard by which trouble might be judged; high levels of threatening letters were less surprising there than in the Meath-Westmeath area just north-west of Dublin city. A word of caution needs to be added, as discussed earlier. The method of counting outrage numbers was changed in 1869; for a period,

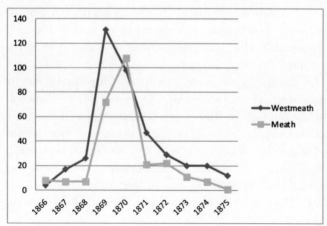

Fig.e 22–
Graph to illustrate the Westmeath/Meath threatening-letter bubble

this led to inflated statistics. If, for example, the same threatening letter was sent to more than one household, then each instance from this date was recorded, rather than simply one letter.[33] That said, it cannot be denied that Westmeath and the adjoining regions were in an unsettled state at this time and that threatening letters increased significantly in consequence.

In Kilbeggan, Magistrate Willam Reade was not particularly helpful in his reply to the new and, as it turned out, ill-fated, under-secretary, Thomas Burke:

> The only threatening letter received within the last 12 months which is in my hands ＿＿＿ I always hand any that are given to me over to the Sub Inspector [RIC]. I have been shown from time to time during the last 12 months several threatening letters to different gentlemen, who have requested me to say nothing about them, and when I had satisfied myself that the writer could not be traced, I did as they wished

In the end, a collection of Westmeath threatening letters was assembled. As new ones were handed into the authorities, they were also added to the collection, bringing the total to well over 100. The coordination work appears to have been undertaken by Samuel Lee Anderson, whose more controversial brother Robert (1841–1918) performed the similar role of countering political crime and Fenianism from an office in the Home Office in London.[34]

What has survived of this exercise is a ledger and Dublin Castle envelopes containing original or, more often, photographs of threatening letters and the envelopes in which most were posted. After the project was concluded, the material was housed, together with an eclectic set of 20 bound volumes of themed newspaper cuttings, in the Chief Secretary's Library in Dublin Castle. Later, the newspaper-cutting volumes went to the National Library of Ireland and the threatening letter volume and accompanying letters were sent across the courtyard to the State Paper Office in the Record Tower and hence eventually to the National Archives in Bishop Street.[35]

The Anderson collection ledger contains 120 pages, numbered pages 10 to 129. After that, there are seven unnumbered pages in the book containing various loose copies of photographs of letters. This volume contains threatening letters glued onto the pages with factual notes about many. Most of the letters in the book are photographs of threatening letters, and there are multiple photographic copies of some of the letters, the idea presumably being to distribute these so matching handwriting could be identified.

In addition to the ledger, there are a large number of Chief Secretary's Office (CSO) rectangular envelopes, each containing original threatening letters. Sometimes the stamps on the envelopes of the threatening letters have been torn out, likely at some later date. Then there are handwritten notes, presumably made by Anderson or his clerk, on the covers of the enclosing CSO envelopes. Most of the threatening letters have a serial number written on them in Indian ink.

It is clear surveying the collection that what Anderson was looking for, and what presumably he found, as the modern researcher will also do, are patterns, repetitions and evidence of conspiracy. The geographic area covered is Westmeath, with some outlying instances such as King's County (Offaly).

So seriously did the authorities regard the threat from the Westmeath area that they eventually put through parliament the Peace Preservation (Ireland) Act, 1870. Inspector Mallon of the DMP's detective division, writing under Superintendent Daniel Ryan's signature, summed up the response to the act: 'It is generally calculated that assassination, threatening letter writing, and offences that can be committed in a secret manner will increase, and will be encouraged with a view to demonstrate how the law may be evaded.'[36]

In June 1871, there followed the Protection of Life and Property in Certain Parts of Ireland Act, what was sometimes termed the Westmeath Act. This neatly covered prime threatening-letter terrain:

- The whole of County Westmeath
- In King's County[Offaly], the baronies of: Ballycowan, Coolestown,

- Garrycastle, Kilcoursey, Lower Philipstown and Warrenstown
- In County Meath, the baronies of: Fore, Lower Kells, Upper Kells, Line, Lower Moyfenrath, Upper Moyfenrath, Lower Navan and Upper Navan[37]

This measure allowed detention, for a limited time, of suspects involved in Ribbonism, under which threatening-letter writing was conveniently taken, correctly or not, to fall. As with so many ad hoc Irish coercion measures, they solved the problem in the short term. The 1870 and 1871 acts, as Figure 22 clearly illustrates, saw the number of threatening letters plummet in Westmeath by 80 per cent between 1870 and 1873 and by 90 per cent in Meath. The King's County decline in that period was 71 per cent.

'Pay no rent'
Figure 23 gives a good illustration of the dramatic rise and fall in the number of threatening letters over the traumatic years 1879–83.

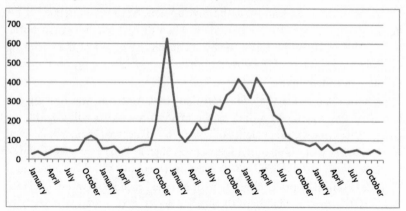

Fig. 23–Threatening letters (general) recorded January 1879 to December 1883

One of the most famous proclamations in Irish history – running to 435 words – was the 'Pay no rent' notice, written and signed by Patrick Egan, treasurer of the Land League, and posted up and distributed throughout Ireland. Neither the concept nor the phrase was new. However, the impact of this campaign was new. Addressed 'To the people of Ireland', the slogan 'Pay no rent' is asserted in bold six times, along with 'Avoid the Land Court' twice and 'Hold the harvest' once. The text contains such clarion cries and assertions as:

- 'war against the people of Ireland'
- 'the ravages of landlordism declared "unlawful and criminal"'
- 'a reign of terror'
- 'a determined passive resistance'
- 'the people now to prove themselves dastards or men'
- 'slavery and degradation'
- 'cast out the person who enters it [the land court] as a renegade to his country'
- 'A short and sharp struggle now, and the vilest oppression that ever afflicted humanity will be wiped away.'
- '[American-Irish] are ready to supply you with unlimited funds'

Such phrases were common in many anonymous threatening letters and notices which related to the campaign against Irish landlords. There are stark differences, however, between this and the more common, localised threatening letter and notice. The threatening communication campaign tended not to be a letter to an individual – though some were sent – but a notice pinned up at chapels, on trees, attached to gateposts or on barn doors. They were often longer in content than the normal threatening letter. They were less abusive, though death was often threatened to those who did not comply. The language used in the campaign notice was invariably literate and phrased in normal style rather than the stilted and pseudo-legalese of the localised threatening letter.

'Pay no rent' notices were frequently not handed into the authorities. In Nenagh, in October 1885, 'Police casually heard that notices were posted ...' Despite the intimidation, either through a sense of loyalty to the landlord or perhaps sheer cussedness, one tenant did break ranks and showed the police a copy of the notice. This was short and to the point: 'Take notice that if you pay rent at this time until the rent afair is settled you may remember the Consequences'. The police reported, 'It is believed that others of the tenants had similar notices posted on their doors, but they would give no information about them'.[38]

The Egan proclamation was by no means the first such pay no rent campaign notice. Similar anonymous notices had been posted up at various times in previous years. A fine example of one was found by Father McDonald on his chapel notice board at Moate in Westmeath in late October 1869. It is worth quoting in full because of the quality of the phraseology and the rhetorical content:

Public Notice. Tenantry of the surrounding District. Slaves of the
soil. It is time you should spring to your feet to grapple with that
two headed monster Landlord tyranny Rack Rents that has ground
your forefathers to the dust of oppression and consigned yourselves
to lives of poverty wretched and woe in few words which must be
complied with as well as attended to. You are requested to withhold
your rents until ample justice is done you by giving your lands at a
fair valuation. Nothing more is requested, nothing less shall be
accepted. Justice Justice to Ireland Faith & Fatherland. Together
together stare landlord tyranny in the face so the Scully landlord
who shall refuse such honourable concession shall be dealt with as
the council hereafter will determine.

We have stopped too long to glaring wrong
Too long in chains were slept
Too long by foreign gold have we
In thraldom base been kept.
By promises fed, by bribes men led,
By fields & factions surrendered
By tythes & taxes robbed & wronged
By landlords plucked & plundered.

Rory War Captain

As was sometimes the case, copycat notices written in more threatening
terms were posted around the same district. In this instance, the following
notice, attached to a tree at Clare, also in County Westmeath, was handed
into the police by one Father Farrelly:

Notice
Let no man on this land pay the last ____ that this ____ got to
Charles Hamilton[39] any man that will pay such rent will be shot at
his own door and his house put on fire the same night.

This notice had, at the bottom, a crude drawing of a coffin and of a flintlock
pistol. Several other such notices threatening death and the firing of the home
if rent was paid were found at Ballinbeg, at Bishopstown near Ballymore, and
at the crossroads at Clare.[40] And more crude notices were to follow. An 1882

threatening notice from the Tulla region of Clare ran:

TAKE NOTICE

Any person coming to pay rent to that son of a hoor, Perry, or
coming to settle with him in any way, I am still thirsty for their
blood; so if you do I will pay the rent for you to the last farthing;
and ye land-jobbers that are in the habit of buying the grass in the
lands of newgrove clear out on the 1st day of March instant, or by
the Immaculate Jesus I will clear ye out. Clear out, clear out.
Captain MOONLIGHT[41]

The Land War and beyond

In 1877, an article in the *Dublin University Magazine* observed, 'Recent
legislation on the land question has done much to abate the nuisance of
threatening letters in the south of Ireland'.[42] That was correct. In 1877, a
mere 190 threatening letters were handed into the police across the whole of
the island. However, matters would soon change and by 1880, the figure
stood at 1,763 and in 1881, at a record 2,862. Parts of rural Ireland were
subject to what the magazine *Nineteenth Century* termed 'agrarian terrorism',
quoting Justice Fitzgerald that some districts had been reduced to 'anarchy
and confusion, differing little, if at all, from civil war'.[43] Although that was
an exaggeration, matters were serious. As Figure 24 well illustrates, these
statistics far eclipsed the Westmeath bubble and indeed the Famine years.

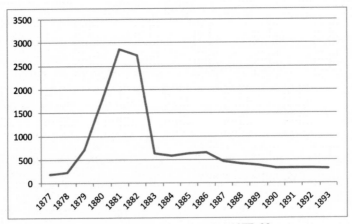

Fig. 24–Number of threatening letters recorded, 1877–93

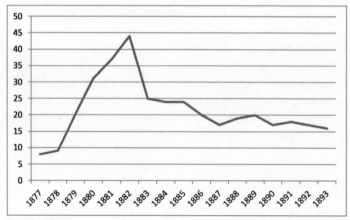

Fig. 25—Threatening letters by percentage of outrages recorded, 1877–93

This increase was unique and needs a specific explanation. The traditional agrarian activities could not explain such an increase, even given the downturn in the agricultural economy. The link between the Land League and the dramatic increase in the number of threatening letters and notices reported to the authorities is largely circumstantial. Outrage was not Land League policy and Michael Davitt went to extreme lengths to denounce outrages, especially attacks on domestic farm animals. However, the rhetoric of the time did not encourage restraint for those inclined to use outrage methods to promote their cause. Occasionally there were also signs that individuals in the Land League, some prominent locally, did indulge in such practices, including writing threatening letters and distributing what were considered subversive leaflets. Superintendent John Mallon of the DMP recorded, in January 1882:

> I have to report that handwriting similar to that on the annexed envelope appeared on several of the envelopes taken from Hugh Gaffrey, the Land League messenger on the occasion of his arrest in Sackville Street.
> It must be admitted that as long as the Women [Ladies' Land League] meet at 39 Upper Sackville Street 'No Rent manifestos' will be distributed despite the police.[44]

The nexus of land agitations and political opportunism in the activities of the Land League was a contradiction in the context of agrarian crime. The

96

Land League both encouraged and restrained agrarian crime. The landed classes and the emerging unionists, though, had little doubt that the Land League and later the National League were key to the rising trouble. They also found the nationalist Irish parliamentary party's denunciations of the acts of outrage disingenuous. As Newton Wallop, Viscount Lymington, the English deputy lieutenant of County Wexford, asserted, 'The Irish members and the Irish party are not afraid of using force. They believe in coercion'.[45] Yet there can be little doubt that Michael Davitt was fervently opposed to the more unsavoury outrage tactics used by agrarian agitators.

These crosscurrents were further stirred by Westminster initially granting limited Irish land reform. This offered the prospect of a new age as well as indicating, as the disestablishment of the Church of Ireland had done a few years earlier, cracks in the ascendency's position. It was a further step towards British disengagement from those who had been the backbone of their establishment in Ireland. In addition, increased literacy, an extending franchise, improved communication and imminent local government reform all released expectations which fed both hope and bitterness, the latter inevitably resulting in political criminal activity.

Boycotting

The activity of boycotting existed in various guises before acquiring the name of the infamous Captain Boycott. The adoption of boycotting as a Land League weapon gave an enormous boost to the number of threatening letters and notices produced. Yet boycotting was by no means confined to persecuting tyrannical landlords. Often it related to the occupation of a farm from which a tenant had been evicted or had been forced by circumstances to vacate. This might have prevented a landlord collecting new rent, but it primarily hit at those tenant farmers who occupied such vacant land. Just the opprobrium of being labelled a land-grabber was sufficient to obviate any mitigating circumstances. Once applied, it became an unanswerable judgement that justified any measure ranging from threatening letters, to destruction of property, to murder. As Professor Comerford so neatly noted in the general context of the Land War, "The 'moral" force of the boycott gave way quite easily in the circumstances to physical violence and its essential accompaniment, the threatening letter'.[46]

There were no rules of combat for those condemned as land-grabbers. Of seven outrage cases mentioned by Arthur Balfour in the House of Commons on 4 March 1890, two related to threatening notices concerning alleged land-grabbers. One of them, Richard Tomkins of Curratubbin in County Wexford, had his cattle and pigs incinerated when outhouses were maliciously burnt to the ground.[47]

As the Land League grew in strength and flexed its muscles, the focus expanded beyond landlords and alleged land grabbers to recalcitrant tenants who were paying the rent requested from them by the landlord. This might have been out of fear of eviction, loyalty to the landlord or distaste at the Land League and its mafia undertones. Of Cork, James S. Donnelly Jr writes:

> All over the county during the autumn and winter of 1880, notices threatening the direst consequences to tenants who paid more than the government valuation were prominently posted in public places, on the doors of catholic chapels, and in the tenants' own houses and farm buildings.[48]

An example of such was posted up around Ballydehob in south-west Cork:

> Notice is hereby given that any farmer who has not paid rent yet, not to pay more than Griffith's valuation. If they do they are sure to be visited by Rory, junior, who is supplied with Notter's [magistrate] powder and ball. He is expected on Wednesday next to meet Sam Jago, agent.[49]

A very common theme of threatening letters and, to a lesser extent, threatening notices was to attempt to bully labourers to stop working for the principal target of an intimidation campaign. This might be domestic servants already working for a landlord or land agent, or a newly hired employee following a dismissal, such as a water bailiff, as in Castleconnor on the Mayo/Sligo border in November 1852.[50] But more often, it concerned a herdsman, or herd as they were termed, a labourer or the servant of a better-off small or medium farmer. Such threats were usually issued in simple enough documents. A typical one emanating from Corkbeg, across the estuary from Queenstown [Cobh] in County Cork, and dating from September 1884, ran as follows:

> Boycott
> If Joan Bibee keeps workin for doyle worse than nice will come to her. This warning is for Kit Cotter too They may repend that worse than the sound of shot will come Conway must take of his nice self also   Captain Moonlight[51]

Some years later, things were not much different with the arrival of the Plan of Campaign and the National League, though the intensity of the Land War somewhat abated. The principal landed estates targeted or places where there was particular trouble, which were therefore subject to their quota of threatening letters and notices, were the Brooke (Donegal); Clanricharde (Galway); Clongorey (Kildare); Coolgreany (Wexford); Coolroe (Wexford); de Freyne (Roscommon); Dillon (Mayo); Kenmare (Kerry); Kingston (Cork); Langford (Cork); Luggacarren (Queen's); Massareene (Louth and Meath); O'Grady (Limerick); Olpherts (Donegal); Ponsonby (Cork); Smith Barry (Tipperary); and Tottenham (Wexford) estates.

Captain Buller, then an Irish magistrate, asserted to Chief Secretary Balfour that 'outrages are really only the means of enforcing the law of the National League that is to say the law of the village tyrant'.[52] Attempts to interfere with employment, attempting to dictate who could employ whom, extended at times to ridiculous situations. In January 1884, a threatening letter was sent to a man named William Hanlon, a painter and foreman working for a man named McMahon who had obtained a contract to paint Borris Castle in Queen's County [Laois] and who had brought in labour from Roscrea, 12 kilometres away across the Ballaghmore bog. A local Borris painter named Michael Horan, who had applied unsuccessfully for the castle contract, was suspected of sending the threatening letter.[53] It was reminiscent of 40 years earlier when a threatening notice had been found on a barn door in Roscommon. It referred to a herd boy who was looking after the farmer's cattle at night and ran:

> Let no person take down this notice
> Must take notice to banish that County Longford Boy. for we dont like Enquire you every County has enough to do to support there own people And if he does not like the nose will be taking of [off] him its no matter who is there he must stay in his own County So let is not come again for if we do you be sorry for it[54]

Campaigns initiated by an evicted tenant or their associates against the landlord, a large farmer or estate owner could very easily result in stalemate. As will be seen elsewhere, by the 1880s, this was sometimes broken by the importing of Emergency men or hired guns. It could also be broken by the collapse or suppression through one of the coercion acts of any tenant rights association. The land purchase acts could facilitate a breakthrough if an adjoining tenant wanted to increase the size of his property. Sometimes, though, the stalemate could drag on for months and sometimes even years.

Periods of heightened political agitation, such as the 1880s, sometimes allowed long-standing grudges to resurface. One example related to an 87-year old bachelor called John Daecon from Rahenarran, Kilmogammy in County Kilkenny, where he had a 'good farm'. On 9 December 1885, Deacon's farm was mysteriously broken into. Nothing was taken. On his front door on 14 December, the following notice, complete with an illustration of two coffins, was pasted:

> Mr Deacon we here [hear] a bad character of that woman. Captain Moonlight.
> Dear Mr Deacon dont be affair Sir we have too much respect but for that bloody woman Kate Disseey to her death or revenge

Kate Disney was aged about 60 years old and kept house for Deacon, something she had done for 19 years. Needless to say, the gossips had had their say. As the police report stated, 'it is alleged that improper relations formerly existed between them'. The report went on to assert:

> I am of opinion that the notice was placed on the door by some of
> Deacons relations. – possibly the Dunicts With a view to
> compelling the old man to get rid of Mrs Disney, as she is not on
> good terms with them and moreover as she seems to have great
> influence over the old man she might turn them against them.

To his credit, Deacon refused to dismiss Disney and the RIC sent out patrols to the farm twice a week, lying in ambush both in and outside the house. The police also surmised, probably correctly, that his relations were concerned that Deacon would make a will giving the farm to Kate Disney and not them.[55]

As the 1880s progressed, the National League emerged from the ashes of the Land League. Its activities, including the Plan of Campaign, were overshadowed by continued agrarian unrest which latched onto the movement. This could take several forms, the most common being the use of outrage and, in particular, threatening notices. League members wrote in the league's name, though in reality, as one RIC report observed, 'written & posted thro' spleen, and not in the interest of the League'. One particular notice, posted up at Ballyneale chapel, in Tipperary, on Sunday 27 September 1885, commenced, 'Notice to the National League. Farmers, labourers, shopkeepers and tradesmen beware of Big Phil Landry (or rotten Phil) ...' It was signed 'A National Leaguer'.[56]

A decade later, a placard written apparently under the aegis of the Errigal Trough branch of the Irish National Federation in Monaghan called for enrolled membership but went on to advocate an end to land grabbing. This referred to a nearby Tyrone farmer called James Brannigan, who had taken some grazing on two evicted farms on the Leslie estate. The county inspector noted, 'He (Brannigan) is not a man likely to be intimidated – as my information goes to show that his neighbours are more afraid of him than he is of them'.[57]

Rebel Kerry in the 1880s

Much has been written about agrarian unrest in nineteenth-century County Kerry, one of the most recent detailed studies being that of Donnacha Seán Lucey.[58] As discussed elsewhere in this study, Kerry holds the dubious distinction of the all-Ireland record for threatening letters recorded by the authorities in the Victorian era, 316 threatening letters (70 per cent agrarian) for the year 1882 alone. Given the lawless state of parts of the county during the Land War years, this number must be regarded as a conservative estimate of the total number of such letters and notices written there. Even in a tiny settlement like Brosna and its neighbourhood, threatening notices were the order of the day. Table 5 records those threatening notices found in or around the village of Brosna between September 1881 and September 1882:[59]

Table 5—Threatening notices found in Brosna, 1881–2

Date	Particulars
9 September 1881	Notice to boycott Wm Murphy Publican Brosna
8 December 1881	Calling on the people to avoid the Land Court
29 January 1882	Threatening the people against paying rent
3 February 1882	Threatening Michael Connor for having paid his rent
26 April 1882	Threatening Dessy Sheehan – should she remain in the employment of one Cotter
28 April 1882	Threatening a Mrs Sheehan for permitting her daughter to remain in the employment of certain people
20 July 1882	Calling on James Connor to give up a certain farm
13 August 1882	To 'Boycott' Michl Murphy
20 August 1882	Calling on the people not to work for F.C. Landes
24 August 1882	Calling on the people not to work for James Molloney
3 September 1882	Threatening any person who would work for James Black

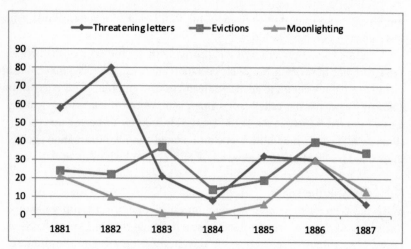

Fig. 26—Tralee, 1881–7: Threatening letters, evictions and moonlighting

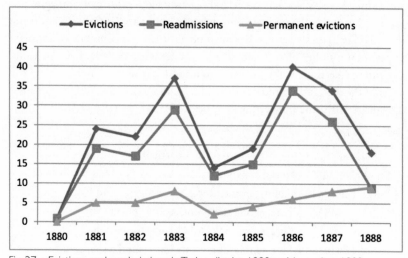

Fig. 27—Evictions and readmissions in Tralee district, 1880 to November 1888

For the district of Tralee in the period 1881–7, the correlation can be seen in Figure 26 between threatening letters, evictions and also, to an extent, moonlighting incidents.

Evictions were, as several modern historians have illustrated, more complicated than nationalist propaganda at the time made out. Figure 27 illustrates the significance of the readmission of tenants, either as tenants or as caretakers in the Tralee district. But nationalist newspaper reports and subsequent public debates tended to concentrate on the initial eviction figures.[60]

Earl Spencer's Kerry outrage map[61]

In the autumn of 1884, the lord lieutenant, Earl Spencer, visited the earl of Kenmare at Killarney House in County Kerry. While in Kerry he requested Dublin Castle to give him a return of the outrages in Kerry since January 1881. These were duly sent to him along with a map setting out the districts and listing for each type and number of outrage. For the period January 1881 until August 1884, these numbered just over 1,000. Overall, the 516 threatening letters and notices constituted half the total number of outrages in the county, with the notorious Castleisland district coming out at the

Table 6–Threatening letters and notices, 1881–4, extrapolated from Earl Spencer's outrage map

District	Number of threatening letters & notices	Number of other outrages	Total number of outrages	Percentage of threatening letters & notices in relation to total number for county	Percentage of threatening letters & notices in relation to other outrages
Listowel	93	103	196	18%	47%
Tralee	131	119	250	25%	52%
Castleisland	145	98	243	28%	60%
Dingle	12	12	24	2%	50%
Valentia/ Caherciveen	17	30	47	3%	36%
Killorglin	18	16	34	4%	53%
Killarney	75	97	172	15%	44%
Kenmare	25	14	39	5%	64%
	516	*489*	*1005*	*100%*	*51% av.*

highest with 60 per cent. These figures have been extrapolated in Table 6. The real value of the Spencer map is that the accompanying handwritten columns list both date and townland, showing when and where these threatening notices and letters appeared.

The northern Kerry districts of Listowel, Tralee and Castleisland were the most disturbed – both in terms of threatening letters and notices, and also other outrages. Killarney was slightly behind in numbers. The other districts – Dingle, Valentia, Killorglin and Kenmare – had relatively little trouble in comparison, a product of more diverse farming and some better farmland.

A word of caution needs to be added to these statistics as the accompanying list of threatening notices and letters does not quite match those given on the Spencer map. In the district of Tralee, there are 173 entries for threatening notices and letters for the 39 months from December 1880 until February 1884. This is 42 more than were entered on the Spencer map. The reason why the full number was not entered is not given in the documentation, but it was probably because only the agrarian notices and letters were included. They number 129, which is only two short of those included in the written list for agrarian crimes. The 173 threatening notices and letters represent 43 per cent of the total of 388 outrages in the county.

It is possible that the figures for threatening letters and notices were slightly toned down as it was realised that they were regarded in nationalist ranks as being of a lesser importance. In seven out of the eight districts, threatening letters and notices were displayed separately; this may be a further indication that the impact of the threatening missive category was being watered down. Equally likely, if not more so, duplicate counting might have been excluded – a problem area when looking at such statistics. If the same notice is posted up in three different townlands, is it to be counted as one or three? Practice seems to have varied depending on the time and place. Or it could simply have been sloppy arithmetic on the part of whoever was set the task of adding all the figures. That said, the percentages in relation to overall outrage figures are approximately accurate.

The following general observations can be made of the Tralee listed threatening notices and letters. Three-quarters (129) were classified as agrarian and a third (44) non-agrarian. Two-thirds (107) were listed as notices and a third (66) described as letters. Documents were listed in four categories: 88 or 51 per cent were agricultural notices; 41 or 24 per cent were agrarian letters; 24 or 14 per cent were non-agrarian letters; and 19 or 11 per cent were non-agrarian notices. It is not surprising that in such a rural area, agrarian threatening notices should dominate.

Royalty

It might be supposed that during the Victorian period, British royalty would have been a prime target for Irish threatening letters, especially in the 1880s, but this does not appear to be the case. Certainly, the Royal Archives at Windsor have no cartons of threatening letters marked 'Ireland'.[62] There are two reasons for such a paucity of source material. First, and most obviously, such communications received would have been passed straight to Scotland Yard rather than simply being archived along with the correspondence of monarchs, courtiers and politicians. It is certainly the case that Scotland Yard did have to deal with the occasional threatening letter.

When the prince of Wales visited Ireland in 1868, it was only a year after the Fenian rising of 1867, so it was hardly surprising that there was some, albeit fairly muted, anger at the event in advanced nationalist circles. At least one threat on the prince's life passed over the desk of the under-secretary, Thomas Burke.[63] An interesting example of a threat against royalty was that which came to trial in May 1882. The writer, an English boy of 17 years of age from Doncaster in Yorkshire called Albert Young, claimed to be an Irish Catholic priest who wrote that he had 50 men in his parish prepared to 'commence operations against Her Majesty's life unless [they were] assisted to emigrate'. For good measure, a threat was also made to shoot Prince Leopold on his wedding day.[64]

Young was from 'a respectable' lower middle-class family and had a job in a railway telegraph office. His story was 'all moonshine'. He had nothing to do with Ireland or Irish revolutionaries. The defence counsel argued that it was a practical joke – 'a lark' – and that he had been put up to it by two other clerks who had dictated the letter, which no doubt was true. Young had asked them to destroy the letter but they had, according to Young, proceeded to post the letter 'by mistake'. It was received at Buckingham Palace on 22 April 1882, a fortnight before the Phoenix Park murders. The harshness of Albert Young's sentence – 10 years – caused some public concern and continued to do so until eventually, he was released two years early. This childish prank, however, occurred at the time the hysteria around the Phoenix Park murders was at its height and the authorities were determined to make an example of the hapless young man. A petition in Young's support and signed by 245 householders of Doncaster, Sprotborough and Hexthorpe met with no concessions, nor did motivations from a clergyman and Young's former school teacher. In contrast, as will be seen in a later chapter, many an Irish offender convicted of writing or sending a threatening letter, even at this time of national excitement, got off with a couple of months in the Bridewell prison.

The second explanation for a scarcity of threatening letters sent to British royalty was the nature of the phenomenon, which rarely had anything to do with high politics and which was essentially a rural phenomenon in Ireland, hijacked at times by Irish nationalist political movements but retaining its rural character. Only in the Edwardian era, thanks to the activities of Ulster unionism and the suffragette movement, is there an increase in purely politically inspired threatening letters. And even then, numbers were not terribly great.[65]

Into the realm of literature

The Irish Victorian threatening letter was well enough known at the time beyond the confines of its recipients and rural settings that it cropped up frequently in literature and contemporary writings. Contemporary memoirs or reminiscences by writers such as Bence Jones, Samuel Hussey, Clifford Lloyd and Steuart Trench refer to the phenomenon. In the contemporary novel, the theme of the agrarian setting nourishing the climate of intimidation was common enough. The three volumes of William Carleton's ponderous 1845 epic *Valentine McClutchy, the Irish agent; or, the chronicles of Castle Cumber* were reissued in 1847 as a single-volume edition. The 20 illustrations were by Phiz, the cartoonist/caricaturist Hablot Knight Brown (1815–1882), most famous for his illustrations for Charles Dickens' novels. Carleton (1794–1869), came from a poor family from Clogher in County Tyrone, his father being a flax-dresser and tenant farmer.[66] He has been criticised both for the stylised portrayal of his characters and his, at times, anti-Catholic stance, having become a Protestant himself. His novels, though, while sometimes pedestrian in story line, demonstrate Carleton's rich background knowledge. In *The Irish Agent*, a Ribbon lodge meeting is called to determine the fate of the local land agent, Colonel Val McClutchy, magistrate and officer in the yeomanry, and his son, Phil. The remote venue, the filtering in of the assembly, the precautions taken, the weapons carried – 'such as they were' – the covering of the windows, and the resolve of the gathering were all described:

> In general they were just as any other number of men brought
> together for any purpose might be. Some to be sure among them
> betrayed strong indications of animal impulse; but taken together
> they looked just as I say ... there was something singularly wild,
> solemn and dreadful, in their comparative quietness; for silence we
> could not absolutely term it ... there is an awful lesson in all this; for
> it is certainly a frightful thing to see law and justice so partially and
> iniquitously administered as to disorganize society, and make men

look upon murder as an act of justice, and the shedding of blood as a moral triumph, if not a moral virtue.[67]

Carleton goes on to describe how 12 men were carried upon to act as jury. After a quiet denunciation of the two absent accused was given by the young inquisitor, a series of questions was posed to the 12, with their silence taken as consent. Needless to say, the determination that the two should be shot was quickly and silently approved. This portrait of how matters were resolved in the Clogher Valley interestingly makes no mention of giving 'fair warning'. The concept of offering the tyrant and oppressor or their agent a sporting chance to escape has tended to form part of popular legend, portrayed as an alternative social justice system and disguising the reality of people, having received threatening letters or notices, being murdered for reasons of rural politics.

We are on safer ground with Anthony Trollope, whose Irish experience did not extend to tenant life in the Clogher valley, but which certainly embraced time in Ireland. His last and unfinished novel, set in the early 1880s and entitled *The Land Leaguer* revolved around the Jones family who, in the immediate aftermath of the Famine, had purchased two adjoining estates on the road between Headford and Lough Corrib in County Galway. As a result, a widower and his two sons and two daughters are caught up in the whirlwind of the Land War. They are boycotted, most of the servants depart and the young son is murdered, all this interspersed with various strung-out romances. The threatening letter, with accompanying art work, quoted elsewhere, has all the appearances of Trollope 'ticking the boxes' of what made up life in rural Ireland at the height of the Land War.[68]

When it came to satire, as well as Patrick O'Conor MacLaughlin's pamphlet *The threatening letter-writer and Irish loyalist companion*, published by M.H. Gill of Dublin in 1889 and discussed elsewhere, there was another relevant pamphlet from an opposing perspective. In 1882, an anonymous 64-page satirical pamphlet was published by Tinsley Brothers of the Strand in London, the full title of which ran: *Practical politics and Moonlight politics. Letters to a Grand Old Man, and certain cabinet ministers, lately our confederates, by Rory-O'-the-Hills, some time National Schoolmaster, now a Moonlighter*. This was written by the larger-than-life figure, Percy Hetherington Fitzgerald (1830–1925).[69] He was born in County Louth and started his career as a prosecutor on the north-east circuit and as high sheriff of Louth. Moving to London, Fitzgerald made his living from writing and as an artist. He also had a close association with the theatre. He was prolific, erudite and knowledgeable, if rather eccentric.

Fitzgerald's pamphlet by a Moonlighter contained five letters and a nine-page catechism with the following approbation:

We have read the above Catechism, drawn from the utterances of our late confederates, Messrs. Gladstone, Bright, Chamberlain, and Foster, and we approve of its being circulated among the peasantry and taught to the children.
(Signed)   C.Moonlight

(+ His mark).
Rory.

This was a satirical comment on the faith that Gladstone and his colleagues had in resolving the Irish question through Home Rule and land reform, while being faced at times with endemic lawlessness in parts of Ireland. The 'Practical Politics' of the title referred to the use of terror and intimidation to reach a state of affairs where conventional politics would accept change which previously would have been unacceptable. So, outrage was excused or played down and soothing words and sophistry disguised reality. As far as threatening letters were concerned, they featured in 'The Moonlighter's Catechism':

Q.–Are letters threatening persons with death and other penalties 'serious criminal offences.'
A.–Nothing of the kind.
Q.–But have not the judges said that they are?
A.–No matter; Gladstone agrees with us in holding the contrary.[70]

Notes

[1] Reilly, *The Irish land agent*, p. 109.
[2] NAI, CSO RP, Outrage papers, Tipperary, Sligo and Roscommon, 26/117, March 1847
[3] NAI, Relief Commission papers, 1845, RLFC 3/1/77, 10 October 1845.
[4] NAI, CSO RP, Outrage reports, Leitrim, January 1846, 3/704/28.
[5] Quoted in Reilly, *The Irish land agent*, p. 96.
[6] BPP: *Outrages (Ireland). Return of the nature of outrages reported to the Constabulary Office, within the barony of Owneybeg. House of Commons, 342, 22 May 1846*, p. 1.
[7] NAI, CSORP outrage reports 1846, 3/704/29; and Quinn, 'Reddington', DIB, vol. 8, pp. 407–9.
[8] PRONI, letter to Christopher Estrange, Temple House, Ballymote, Sligo, 4 July 1881, T3905/5.
[9] NAI, CSORP outrage reports 1846, 3/704/29 and 3/704/28.

10 To be sung to the air 'Granuaile'. CSORP outrage papers 1846, 3/704/29.

11 Donnelly, *The great Irish Famine*, p. 139, quoted in Reilly, *The Irish land agent*, p. 135.

12 NAI, Anderson collection of threatening letters, 3/719/5.

13 *Hansard*, 15 February 1870, vol. 199, col. 347.

14 Davitt, *The fall of feudalism in Ireland*, p. 100.

15 Vaughan, *Landlords and tenants in mid-Victorian Ireland*, Appendix 1, pp. 229–31.

16 Becker, *Disturbed Ireland*, pp. 227–8.

17 NAI, CSORP, Outrage papers, Armagh, 1851, 3/705/20.

18 McCracken, *Inspector Mallon*, pp. 6–7.

19 Beames, *Peasants and power*, p. 66.

20 Trench, *Realities of Irish life*, p. 47.

21 Bussy, *Irish conspiracies*, p. 12.

22 NAI, Fenian papers, box 15, file 7241, 16 March 1871 box 12, file 5720, 23 March 1870, quoted in McCracken, *Inspector Mallon*, pp. 6–7.

23 Madden, *Forkhill Protestants and Forkhill Catholics*, p. 132.

24 Becker, *Disturbed Ireland*, p. 37.

25 *Examination of some recent allegations concerning the constabulary force of Ireland*, p. 49.

26 Vaughan, *Landlords and tenants in mid-Victorian Ireland*, pp. 154–6.

27 NLI, Report on the state of Ireland in 1863, ms 915, ff. 190–1.

28 BBP: *Abstracts of police reports of some of the principal outrages in the counties of Tipperary, Clare, Limerick, Leitrim, and Roscommon in the year 1845*, p. 19.

29 NAI, CSORP 1881, 16798, 3/638/31.

30 The 'Redheaded Earl' was twice lord lieutenant, first, from December 1868 until 1874; then, perhaps more famously, from 1882 until 1885.

31 NAI, CSO, 14,195, 22 September 1869; and CSO RP, 1870, 3/630/17, file 15046/69, 8 October 1869.

32 Gregg, 'The Irish cauldron', pp. 265–6.

33 *Agrarian outrages (Ireland), Memorandum as to the principle upon which outrages are recorded as Agrarian, and included as such in the returns laid before parliament.*

34 Richard Hawkins, 'Sir Samuel Lee Anderson', *Dictionary of Irish Biography*, vol. 1, p. 111.

35 NAI: CSO Library. Threatening letters & notices (+ photos). 1869–1872 3/719/5.

36 NAI, Fenian papers 'R', box 12, Peace Preservation Act, 30 March 1870.

37 *House of Lords. [Bill 129.] Protection of Life and Property in certain parts of Ireland [H.L.], brought from the Lord's 5 May 1871, ordered by the House of Commons to be printed, 8 May 1871*, p. 2.

38 NAI, CSORP 1886, 4146, February 1886, 3/646/35.

39 C.W. Hamilton of 40 Dominick Street, Dublin.

40 NAI, CSO RP 1870, 3/630/17, three letters by William Redae dated 26 October 1869 to the under-secretary at Dublin Castle.

41 *Special Commission Act, 1888*, p. 455.

42 Prester John', 'Terrorism in Ireland', p. 390.

43 Wilson, 'The present anarchy', pp. 38–9.

44 NAI, CSORP, 1882, file 4554, 26 January 1882, 3/639/2.

45 *Hansard*, House of commons, Viscount Lymington, 28 March 1887.

46 Comerford, 'The land war and the politics of distress', p. 45.

47 BPP: *Outrage and intimidation (Ireland). Return of certain cases of outrage and*

intimidation referred to by the chief secretary for Ireland in a speech in the House of Commons on 13th February 1890, 85, House of Commons, 4 March 1890, p. 1.

48 Donnelly, Jr, *The land and the people of nineteenth-century Cork*, pp. 271 and 274.

49 Townshend, *Political violence in Ireland*, pp. 111–12.

50 NAI, CSORP 1852, 3/705/27.

51 NAI, CSO RP, 1884, 3/644/27, file 21594.

52 BL, Add Ms 49 807, Buller to Balfour, 1 April 1887.

53 NAI, CSORP 1884, 20739, 23 January 1884, 3/644/26.

54 NAI, CSORP 1846, Outrage papers, 25/4679, 3/704/29. For claims dating back 10 and 20 years, see Herlbert, *Ireland under coercion*, vol. 2, pp. 120 and 155.

55 NAI, CSORP 1886, 4157, 3/646/35.

56 CSORP, 1886, 4123, 3/646/35.

57 CSORP, 1894, 11267, 3/657/4.

58 Lucey, *Land, popular politics and agrarian violence in Ireland: The case of county Kerry, 1872–86*, University College Dublin Press, 2011.

59 NAI, Police and Crime, Crimes Act 1882, carton 6, 3/714/5.

60 The figures might be modified somewhat by unofficial and unrecorded evictions, but the figures are too stark to alter the fundamental conclusion. *Special Commission Act, 1888*, pp. 331–3.

61 NAI, CSO RP, 1884, 3/644/26, RIC file 20904, Kerry, 5 September 1884.

62 Ms Derrett to D.P. McCracken, Royal Archives, Windsor Castle, pers corr, 3 October 2016.

63 NAI, CRB, Fenian R series, 2033R, Burke to Larcom.

64 TNA, HO 144/99/A17173.

65 See, for example, TNA, MEOP, 3/2767.

66 Ó Gallchoir, 'Carleton, William (1794–1869)', *Dictionary of Irish Biography*, vol. 2, pp. 347–9.

67 Carleton, *The Irish Agent*, pp. 370–9.

68 Trollope, *The Land Leaguers*, p. 203 and Dungan, *Mr Parnell's rottweiler*, p. 1.

69 Frances Clarke, 'Percy Hetherington Fitzgerald', *Dictionary of Irish Biography*, vol. 3, p. 907.

70 Anonymous, *Practical politics and Moonlight politics. Letters to a Grand Old Man, and certain cabinet ministers, lately our confederates, by Rory-O'-the-Hills, some time National Schoolmaster, now a Moonlighter*, p. 58.

5. The urban setting

Part I: The urban threatening letter and placard

The vast majority of threatening letters and notices in Victorian Ireland that were reported to the authorities emanated from the countryside and the market towns. Even those found in towns invariably referred to rural land ownership and use, or were linked to the countryside through tenant debt or shopkeeper ownership or subletting rural land. It is an interesting feature of this means of intimidation that nineteenth-century rack-renting in Ireland's cities and towns did not produce a similar outpouring of rage and sympathy in the nationalist establishment.[1]

Irish poison-pen letters written by someone with a personal grudge unrelated to farming were extremely rare. It must therefore have raised great curiosity among the constabulary in Sligo in 1852 when a continental foreigner posing as St Helliers, alias Dr Tucker, alias Allessandro Dominico Viniano Bonomes Duke of Garibaldi received a threatening letter with a Sligo postmark. The letter was complete with a coffin with 'Death' written inside it and a drawing of three circles intersected by a single line. Written in English, it warned the recipient not to lecture and to leave town within 48 hours.

Although Tucker/St Helliers had come to the Sligo police barracks, he had been most reluctant at first to show anyone the threatening letter. A visit by the police to the 26-year-old's lodgings followed, when he said he was really the duke of Garibaldi and had fled Padua in Italy following the 1848 revolution. Sir George Grey (then governor of New Zealand) had apparently told Tucker that he could stay in the United Kingdom if he remained quiet. He therefore sought out Sligo as a refuge where he hoped to make a living as a homoeopathic doctor. Foolishly, during a lecture on the revolution in Rome, Tucker denounced the cardinal. For this, he was censured from the Sligo pulpit by Father Phillips, who said that Tucker was 'one who wishes to shoot the Pope and drive him out of Rome'. The circle symbol in the threatening letter, Tucker claimed, related to a secret society in Italy, which he had left after several murders had occurred. Royal Irish Constabulary (RIC) investigations revealed that Tucker had 'kept a French academy in the town of Bradford and passed there as a French-man'.[2]

Nothing more is heard of this strange matter, ironic in some respects given the mafia-style nuance of the whole Irish threatening-letter phenomenon.

Crank letters

Many rural threatening letters were near comical in their presentation and content, but this was unintentional. Crank letters, in contrast, appear to have been rare, if non-existent in places. Generally, Irish threatening letters had a rational underlying demand or purpose, usually relating to land – except in Dublin.

In 1842, there was something of a stir when a sapper and miner called Private Hickey was brought to court having been accused of sending a threatening letter to Captain Thomas Larcom, the eminent head of the Ordnance Survey in Ireland.[3] The nature of the threatening letter was one well known in the countryside – attempting to get an employer to dismiss an employee. In this case, the employee was an engraver in the Ordnance Survey office named John Stait, 'a bloody orangeman'. Stait was also sent a threatening letter, in this instance referring to Stait's father also as a 'blody orangeman' but refraining from threatening to attack him as 'he is two old'. Stait junior was warned on pain of death to leave his employment. Larcom sent both letters to the Dublin Metropolitan Police (DMP).

Larcom had encountered Hickey shortly after receiving the threatening letter and found him in a very excitable state. He thought Hickey 'not quite right in the head'. Hickey was also said to have a drink problem. A comparison of his handwriting drew further suspicion. It appears that Hickey had worked for Larcom for a while. Larcom tried to distance himself from the issue, making Stait press the case with the authorities. The solution seems to have been that long adopted by the DMP when facing an awkward issue. The problem (Hickey) was sent to England – where no doubt, as far as the DMP was concerned, he could write as many threatening letters as he wished.

Another anonymous letter was posted in Dublin in May 1893 after a small bomb went off along the railings of the Four Courts on the eleventh anniversary of the Phoenix Park murders. The letter was sent to the Press Association in London with a version also sent to William Gladstone, the prime minister. It ranted about religion which, perhaps ironically, was unusual in an Irish threatening letter. It was clearly not written by those who had actually planted the bomb. The letter read:

Sir,

We decided on blowing up the Four Courts on Saturday night after reading in the morning papers of the passing of the second reading of the Irish Sunday Closing Bill in the House of Lords. The fact is that the Irish people have much less liberty now than twenty years ago, and we won't tolerate any more restraints on our liberties. The idea of imposing restraints in regard to food [_] a whole day by legislation is simply insanity. Early closing on Saturdays would be tolerable enough, but total closing on Sundays drives us to rebellion.

What makes Sunday closing doubly galling is on account of it being a religious restraint. No parliament in the nineteenth century should think of imposing religious restraints or religious duties on the people.

We hate religion. A great number of the intelligent workmen of the present day are either infidels or sceptics. They only laugh at the religious legends of the ignorant fishermen of galilee which have become fossilised into religious truths because they were adopted by the learned fathers of the Church, though these legends or Gospels contradict one another materially.

How is it to be explained, supposing Christ really desired the salvation of us all, that he did not declare his doctrines in a way that all his followers would understand him rightly, Protestant as well as Catholics, – though he must have foreseen that his words would cause dissensions.[4]

At the same time, Mrs Gladstone also received a threatening letter of Irish origin warning her that she 'would soon be a Widow'.

Urban Fenians were not averse to using the weapon of the threatening letter. The detective division within the DMP frequently received anonymous tipoffs through the post and sometimes a threatening letter. John Mallon, who rose from office boy to assistant commissioner of the DMP, was no stranger to this. Not that it seems to have affected him in the slightest – he was as tenacious in his pursuit of 'the men of violence' as an assistant commissioner in 1900 as he had been as an inspector in the 1860s.

Mallon made his name as the key figure in tracking down the Invincibles, the Phoenix Park murderers, and bringing the perpetrators, though not their handlers, to the gallows. The murders caused a general panic in the British administration in Dublin Castle and a greatly increased security bureaucracy was drafted in. This included a team to deal with the flood of anonymous letters which were received giving largely useless information about the crime.[5] Most of these were not threatening. Though in times of security crises, such as that following the Phoenix Park murders, and earlier in 1848 and 1867, threatening letters were received relating to the unrest, they were not a key element of these crises.

The placard war
The Crime Branch Special files in the National Archives of Ireland contain a large number of leaflets and posters which the constables of the DMP regarded as seditious placards and removed whenever encountered. These included posters for public meetings opposing recruitment to Irish regiments and Irish pro-Boer propaganda. Assistant Commissioner Mallon recorded in October 1899, 'The leaflets were thrown about the streets in bundles of six or eight, but the police have not heard that they were handed out to people except in one case ...'[6] Inspector Considine was of the opinion that leaflets were of one of four varieties: those trying to prevent army recruitment; those aimed at corrupting the loyalty of soldiers; those trying to induce young men to join Irish brigades in foreign countries; and lastly: 'General seditious language or documents tending to inflame the minds of disaffected persons and prepare them to join a revolutionary conspiracy against the Government.'[7]

These posters were essentially an urban phenomenon, but they could also be found in rural areas in market towns and in villages, often left by a former Ballygawley schoolmaster called Henry McAteer, the sometime travelling agent of the Irish Transvaal Committee.[8] The sergeant of police in Balla, County Mayo, which had a population of 400, reported: 'I found attached notice posted up at the Courthouse Balla, another was posted up on the market square (on the weighing machine) and one on each of seven of the telegraph poles on Kiltimagh road from Balla.'[9]

As with their counterparts in the Royal Irish Constabulary (RIC), the DMP removed any Land League poster, considering them subversive. This included the poster carrying Davitt, Dillon and Parnell's repudiation of the Phoenix Park murders, despite Dublin Castle's objections.[10] The DMP even had little hesitation in confiscating editions of advanced nationalist newspapers such as *The Nation* or *United Ireland* when their officers considered they had crossed the line to subversion, even when the chief secretary has advised caution or prohibited such action.[11] All this said, there was very little in the way of urban threatening notices compared with the extent of the problem in the countryside.

The placard war was not, of course, limited to supporters of nationalism. In many of the northern towns, the constabulary had to deal with anti-Catholic sectarian placards. These were frequently classified in the press as orangeism and even the DMP sometimes had to deal with such occurrences. In 1851, the police had, on three occasions, removed placards attacking Cardinal Cullen and the pope from 42 Wellington Quay which, not surprisingly, were causing 'a slight disturbance' outside on the quays.[12]

Back in the Famine years, there had been a tendency, for a while, for placard to be met with responding placard. In 1844, the Mining Company of Ireland had taken over the lease of one of the Slieveardagh coal areas at Earlshill and Ballyphilip, east of Thurles. During the 1848 insurrection, the area was disturbed and indeed, the coalminers and William Smith O'Brien were in contact with each other. But even before that, there was trouble. The shooting and wounding of the company's steward, Martin Morris, elicited rewards of £300 from the company and a further £100 from the Dublin authorities for information leading to any arrest and convictions. This produced no result and matters deteriorated, with workers receiving threatening notices warning them to stop work. On 26 November 1845, the company secretary, Richard Purdy, on behalf of the company board, announced that operations would be suspended from 20 December. He cited the Morris shooting and 'the threatening Notices subsequently served on those well-disposed workmen who are desirous to work under the Company and earn support for themselves and families, but whose lives are too highly valued by the Board to be risked by continuance of the Works, until sufficient protection can be afforded to them'.[13]

Even more retaliatory was a notice issued on 1 December 1846 by the Famine relief committee at Athboy in County Meath, west of Navan, under the name of Lambert Disney:

NOTICE
In consequence of the disgraceful outrages, which have taken place in the Barony of Lune, within the last few days, the Relief committee hereby give NOTICE, that they will discontinue to issue any more Tickets for cheap meal, in case of any further outrage in this district.

Disney, on sending a copy of this notice to the authorities, commented that he hoped it 'may have a salutary effect'.[14]

The magistrates were not slow to enter this placard war. A good example, under the names of three magistrates at Carrick-on-Suir in Tipperary, in September 1846, denounced 'some evil minded Persons [who] posted a number of illegal Notices'. While Messrs Thomas Lalor, Henry Briscoe and Harrison Briscoe 'deeply commiserate and feel for the sufferings of the labouring classes & poor, & are determined to alleviate their distress', the substance of their poster was clearly spelt out: 'we are determined to preserve order [in the town] at all risks'.[15]

An interesting case of the urban placard linking town with agrarian unrest related to the Francis Hynes murder trial and its aftermath. Hynes was a young farmer outside Ennis who had employed James Doolaghty, a married man with seven children, as a herd. Hynes sublet the farm to a James Lynch, with Doolaghty transferring to his employment. In about 1880, Hynes was evicted from the farm and Lynch formally took it over as full tenant, still employing Doolaghty. Intimidation of Doolaghty then began, urging him to resign as herd. This he refused to do. Unlike most such tenant-on-tenant or tenant-on-labourer cases, the matter escalated to violence. On 9 July 1882, after attending mass, Doolaghty was shot full in the face with a shotgun charge. Hynes was arrested. The case was tried under the special commission court set up under legislation passed after the Phoenix Park murders, the first such case to be heard in Dublin, far away from the scene of the crime. Judge Lawson presided. Inevitably it soon became a *cause célèbre* including accusations of jury packing being made. Despite intense public and nationalist political pressure, Earl Spencer, the lord lieutenant, and the Irish government declined to give clemency and Hynes was hanged at Limerick jail on 11 September 1882.

In January, the lord lieutenant and Lady Spencer visited the 3rd earl of Portarlington at Emo near Portarlington in the Queen's County [Laois]. The following notices or placards were printed in Dublin and a large number posted to 'different residents in this town [Portarlington]':

You are desired to give welcome to SPENCER THE MURDERER
OF FRANCIS HYNES with barred doors and closed blinds.
By order of
'Blood Avengers'[16]

Spencer was, by then, the constant subject of often crude abuse. One just has to survey the cartoons attacking the lord lieutenant in *United Ireland* to see evidence of this.

Whistle-blowing

One category of anonymous communication, threatening or otherwise, restricted to the urban setting was what is today called whistle-blowing – and as with the modern equivalent, this might be true, full of half-truths, or simply malicious. In 1887, the Dublin *Daily Express* and *The Irish Times* referred to two anonymous whistle-blowing letters. One was sent to Chief Inspector Hughes of the DMP, and a second to David Harrel, the under-secretary at Dublin Castle, under whom the DMP fell. Both attacked Hughes and the detective division of the DMP. An official minute noted:

> These letters were shown to the men of G Division (the detective),
> who, one and all, repudiated in the strongest terms any sympathy
> with their object, and protested against any idea of dissatisfaction or
> discontent, existing among them.
> Chief Inspector Hughes is an officer of the highest integrity and
> respectability.
> The anonymous letter was evidently the work of some outsider,
> who, for personal or other malicious reason, wished to injure Chief
> Inspector Hughes and the detective staff.[17]

Two years later, in September 1889, a classic example of malicious anonymous whistle-blower allegations arrived at the under-secretary's home at 10 Ailesbury Road in the Donnybrook suburb of Dublin. It also related to the DMP. It ran to four tightly-written foolscap sheets, and was about 1,400 words long. It was neatly written, clearly by someone used to writing. It was an attack on the legendary head of the DMP's detective division, Superintendent John Mallon. It began:

> Sir, I beg to convey to you a few facts which have come to my
> knowledge some time ago and of which I believe you are not aware
> as your words and acts do not show that you are in any way
> conversant with the surroundings of the case. A great many are
> aware that you have been warned on different occasions to be
> cautious and guarded in your dealings with Chief Supt Mallon but
> these warnings seem to have fallen on you as seed upon barren soil.
> For the last time however you are now put on your guard and if you

close your ears to the voice that calls you must only put up with the consequences that will ensue

It is only right to tell you that Mr Mallon whom you have described as an honest officer is none other than a traitor and a knave. He has lead you round the Castle even without a silken thread and turn you at any point where he desires. His period of services whether we look at it from a public or private point of views has been one long series of frauds but with these we will not now trouble you.[18]

The disgruntled colleague or former colleague proceeded to make accusation after accusation, which included allegations that he had set up his former superior, victimised those who found out about his misdeeds, and even that his wife was a fraud and a drunk. Nevertheless, the police's shining star survived and several years later, he became the first Catholic duty commissioner of the DMP.[19]

Clubland
Even Dublin's clubland was not immune from threatening letters. The Kildare Street Club, the bastion of the landlord ascendency class, was not hostile to gentlemen of political persuasions other than their own being members – though there were limits. The eccentric and future president of Sinn Féin Edward Martyn (1859–1923) was a member and regular visitor. He had been provided by the club secretary with a writing desk used when standing, or a Disraeli as it was sometimes called. All was well for a number of years until he expressed himself strongly in favour of the Boers during the South African War. Then he received an anonymous note on a club card which read: 'Had you not better resign your membership here before you are expelled'. He was not cowed by such tactics and remained a member, even later when an open attempt to expel him resulted in a court case, which he won. After that, the club returned to normal, with Martyn continuing to have his expansive dinners in what today are premises occupied by the National Library of Ireland.[20]

When country comes to town: The rural overflow
Irish rural politics and the urban scene did not tend to mix much, especially from a Dublin-centric point of view. However, an interesting postscript to the Boycott affair occurred when Captain Boycott arrived in Dublin after the stirring events in Mayo and booked into the Hamman Hotel and Turkish

Baths in O'Connell Street. A series of threatening letters to the hotel's proprietor did the trick and the Boycotts had to leave for England. One of the letters read:

> We warn you that if you keep Mr Boycott in your hotel another day
> your life is in danger. As a friend i give you warning. You are marked
> for vengeance already; and as for boycott he need not crow till he
> gets out of the wood. There were closer watched men than he shot
> in Dublin: and i do not think he will bring his life out of it. Rory[21]

Much more common were threatening letters received in towns which originated from the countryside and which were concerned with land matters. So, one finds that Joseph Lowry, an auctioneer in Kells, County Meath, received the following, dated 17 November 1867:

> Sir we hereby give you as well as all other Auctioneers notice to quit
> that danmed sistyem the letting of grass lands for the futher So it if
> you insist depene withit will be at the cost of your lives

The same day another Kells auctioneer, Michael Freeman, living in Cross Street, received the following:

> Sir we understand that you intend holding the annual Sale of grass
> land upon next Friday Therefore we give you timely notice not to
> attempt letting it or any other grass land for the season or if you do
> we will leave you an example to Brother Auctioneers if powder and
> ball does it so this is our last notice and beware for it is as true as
> true can be for if we intended to let any one acer be set in the
> county I am sure the most noble the Marquis of Headfort would be
> the last man in Ireland we would prevent
> No more at present but i hope you will save your own life and save
> us the trouble of taking it

An interesting urban threatening placard campaign occurred in Millstreet, north-west of Cork city 11 years later. Jeremiah Hegarty was a well-to-do merchant and farmer. When a branch of the Land League was established in the town, Hegarty was invited to join. He refused. This resulted in the following boycott placard being posted up throughout the town on 22 December 1880:

Take notice you are cautioned against having any dealings with John [meaning Jeremiah] Hegarty, of Mill Street, or his family; neither buy nor sell them anything; shun them as you would lepers. If you disobey this order may the Lord have mercy on you.

Hegarty, however, was not so easily intimidated and the matter escalated. He published his correspondence with the Land League and took out a case against two leaguers, who subsequently received prison sentences. The matter spilled over into the National School, where a witness in the trial taught. A rival school was established. The future Cork City MP, Dr C.K.D. Tanner described Hegarty as 'a low creeping reptile'. Hegarty was shot at and his home burnt. Needless to say, the case featured in the Parnell Commission of 1889, as did several other cases where there were posters put up in towns calling for boycotts of individuals, who though usually urban tradesmen, had links with the countryside.[22]

At a lower level, tradesmen trying to extract payment from tenant farmers could and did run into trouble. One Armagh magistrate reported:

I will state a case: a man went out [to the countryside] to collect his debts who was a baker in Newry, and he was served with most desperate notices because he asked for the debts; he was told if he sent his bread cart again he would have other news to bring back with him.[23]

A more serious case of the country threatening a townsman was that of the shopkeeper and gombeenman or moneylender John O'Reilly from Ballyjamesduff in County Cavan, who also owned property in the countryside and had twice evicted a tenant farmer called Simon Flynn of Behermagh near Virginia, once on 24 August 1880 and a second time on 17 February 1884, presumably after Flynn had been reinstated, for a debt of £388 owed.[24] Mrs Alicia Fynn had the boldness to try and involve the local police in the matter. Sergeant Lysaght, though, became suspicious and came to the conclusion that she had written the threatening letter as a means of intimidating O'Reilly into reducing the debt. Mrs Flynn's brother was a priest in America who had sent her £200, so there was some chance of hanging onto the farm. O'Reilly meanwhile had suspected that Simon Flynn's brother, Owen, had been the instigator of the threatening letter, Simon being unable to write. Though the sergeant tricked Mrs Flynn into writing something for him and so giving a sample of her handwriting, it was felt that a case against her would not succeed. Interestingly, O'Reilly did compromise; the £200 was paid to O'Reilly with a promise of a further £100 in a month's time, and there the matter rested.

The imprisonment of fiery newspaper editor William O'Brien in 1889 had an unusual sequel – the arrival at the vice-regal lodge in the Phoenix Park of a politically driven urban threatening letter. Posted in Dublin on 10 February, and addressed; 'My dear Londonderry', the communication, written in a neat hand and complete with skull above two bones in a V-shape, advised the lord lieutenant as follows:

> do not get excited over these few lines. you or your comrades shall
> receive a fatal shock in the ____ but not very far distant.
> We are resolved to take any le____ to prevent cruelty to our pat___
> Mr William O'Brien in Co[rk] jail, I give you timely warn[ing]
> Good bye
> Yours
> A revenger[25]

The matter was placed in the hands of Superintendent William Reddy of the G Division of the DMP, but there is no evidence that the culprit was tracked down.

Small town and village disputes occasionally involved threatening letters or notices, though admittedly these were few in number, and generally had an agricultural source. Posting boycott notices could very well have a ripple effect and seriously interfere with the lives of people unconnected with any perceived ill-doing. A case in point was a series of boycotts initiated by Hugh McBride, a 60-year-old small farmer in Magheraclogher in west Donegal. This, according to RIC Inspector Davies, resulted in the following: 'Bunbeg store was closed up, servants at Gweedne Hotel and in private houses left. Fishery men left – and yarn for stockings etc was returned by the Knitters to local Agent.' Hugh McBride, who had a wife and six children dependent upon him, was rounded up under the 1881 coercion act and packed off for a spell in Dundalk Jail.[26]

Resisting such boycotting could tempt retaliation in even the smallest communities, as a case in the small, remote and picturesque village of Moneree near Dingle in County Kerry showed. In late December 1885, a threatening letter was posted up on the door of Denis Slattery. The notice was clearly written on a page torn from a note-book. The district inspector of constabulary was convinced the matter was centred on the village and sent his head constable and a sergeant to call on all the houses and to keep an eye open for any notebooks lying around. In Denis McCarthy's house, the head constable found such a notebook, which belonged to Timothy, McCarthy's 15-year-old son. It was soon established that the jagged edges of one side of the threatening notice corresponded with those remaining in Timothy McCarthy's notebook. The local schoolmaster refused to give the RIC any of Timothy's books which were at the school, stating that they were private property. However, a handwriting expert, John Shaw Peaks, was employed to compare the writing in the notebook found in Timothy's home with that on the note and asserted them to be the same.

The morning after the threatening notice was posted up another incident occurred. A lynch-pin on the Slattery's cart had been removed and as they travelled into Dingle for mass on Sunday morning, the wheel came off. Fortunately, Denis McSlattery and his wife were not injured. Slattery strongly suspected the McCarthy, Griffith and Fitzgerald families, all of Moneree, 'of this piece of blackguardism'. Slattery had seen a group of members of these families in his yard the night before the threatening notice was posted and a stone had also been thrown at the Slattery house that evening. Slattery gave the police as possible explanation that he had spread a story that Timothy Griffith, 'had made a bill of sale of all his property over to his son in order to defeat his auditors'. However, the police were not convinced by this and rather favoured the idea that Slattery had entered the boycotted shop of a man named Atkins. A constabulary report concluded: 'This is not the first instance in which persons have been threatened for going into this shop, but hitherto the threats have been oral and the parties threatened have, through terror, refused to come forward & give evidence.' This summation is confirmed by the fact that when the case came to the Kerry assizes, the jury, despite the evidence of the notebook, the handwriting of the boy, and the known enmity against Slattery, found young Timothy McCarthy not guilty.[27]

Part II: Newspapers and 'printed intimidation'

In recent years, much attention has been given to attempts at curbing the Irish press directly, usually through ineffectual warnings or sometimes the use of coercion legislation thanks, in no small part, to the excellent work of the Newspaper and Periodical Forum of Ireland and such historians as Myles Dungan, Colum Kenny, Felix Larkin, Patrick Maume, Mark O'Brien, Simon J. Potter and Kevin Rafter.[28] This is part of the emerging sub-discipline of

Irish historiography surrounding the history of Irish journalism and the Irish press.[29]

Not so much has been written concerning the negative aspects of newspaper content, in other words, answering the question: To what extent did newspapers set out to do harm and, indeed, to intimidate?

Myles Dungan has meticulously traced the cat-and-mouse game which Dublin Castle and William O'Brien pursued in the 1880s, with prosecutions, imprisonments and seizures of copies of *United Ireland*. The end result was probably more of a victory for O'Brien than for the Castle, whose Law Office increasingly came to the pragmatic view (one not held by the DMP) that, in Dungan's words, they would 'leave well alone when it came to the *United Ireland*'.[30]

The Irish press, and the Anglo-Irish or unionist press, in particular, carried short snippets reporting various threatening letters or notices, especially as the century progressed.[31] These tended to be purely informative and, in most cases, must have been information supplied to journalists by the authorities, sometimes because a reward had been offered for information leading to an arrest and conviction.

Monitoring the press[32]
Irish newspapers were printed in many of the island's provincial cities and towns, so ensuring the drama of newspaper publishing was played out widely. Closing down of 'recalcitrant' newspapers through coercion acts had its drawbacks. More often than not, other methods were employed to try and limit the advanced nationalist press. In addition to the libel laws, various methods of intimidation were refined, especially by the Dublin police. These included such simple devices as the use of informers. Surveillance, or shadowing as it was termed, was a procedure that was strongly denied but was common practice, especially later in the century. The authorities also paid minute attention to what was being printed in the advanced nationalist press.[33]

As mentioned, the National Library of Ireland holds 22 thick volumes of newspaper clippings which were originally kept in the library of the chief secretary in Dublin Castle. These are as invaluable a source to the modern historian as they were to the security authorities 125 years ago. The Victorian newspaper habit was to record detail, including as many names as possible of people who attended public and semi-public meetings. As a result, this saved the Dublin detective force, the G men, much effort and leg work.

Every morning, Inspector Mallon, the head of the approximately 30-strong detective division in Exchange Court beside Dublin Castle, would go through selected newspapers with a pair of sharp scissors, a pen and a bottle of red ink, underlining names of subversives, details of meetings and comments which might have significance.[34] Mallon's expenses claims regularly included 10 shillings for newspapers, 'for evidence if required'. A hundred metres away, a clerk in the chief secretary's office was also cutting up newspapers, but working on a much larger pile. Mallon, a Catholic and moderate Irish nationalist himself, in his relentless pursuit of those who were or might be inclined to violence, concentrated on the advanced press, including the Irish-American newspapers. The chief secretary, though, was more interested in seeing the full scope of opinion, not just the advanced nationalist outpourings, but also that in the moderate nationalist press, such as *The Freeman's Journal*, as well as the advanced and moderate Irish unionist press, in particular the Belfast newspapers such as the *Belfast Newsletter* and *The Northern Whig*.

We know, for example, that in the five and a half years between November 1887 and June 1893, Dublin Castle subscribed to no fewer than 60 different Irish, British and American newspapers. In the region of 350 issues of these newspapers were received in Dublin Castle every month, representing about 35 different titles at any one time. Very often, two copies were ordered and sometimes as many as four. For example, in January 1888, Dublin Castle took 433 copies of newspapers, being 327 issues (daily, bi-weekly or weekly) of 35 different newspapers. Some papers were taken for only a short while. These included the *Celtic Times*, *The Gael*, the *Labour World*, the *Limerick Reporter*, the *New York Herald*, the *People's Advocate* and the *Tipperary Advocate*. Other newspapers, such as the *Western News*, ceased publication.

Some of the newspapers folded because of legal action or just a lack of funding. The *Suppressed United Ireland* lasted for two editions to be replaced by the *Insuppressible*, which Dublin Castle managed to get a copy of in December 1890 and which appears to have ceased publishing on 24 January 1891. Tactics by journalists such as Bodkin and O'Brien served at once to annoy both Dublin Castle and their nationalist enemies. This was reminiscent of the actions of Arthur Griffith some years later when serious press control was initiated and he would close one paper or have it closed by the authorities and reopen with another, *Scissors and Paste* being an example (1914–15).

The principal newspapers taken by Dublin Castle in the early 1890s were mainline papers such as:

Daily Express (Dublin)
Daily News (Dublin)

The Freeman's Journal
The Irish Times
The Morning News (Belfast)
The Pall Mall Gazette
The London Star
The Times

There was also a cohort of weeklies which frequently were radical or advanced nationalist, such as *The Nation, The People of Ireland* and the short lived *Workers' World*, which ceased publication in May 1891. New newspapers emerged and were added to the authorities' list, such as the *National Press* in 1891. Then the influx of funding for the Fenian revolutionaries from the United States and the subsequent bombing campaign in Britain and Ireland necessitated Dublin Castle subscribing to the *Irish World*, the *Chicago Tribune* and *The New York Herald*.[35]

Threatening copy

The alleged nexus between the nationalist press and the phenomenon of the Irish threatening letter and notice consisted of two known threats. The first was the extent to which newspaper agitation encouraged the phenomenon. The second was the fact that newspapers were, on occasion, involved in the criminal activity of printing and distributing threatening notices.

How far newspaper content encouraged this form of intimidation is difficult to ascertain in practice. In 1883, at the time of the trials relating to the Phoenix Park murders, the chief secretary, George Trevelyan, remarked that the leading articles in *United Ireland* were 'forming as essential a part of the machinery of assassination as the daggers and the masks'.[36] Even the editor of *United Ireland* described the editorial office as 'that tabernacle of treasons'.[37] It cannot be denied that, as the expansion of the land issue took centre stage in political activity in the 1880s, there was a concurrent increase in reported outrages and in particular, the number of threatening letters and notices. It is difficult to deny that land agitation was encouraged and promoted by the advanced nationalist press, in particular through the outpourings of the weekly newspaper *United Ireland*.

William O'Brien's *United Ireland* was a strange beast of a newspaper. Much of its content was pedestrian enough and worth buying as a weekly newspaper simply for its news coverage. But the commentaries would, on occasion, erupt into an explosion of indignation and insult, verging on corner-boy abuse. This made the newspaper alluring and exciting for the nationalist readership. There is also a little evidence to suggest that even the enemies of the newspapers – or at least the more mature and worldly, such as the wise Earl Spencer, who as lord lieutenant was lambasted in *United Ireland* issue after issue, were quietly amused. The cartoons, which were at first black and white, within the body of the newspaper from the end of 1883, became lavish coloured artworks by John Dooley Reigh (*c.* 1851–1914). These were frequently kept by the purchaser. The author has one such, entitled 'The political gamble', featuring Lord Salisbury, which the celebrated special magistrate Major R.G. Traill carefully pasted into the back inside cover of his personal scrap book.[38] Advertisements, such as for Clery's department store, were another example of the mundane and ordinary, alongside the political placard.

O'Brien was very much fixed in his niche at *United Ireland*, clearly enjoying cavorting with the politically powerful and being rude in print under the guise of nationalistic endeavour. Yet despite the bravado, O'Brien was somewhat insecure. It is significant that he turned down Parnell's once-in-a-lifetime offer to edit the big-circulation nationalist mainline daily, *The Freeman's Journal.*[39] Certain themes and topics emerged in *United Ireland* with great regularity. Between September 1882 and November 1890, magistrates were attacked by name in the paper 137 times.[40] To what extent was *United Ireland* a radical advanced nationalist organ within the Parnellite fold and to what extent was it a vehicle for incitement and threat? Or, to put it another way, was the newspaper a weekly threatening letter?

The tone of *United Ireland* was certainly out of kilter with other advanced Irish newspapers of the latter half of the Victorian era and early twentieth century. Griffith's *United Irishman* or Connolly's *Workers' Republic* did not exude such erudite ferocity, spite and vitriol. *United Ireland* was a mixture of a good weekly partisan but news-packed Irish nationalist newspaper and a European continental political scandal-sheet. It is hard to deny that it was the prime promoter of boycotting in print, and, as Conor Cruise O'Brien observed, boycotting was not only at the heart of the Plan of Campaign but the 'whole national-agrarian system'.[41] Given that threatening letters were the keystone to boycotting, there was also, inevitably, some relationship between *United Ireland* and the posting of boycott threatening notices.

Newspapers, indeed, were not immune from running what might be termed threatening copy, which can be seen as likely to incite violence against a person. An example appeared in the *Galway Observer*:

AN EXTERMINATOR COMING HOME

You are all aware that the greatest of all exterminators, Lord
Dunsandle, has been spending the people's hard earned monies
abroad for some years past. The latest news from Dunsandle declares
that his lordship is about coming home to Dunsandle. There is no
need to make any reference to this man's bad acts. Since history
records them and tells of the thousands of human beings he cast on
the roadside, and of the number of our fair daughters he sent on the
destructive path. Can it be that Dunsandle is coming home to aid
his son in destroying the few remaining on the property.[42]

Dunsandle, who received a copy of this newspaper piece in advance of
his return, considered it an incitement to murder. Staying at the Kildare Street
Club in Dublin, he pestered the police and Dublin Castle, demanding 'to
know whether the government propose to take any steps in the matter'. The
attorney general's office, however, was cautious:

> It contains very gross personal abuse of Lord Dunsandle. I am
> however quite clear that no prosecution cd be maintained against
> the editor on the ground that it amounts to an incitement to
> murder – In such cases as the present i.e. cases where a person is
> slandered the person slandered must himself proceed.

There followed a series of attempts to persuade Lord Dunsandle to accept
police protection, something he opposed. In the end, this was provided in a
discreet fashion.[43]

Even more free spoken than the *Galway Observer* was the *Tuam News and
Western Advertiser*, the popular paper of north Galway and Mayo. Week after
week during the Land War, it published articles in support of anti-landlord
activity and virulently attacked individuals. It is difficult to judge how much
impact such denunciation had on the local population. For many, they must
have been regarded as something of a sporting good read. A lengthy poem
on landlord hunting entitled 'A hunting we will go' can hardly be taken too
seriously. Of course, as with other newspapers which drew the eye of the
authorities, including *United Ireland*, these local publications were something
of a curate's egg. Within the same edition, a ranting denunciation would be
found alongside the mundane news reports of a country newspaper. While
the authorities were generally more restrained than they have been credited
with, there was a limit. In January 1883, the proprietor of the *Tuam News*,

John MacPhilpin,[44] was convicted under the 1882 Crimes Act of three counts of publishing intimidating and inciting material. For this, he received three sentences, one of one month and two of 14-days' imprisonment. That advanced men were stirred into action by the *Tuam News*' denunciation is, of course, possible and the case of Shawn Beagh comes to mind. On 14 April 1882, the newspaper carried the comment:

> In this very town the fearful spectacle of eviction has been witnessed on the property of that execrable tyrant 'Clanrackrent' by the edict of that cruel shaking, shivering old exterminator, Shawn Beagh, and under the immeadiate super-intendance of the crooked cadaverous sneaking bailiff

Shawn Beagh was land agent to a man named Blake. Shortly after the article appeared in the *Tuam News*, Beagh and his driver were murdered, while his unfortunate wife was shot in the hip.

Another newspaper editor who found himself rounded up under the 1881 coercion act for intimidating and printing threatening notices was Jasper Tully of Boyle, the 23-year-old editor of the *Roscommon Herald* and leading light in the Roscommon Land League.[45] He put Inspector H.B. Lynch to a lot of trouble, first going to ground and ensuring his friends said he had gone to America. Some Land Leaguers claimed Tully had absconded and that, in indignation, they were returning copies of the *Herald*. Two weeks later, however, this was all exposed as a red herring and Lynch had his man. Touchingly, Lynch allowed the young editor to spend a 'last night' in his mother's house with a police presence. She owned the town's Royal Hotel. In the morning, he managed to get his prisoner to the nearby railway station before a crowd of about a thousand assembled. Securing Tully in the second-class waiting room, Lynch decided to miss the first train through, as it was full of travelling harvestmen and he feared trouble. Finally, he installed his prisoner, the future MP for South Leitrim (1892–1906), and the police escort in a second-class compartment and sent him on his way on the 12.20 a.m. to mix with Parnell and associates in Kilmainham Jail.[46]

Generally, though, the Irish press began to see threatening letters as part of their news agenda. They were not slow to comment upon – or indeed, when the reporter could get copy, to reproduce copies of – threatening letters and notices. And it was not just the nationalist press which commented upon and reproduced them. *The Irish Times* was addicted to the phenomenon. Interestingly, the newspaper subeditors had a habit of regularly correcting the

English, probably to make it more legible for their readers. However, as the printing press rooms of Ireland were hot beds of insurgency and advanced nationalist thought, it might equally have been not to show up the poor English of their compatriots. Whatever the reason, these authorised versions largely destroy the regional accents and cultural nuances often contained in such missives.

This reportage spans the Victorian era. Often there was just a short note, as in the *Roscommon and Leitrim Gazette* for Saturday 13 January 1844: 'A Rockite notice has been served on Dean Hawkins, of Dunkerrin, threatening his life'.

Some nationalist newspapers even published boycotting notices. This could be interpreted either as news reporting or spreading the word about whom to boycott, and as such acting as a very public threatening notice.[47]

Printers and printed notices

Beyond the newspapers and equally well known to the police, the printing trade was generally packed with Fenian members and sympathisers who were not slow to use the facilities they operated for the national cause, and sometimes this involved printing threatening notices. This particularly applied to the pay no rent campaigns.[48] But even earlier printed notices popped up now and then, especially in relation to the Molly Maguires. A good example, entitled 'Address of "Molly Maguire," to her children', was from Cloone in County Leitrim in July 1845. Commencing, 'My dear children', it denounced landlords and set out 12 rules to be observed. These included such usual items as: fair rent; no rent until harvest; demanding a rent abatement; and no undermining of tenants. It also included what in the context might be regarded as moderated demands and actions, such as:

- No evictions unless two years' rent due
- Assist a good landlord to get his rent
- 'Cherish and respect' the good landlord and agent
- Do not travel at night
- Do not steal arms: '... from such acts a deal of misfortune springs, having, I trust you have, more Arms than you ever will have need for'
- Avoid contact with the military and police
- Make no distinction on grounds of religion
- 'Let bygones be bygones, unless in a very glaring case; but watch for the time to come'[49]

The first arrest made under the 1870 Peace Preservation (Ireland) Act was of John Mathews, a printer from Dundalk in Louth. As will be seen below, in Kerry, printers were caught red-handed having printed threatening notices in a famous case involving a Tralee newspaper. It is hard not to believe that Bernard Doyle and his presses a 9 Upper Ormond Quay in central Dublin were not doing exactly the same thing. At the turn of the century, they were certainly printing the Irish Transvaal Committee's pro-Boer propaganda posters and leaflets.[50] Superintendent Mallon had no illusions but that the printing presses for even mainline nationalist newspapers were, at times, involved in nefarious goings-on. Writing to the solicitor general, Hugh Holmes (1840–1916), in November 1879, in typical Mallon fashion, he both advised and then cautioned his superior:

> I have to report that there is not the slightest chance of getting the evidence alluded to as A [a query as to obtaining evidence as to who printed or posted a placard]. It is probable that the placards were printed in the Freemans Journal office but of course no inquiry in that direction could be attempted[51]

The solicitor general's comment was a brief, 'Nothing can be done'.

The *Kerry Sentinel* [52]

Thanks to the implementation of several nineteenth-century Irish coercion acts, we have some impression about what an Irish newspaper office was like. The dramatic DMP midnight raid on the night of 15/16 September 1865 on the offices of the *Irish People* in Parliament Street between Dublin City Hall and the River Liffey is a case in point. Then, a generation later, in the town of Tralee, another police raid on newspaper offices also divulged hidden secrets. If *United Ireland* and *The Nation* were the standard by which Dublin Castle judged trouble from the capital's press, then the *Sligo Champion* and the *Kerry Sentinel* were the provincial equivalents.

As can clearly be seen in Figure 28, there was a sudden upsurge in threatening letters reported to the authorities in Kerry in the early 1880s. In 1882, this amounted to 316, slightly less than one a day. This was the highest quantity recorded in any one year in any Irish county in the Victorian era. Clearly the emergence of the Land League and the Land War were key factors. Not only were there the usual tenant-on-tenant threatening letters, as well as letters to landlords of that county, but there was also an additional large number of threatening notices or proclamations, many demanding that tenant farmers cease to pay any rent. What was interesting about these 'pay no rent' notices, which were certainly regarded as threatening by Dublin Castle, was that many were printed. In a county like Kerry, there were a limited number of places where such notices could have been produced. As mentioned above, the printing trade was considered to be 'knee deep in Fenianism'. Not surprisingly, attention was focused on the *Kerry Sentinel*, the new local newspaper which had recently replaced the *Kerry Vindicator*.

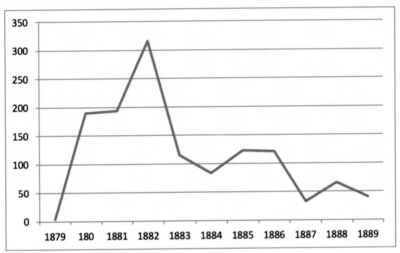

Fig. 28—Threatening letters reported in Kerry, 1879–89

Behind the *Kerry Sentinel* were two able brothers, Edward and Timothy Harrington. Both were fervent Land Leaguers and both later represented the nationalist Irish parliamentary party at Westminster. Timothy, the more famous of the brothers, was a close associate of Parnell. He sat for the equally unsettled county of Westmeath from 1883 until 1885. Then from 1885 until his death in 1910, he represented the Harbour constituency of Dublin. Edward, who edited the *Kerry Sentinel*, represented West Kerry in parliament from 1883 until he was defeated by the anti-Parnellite nationalist Sir Thomas Esmonde in the bitter election of 1892.[53]

The *Kerry Sentinel* was published in Nelson Street [now Ashe Street] in Tralee, a town with a population of under 10,000 people. It was noticed by the police that a number of notices were pasted up around the small town as well as in adjoining small towns such as Castleisland and Brosna. The former was notorious during the Land War. As an RIC tourist guide to Ireland observed succinctly of Castleisland a decade after the Land War, there were 'many agrarian murders committed in vicinity; was anciently a stronghold of the Desmonds'.[54]

One notice posted up around Tralee called on the inhabitants to enrol in the Invincibles, the secret society which had carried out the Phoenix Park murders on 6 May 1882. The notice ran as follows:

To the men of Tralee
Castleisland to the front
To Hell with the Queen

Take notice that we (the men of Tralee) are now ready to form a branch of the Invincibles in this town and any person desirous of connecting himself with it will kindly make every active and secret enquiries at the upper part of Boherbee where weekly meeting and drilling will be carried on. And you must also take notice that any person or persons acting Contrary to the orders of his Superior Officers will as sure as he has breath in his body, meet with a worse death than Lord Cavendish and Burke got, as we intend to make history.
We must remove all Tyrants, Blood for Blood!
Poff and Barrett were unjustly executed by the bloody Government of England and we must have satisfaction.[55]
Death to Landlords, Agents and Bailiffs
By Order of the Tralee Invincibles
God save Ireland from informers.

Some good police work followed. The local magistrate wrote to the under-secretary at Dublin Castle on 31 May 1883:

on examining the document we noticed that certain words, evidently belonging to some letter of Michael Davitt, had been accidentally printed at the head of the notice. We immediately instituted a search in all the recent files of the Kerry Sentinel, as from our knowledge of that paper & the persons employed in the offices, suspicion at once turned toward it.

The print was very faint on the notice where the extraneous material was to be found but with a strong magnifying glass, various words were discernible.

It was then found that the *Kerry Sentinel* of 22 May 1883 contained such words, 'and positions of words, corresponded exactly with the last portion of a letter from Michael Davitt'. In other words, the type from a printing of a copy of the newspaper had not or had not completely been broken up, resulting in the text appearing at the head of the threatening notice. In addition, the typeface used was long primer, which was not to be found in any other office in Tralee, and the notices came off a roller press of a type used only for newspapers. This information was (no doubt enthusiastically) given by the rival *Kerry Weekly Reporter*. The informant also, not surprisingly, requested that the authorities not disclose his name.

The offices and printing presses of the *Kerry Sentinel* were raided on the evening of 23 May 1883 by the police with a warrant issues under the provisions of the Prevention of Crimes Act of 1882. This act had certain catch-all provisions (section 13) which specifically dealt with newspapers:

13. (1) Where after the passing of this Act any newspaper wherever printed is circulated or attempted to be circulated in Ireland, and any copy of such newspaper appears to the Lord Lieutenant to contain matter inciting to the commission of treason or of any act of violence or intimidation, the Lord Lieutenant may order that all copies of such newspapers containing that matter shall, when found in Ireland, be forfeited to Her Majesty, and any constable duly authorised by the Lord Lieutenant may seize the same.
(2.) Where it appears to the Lord Lieutenant that such newspaper was printed and published in Ireland, the order of the Lord Lieutenant shall indicate the part of the newspaper on account of which the order is made, and if the newspaper specifies the office in Ireland at which the newspaper is printed and published, the order shall, as soon as practicable, be served in the prescribed manner at the office so specified.
(3.) Every order of the Lord Lieutenant under this section shall be published in the 'Dublin Gazette,' and shall be laid before Parliament within thirty days if parliament is then sitting, and, if not, within thirty days after the next sitting of parliament.[56]

Two journeymen printers admitted to printing threatening notices and each received a sentence of two months. Several others appealed successfully against their convictions. Edward Harrington and his foreman printer James Brosnan each received six months, without hard labour, though neither were on the premises at the time of the printing. Harrington was regarded as having overall responsibility for what went on in the printing room and indeed of 'having caused to be printed' the notice, and Brosnan was considered to be the man behind and probably the author of the threatening notice. However, Mr Justice W. O'Connor Morris was adamant: 'I confess it would take a great deal of argument to satisfy me that these two boys could have concocted that document, with only one mistake, on the spur of the moment, without a suggestion from a soul, and could have launched it in that way'.

At the appeal, the journeymen printers stated that they had done the printing without the knowledge of Edward Harington, which, as the chief secretary pointed out in parliament, they had not claimed in the original trial. The legality of the printers serving both as witnesses and accused in the initial trial was disputed by Harrington's defence counsel. Be that as it may, it is difficult not to believe that Edward Harrington, the ardent Land Leaguer, editing a newspaper which rivalled *United Ireland* in its outspoken virtuousness, did not know what his printers were up to.

Out of the *Kerry Sentinel* trial came the only account we have by a perpetrator of the posting up of threatening notices. This was given by one of the convicted printers, Robert Fitzgerald. What strikes one is how casual it all was:

> Met Maurice Keane in the street some time after, and he said,
> 'Come and we'll put up the threatening notices,' and I said all right.
> He did not tell me that he'd meet me. He had the notices and the
> paste, and I had nothing. The first place we went was up Nelson-
> street [Ashe Street] and posted two notices in Courthouse-lane, and
> then we went to the railway and posted another there. Maurice
> Keane was the only person with me. Did not ask him anything
> about the notices on Sunday. I think there were only five altogether.

The *Kerry Sentinel* case was a major coup for the authorities. Not only did they secure a conviction, they also embarrassed a newspaper which was one of their most fervent opponents. On top of this, they also got a conviction for the forged Sheehan threatening letter they had discovered among the six large sacks of documents which the constabulary had carried off as a result of the raid.

This forged letter, signed by Mortimer Sheehan, was dated 24 August 1882, so it was nine months old when the RIC raid took place. In itself, it was not a threatening letter as it was a request relating to the provision of threatening notices. It discusses action against Trench, 'the landshark' – 'the wolfe seldom changes his nature' – concerning the issue of arrears of rent and a new rent settlement in the Brosna area. There were, the letter went on, some weak-kneed lads who were not amenable to holding out. The request therefore was that Harrington print some threatening notices 'directing the tenants one and all how they should act which notices I will surreptitiously post up'. Some were to be signed Captain Daylight.

Timothy Harrington, brother of Edward, described as the proprietor of the *Kerry Sentinel*, gave evidence with an air of authenticity and frankness about him

> I received the letter signed 'Mortimer Sheehan.' I simply threw it away in the in the [sic] office and took no further notice
> [of] it. I know Mortimer Sheehan to reside at Brosna and I saw him once or twice; I threw it in the waste paper basket as I did with a lot of my correspondence; I did not think it necessary to give it to the police; I sent no reply to the letter, and so far as I know no notices were ever sent from my office; at the time I saw the letter I thought that it was a forgery, and I think so now too; my brother Edward never saw it ... I get many foolish documents like most newspaper editors; I get very few letters showing that the writers are members of the criminal association; I thought that was a serious criminating letter; that letter looks like a trap to inveigle me into something in reply I might send to it; the letter appeared to assume that threatening letters would be printed in my office; I didn't think it necessary to repudiate ...
> I wish distinctly to state that neither by writing or printing I never in my life had a connection with threatening notices, though I read many, some for condemning outrages in Kerry and threatening my life.

The authorities accepted that Sheehan was not the author of the notice – perhaps because they doubted if he could spell surreptitiously properly, but also because they had, very likely, information from an informer on the subject. They certainly suspected a man named John Riordan and obtained the evidence of the professional expert on hand-writing, John Shaw Peake. Riordan was a relative of Sheehan, but more interesting was that he admitted to John Maxwell, the local magistrate, that 'it was his way of living by "writing for people"'. This would appear to mean that, among other services, John Riordan wrote threatening letters and that he had merely been doing as his relative requested. This might explain why Riordan received the relatively light sentence of eighteen months in jail.

There was also another letter found by Magistrate Maxwell in the newspaper's premises. This unsigned letter was dated 2 September 1881 and discussed a journey the writer had made around Kerry where 'I made the people acquainted to the rules of the Irish National Land League'. There followed a bitter complaint about a land dispute with two brothers also called Sheehan, David and John. The letter concluded, 'I must introduce Capt Moonlight and his men to clear them out'. *The Cork Examiner* of 5 June 1883 commented, perhaps incredulously, that 'It was a remarkable thing that no document appeared to have been carefully destroyed in the office'. This was a lesson that advanced Irish nationalists were to learn the hard way. Ultimately, though, there can be little doubt that the presses of the *Kerry Sentinel* were used and had been used to print notices threatening and otherwise in support of the Land League.[57]

An interesting footnote in the case was the following paragraph which was among documentation published for internal Irish Office circulation in London:

A remarkable feature in the evidence in this case was a letter which was found amongst the documents seized in the office of this paper, signed 'Mortimer Shehan' asking for a supply of threatening notices to be sent to him. This letter was commenced 'Respected Sir,' and appeared to have been addressed to Mr Harrington.[58]

Such activities and, perhaps, over-monitoring, helped create an underlying perception in the mind of Dublin Castle that advanced nationalist newspapers were involved in overt intimidation. Despite pressure for restraint by Dublin Castle, which at times brought the police into conflict with the under-secretary's office, by the time of the plan of campaign, press prosecutions were becoming frequent. Under the provision of the Criminal Law and Procedure Act of 1887, in the 27 months between October 1887 and December 1889, 20 newspaper prosecutions were brought against 14 different newspapers. These were:

Carlow Nationalist and Leinster Times
Cork Daily Herald
The Cork Examiner
Kerry Sentinel (x3)

Leinster Leader
Limerick Leader
Midland Tribune
Munster Express (x2)
The Nation
Sligo Champion (x2)
Tipperary Nationalist (x3)
Tipperary Sentinel
Waterford News
Wexford People

Though all were convicted, three, the *Leinster Leader*, *Munster Express* and *Wexford News*, each had its conviction quashed on appeal.[59]

Ironically, a number of newspaper proprietors were magistrates. These included William Baird (*Belfast Evening Telegraph*), John Robinson (Dublin *Daily Express*), and Edmond Woods (*Clonmel Chronicle*), who were all conservative in outlook, as well as others such as Jerome Counihan (*Munster News*) and Maurice Lenihan (*Limerick Reporter and Tipperary Vindicator*) who were not.[60]

Irish World

A note needs to be added concerning the New York-based *Irish World*, which had a reputation in Dublin Castle and unionist circles for irresponsible and dangerous extreme language. Of course, being printed in America, the RIC could not interfere with its publication, although its distribution in Ireland was vulnerable. A worthwhile study would be a comparison between the *Irish World* and *United Ireland*.

On the other hand, Arnold Forster, the son of the former chief secretary of Ireland, 'Buckshot' Forster, viewed matters in a slightly different light from many of his contemporaries. Writing in 1883, in his famous pamphlet 'The truth about the Land League. Its leaders and its teaching', Forster comments:

> It should be stated in justice to the Irish World that the greater
> proportion of the objectionable matter which it contains as
> connected with Irish subjects, and usually furnished by contributors
> on this side of the Atlantic. Much of what appears in the paper on
> other topics is comparatively moderate; and unlike the contributions
> to United Ireland mentioned in following chapters, is often very
> ably written.[61]

Whether Forster would regard the following from the *Irish World* edition of 23 December 1876 as 'ably written' or 'comparatively moderate' is uncertain:

> One very great mistake our suffering countrymen make in dealing with the petty tyrants of Ireland is that of sending 'threatening letters' to the heartless fiends. Stop that practice, friends! When a petty tyrant plays fantastic pranks upon a peaceful tenant, instead of alarming the tyrant by sending a threatening letter through the mail, it should be wrapped around a bullet – and aim low.[62]

Notes

[1] For an interesting article on town tenant protest, see Moran, 'The Land War, urban destitution and town tenant protest, 1879–1882', *Saothar*, 1995, 20, pp. 17–31.

[2] NAI, CSORP 1852, 3/705/27.

[3] NLI, Larcom papers, Ms 7519; Doherty, *The Irish ordnance survey*, p. 17.

[4] TNA, Kew, MEPO 3/2767, Special Branch letter book, May 1893.

[5] Malony, *The Phoenix Park murders*, p. 87.

[6] NAI, Crime Branch Special, box 16, s/20246, 24 October 1899.

[7] NAI, Crime Branch Special, s/23187, 17 October 1899.

[8] NAI, Crime Branch Special, (McAteer file), s/23178, February–April 1900.

[9] NAI, Crime Branch Special, s/20393, n.d. (27 October 1899).

[10] Townshend, *Political violence in Ireland*, p. 176.

[11] McCracken, 'The imperial British newspaper, with special reference to South Africa, India and the 'Irish model', *Critical Arts*, vol. 29, no.1, 2015, pp. 5–25.

[12] NAI, CSORP Outrage papers, 1851, box 1196, 3/705/20.

[13] NAI, CSORP outrage reports, Tipperary, 1845/1846, 3/704/29.

[14] NAI, CSORP outrage reports, Meath, 1846, 3/704/29.

[15] NAI, CSORP outrage reports, Tipperary, 1846, 3/704/30.

[16] NAI, CSORP 1883, box 2875, 3/641/14.

[17] TNA, CO 903/2.

[18] NAI, Crime Branch Special, carton 5, 1889.

[19] McCracken, *Inspector Mallon*, Dublin, 2009.

[20] Bence-Jones, *Twilight of the ascendency*, pp. 110–13.

[21] Dublin *Daily Express*, 1 December 1880 and Marlow, *Captain Boycott and the Irish*, p. 218.

[22] *A verbatim copy of the Parnell Commission report with complete index and notes*, Irish Loyal and Patriotic Union, London and Dublin, 1890, pp. 54–8 and 78; *Special Commission Act*, p. 115.

[23] *Report from the select committee on outrages (Ireland)*, 1852, pp. 9 and 23.

[24] NAI, CSO RP, 1884, 3/644/28.

[25] NLI, Joseph McCarrity papers, Ms 17 574, threatening letter to Lord Londonderry, posted 10 February 1889.

[26] NAI, CSORP 1881, 3/638/4.

[27] NAI, CSORP 1886, 4295c, 3/646/35.

[28] See, for example, 'Dublin Castle and the press: Under Secretary's warning', NLI, Anderson, ILB 300, p. 11.

[29] These include such books as Dungan, *Mr Parnell's Rottweiler*; Larkin, *Terror and discord: The Shemus cartoons in the Freeman's Journal, 1920–1924*; O'Brien, *The Irish Times, A history*; Potter, *Newspapers and empire in Ireland and Britain*; Rafter (ed.), *Irish journalism before independence*.

[30] Dungan, 'Mr Parnell's rottweiler' in Travers and McCartney (eds), *Parnell reconsidered*, p. 107.

[31] See, for example, *Armagh Guardian*, 29 July 1845; *The Irish Times*, 11 March 1870.

[32] Unpublished research paper by Donal P. McCracken, 'Freedom of the press in Victorian Ireland', International Association for Media and Communication Research conference, Dublin City University, 2013.

[33] See, for example, NAI, Crime Branch special, report on the *Irish Republic* s/13989, 4 August 1897; report on the *Workers' Republic*, s/17376, 7 October 1898.

[34] See, for example, Mallon's cuttings from *The Freeman's Journal* and the *Irish Daily Independent* on the funeral of William Rooney, NAI, Crime Branch Special, s/24651, 7 May 1901

[35] Newspapers received at Dublin Castle, 1887–1893, NAI, Chief Secretary's Office, ICR 7 (location 3/754).

[36] O'Brien, *Evening memories*, p. 2.

[37] Ibid., p. 90.

[38] *United Ireland* coloured cartoon dated 4 July 1885.

[39] O'Brien, *Evening memories*, p. 352.

[40] TNA, CO 903/2.

[41] O'Brien, *Parnell and his party*, p. 213.

[42] *Galway Observer*, 31 May 1884.

[43] NAI, CSO RP, 1884, 3/644/26, file 20403.

[44] The RIC report gives the name as Macpherson.

[45] NAI, CSORP 1881, 3/638/4. The Tully family owned the *Roscommon Herald*.

[46] Wheatley, *Nationalism and the Irish party*, pp. 99–100.

[47] *Hansard*, House of Commons, Arthur Balfour, 28 March 1887.

[48] An example is mentioned in the PRONI, Verner papers, D236/488/2, James Crossle to Lady Verner, letter book, p. 404, 26 January 1882.

[49] NAI, CSO RP, 3/704/28, Outrage papers, Leitrim, 16/617, January 1846.

[50] NAI, Crime Branch Special, s/20142, 16 October 1899.

[51] NAI, CSORP 1879, 20696, 26 November 1879, 3/636,21.

[52] NAI, Police and Crime, Crimes Act 1882, carton 6, 3/714/5 containing: *Cork Examiner*, 5 & 6 June and 10 & 11 July 1883; *Kerry Sentinel*, 22 May 1883; *The Times*, 31 July 1883.

[53] Walker (ed.), *Parliamentary election results in Ireland*, p. 146.

[54] Dagg, *Devia Hibernia: The road and route guide for Ireland of the Royal Irish Constabulary*, p. 91.

[55] Sylvester Poff and James Barrett were hanged on 23 January 1883 for the murder of Thomas Browne.

[56] *Prevention of Crime (Ireland) Act, 1882*, 45 & 46 Vict., Ch. 25, section 14, p. 8.

57 The author was once told by Arthur Griffith's son, Nevin, that his father kept very few papers because of the threat of a raid by the British authorities.
58 TNA, CO 903/2.
59 TNA, CO903/1, Press prosecutions.
60 http://irish.victorianperiodicals.com/series3/index.asp (accessed 6 January 2017); *Commission of the Peace (Ireland)*, pp. 117, 119, 124–5 and 128. See also, Irwin, 'Maurice Lenihan', *Dictionary of Irish Biography*, vol. 5, pp. 448–9.
61 Forster, *The truth about the Land League*, p. 40.
62 Quoted in 'Prester John', 'Terrorism in Ireland', p. 393.

Section 2

ANSWERING THE MAIL

6. Landlords and land agents in the firing line

Practically the whole of rural Irish society was drawn into the phenomenon of threatening letters and notices. Table 7 identifies 18 categories of occupation which were the most affected by the threatening letter and notice phenomenon.

The perpetrators, however, were confined to a fairly narrow social base centred on the small tenant farmer. The largest numbers of threatening letters were mainly sent by just four groups: tenant farmers, sons of tenant farmers, subtenants and labourers. Seventeen categories can be identified as recipients of threatening letters and notices, including tenant farmers, subtenants and labourers, but excluding sons of tenant farmers, the only one of the 18 categories for whom no evidence has emerged of their being recipients of threatening letters and notices.

Several categories have been omitted from the list, such as threatening letters sent to the Royal Irish Constabulary (RIC); sectarian threatening letters; threatening letters centred on parliamentary party politics; rural secret societies; and members of the Irish Republican Brotherhood (IRB) or Fenians operating in a rural context. With the sole exception of the ubiquitous rural secret societies, none of these groups was prominently involved in the threatening-letter phenomenon.

The police did occasionally receive threatening letters, but these were occasional rather than regular. There is an anomaly relating to the RIC and the various political and quasi-political struggles in nineteenth-century Ireland. The Irish Constabulary was not particularly liked in the pre-Fenian era but was accepted and tolerated, if grudgingly. To an extent, this changed later; yet, despite the RIC presence at emotive eviction scenes, the Irish police forces retained a tacit support from moderate Irish nationalists. This was no doubt mainly based on the pragmatic sense that without them there would be English military rule and even that once Home Rule was granted, the police would be needed to keep the wild men in check. Whatever the reason, the RIC was not the subject of a sustained threatening-letter campaign.

Sectarian threatening letters were sent, more particularly in the earlier part

Table 7–Senders and recipients of threatening letters and notices

Category	Sender	Recipient	Notes
Landlord and family members		X	
Land agent and family members		X	
Employees in domestic service or on a domain farm of landlords and land agents		X	
Large farmers		X	
Tenant farmers	X	X	
Landless sons of tenant farmers	X		
Middlemen		X	Mostly pre-Famine
Subtenants	X	X	Such as conacre plot occupants, mostly pre-1860s
Tenant occupiers of land vacated due to eviction or 'forced emigration'		X	'Land-grabbers' fall into this category
Graziers/herders		X	Letters sent to their employer demanding their dismissal
Agricultural labourers	X	X	Letters sent between labourers and from labourers to their employers demanding the dismissal of fellow labourers
The number of agricultural labourers declined as the century progressed.			
Credit providers to the agricultural sector		X	Often market town-based, including shopkeepers and moneylenders (gombeenmen)
Retailers, usually boycotted		X	
Auctioneers		X	Market town-based, sometimes acting as land agents
Assize and petty session judges		X	
Magistrates		X	
Bailiffs and summons' officers		X	
Emergency men		X	
Totals	4	17	

of the nineteenth century than the latter. An 1842 threatening letter held by the National Library of Ireland was included in a project to sum up Irish history in '100 objects'. It runs:

> If you do not leave your situation against Saturday, the 3 of July you shall have a visit from Captain Rock.
> We would wait on your father the blody orange man but he is two old but we are determined to visit you and if you do not leave Look to the bottom of this letter [drawing of a skull and crossbones and coffin] we will at some time to Larkum threatening him with the same fruit
> You have till the 3
> to save your life
> Capt Rock
> Rockhall[1]

As the century progressed, sectarian threatening letters in the rural context tended to be a cover or closely associated with a more mundane land-owning dispute. Playing the religion card was an easy ploy in the game of land possession.

The Irish land agent

It might seem strange to discuss the category of land agent before that of landlord, but the truth of the matter was that the Irish land agent took the brunt of agrarian agitation aimed at the landed classes. There were also, certainly in the earlier part of the century, often middlemen who sublet to under-tenants and who were frequently drawn into conflicts with tenants, receiving their own fair share of threatening letters.

The *Daily News* journalist Bernard Becker, when he visited Ireland in early 1880, noted:

> Personally I must confess that I am favourably disposed towards the much vilified agents. They are in many respects the most manly men in Ireland. Nearly always well-bred, they excite sympathy by the position they hold between the upper and nether millstone of landlord and tenant. Perhaps they have made a good thing of it, but if so they have earned it, for their position always reminds one of that assigned to Lord Macauley to the officers of the East India Company, such as Clive and Warren Hasting. To these founders of

our Eastern Empire 'John Company' said, 'Respect treaties; keep faith with the native rulers; do not oppress the people; but send us the money' ... for the last quarter of a century, since the younger sons of Irish families took to land agency as a profession because there seemed nothing else in Ireland for them to do. Nevertheless they are hideously unpopular.[2]

Stories were told in Ireland of how when certain land agents or indeed landlords died, be it from natural causes or having been murdered, bonfires were lit on the hillsides around by the rejoicing peasantry. This certainly happened at Strokestown and at Carrickmacross and the fact that these were isolated occasions symptomatic of local circumstances is neither here nor there. Despite a generation of research and publication by professional historians and serious journalists, the popular image of the Irish Victorian landlord and land agent has not fundamentally changed in 200 years: they are still seen as a bad lot.

Threatening letters were often the harbinger of more serious criminal agrarian unrest and activity. Often the danger came out of the blue. In the 1880s, the Irish Patriotic and Loyalist Union (IPLU) was not too far off the mark when it claimed that outrage tended to follow the establishment of a branch of the Land League. The landed classes might be targets for a range of reasons from a standing grudge to eviction of tenants. Murder was usually justified by circulating stories, frequently without foundation, to justify the action. In Trollope's *The Land Leaguers*, Philip Jones's experience was fairly typical of a landlord destined to be boycotted and victimised:

'Twelve months ago I thought there was not a man about the place who would raise his hand to do me an ill turn. I have done them [the tenants] many good turns in my time.'
'You have father,' said Ada.
'Then this man came to me and said that because the tenants away in County Mayo were not paying their rents, he could not pay his. And he can sell his interest on his holding now for £150. When I endeavoured to explain this to him, and that it was at my cost his interest in the farm had been created, he became my enemy.'[3]

In the saga of the Irish threatening letter and notice, the land agent and landlords, along with under-agents and stewards, might be expected to shoulder the brunt of this form of retaliation against 'oppression and exploitation'. As Thomas Murray, land agent at Edenderry in King's County, recounted, there is hardly a day I don't get a coffin or deaths head to me'.[4] However, the reality was, as already pointed out, that the bulk of anonymous threatening letters were delivered class-on-class, or within a section of classes below that of the proprietor property zone. This is not to deny that the ruling agricultural elite, absentee or not, and their functionaries received their fair share of threatening letters and a steady number were murdered and suffered from assault with intention to murder. But reality and perception did not always coincide.

The 1861 census in Ireland gives the number of landed proprietors as 5,789. In addition, it lists 550 land agents, 2,314 land stewards and 413,309 farmers.[5] The dividing line between the land agent and the land steward was frequently crossed. Land agents were usually Irish, though some were Scots and a few English. Being Irish was a great advantage in their work because while of a different class from the tenants and labourers, they understood Irish society better despite the image of continuous confrontation. More often than not, land agents charmed, cajoled, persuaded or, thanks to small compromises such as supplying an iron gate or material to mend a roof, extracted some rent from any truculent tenant farmer down on his luck.

Being a land agent was not an easy life. It was stressful and at times dangerous. Some land agents were minor gentry or substantial farmers in their own right with their own tenants or labourers. They were often aware of the need to increase productivity by improving land, such as by clearing stones and rocks, draining extensively and constructing roads to make places more accessible. They often also tried to rid the countryside of the ubiquitous cabin and replace it with solid stone structures, sometimes reinforced by concrete, although these attempts were frequently thwarted by the occupants. The irony is that these men were entrepreneurs who changed rural Ireland very much for the benefit of those who allegedly hated them. Tenants, however, were often conservative and showed little interest in anything which smacked of more modern agricultural farming practices. Indeed, such efforts by Jonathan Darby of Leap earned him a threatening letter warning him he would end up 'in a coffin' if he continued to push his new farming methods.[6]

Land agents were also often magistrates, making up 9 per cent of all magistrates in 1884 or some 448.[7] In 1861, about 20 per cent of Irish land agents in Ireland were Catholic. They were usually paid on commission, receiving 5 per cent of rents collected. This distanced them from the ascendancy milieu but made it easier for them to soldier on in a pragmatic fashion in what was sometimes a seemingly impossible position. That said, the Irish land agent held a higher status than his equivalent in English society. More often than not, the agent did retain the eccentricity, the mannerisms, the accent and the characteristic of behavioural excess which were hallmarks of the ascendancy. Frequently, they were men of great character and, according to several references, often jovial. While personality and flexibility might count for a great deal when handling such a job, an agent who did not carry an air of authority was not going to last long against a conservative peasantry and it would also have helped them to deal with those above them in society. Aloofness, arrogance and bullying were characteristics likely to gain a hostile response from tenants, so a combination of firmness, courtesy and pragmatism was the best approach for most land agents. Samuel Hussey makes the legitimate point that as it became more difficult to collect rents, 'more competent men of experience and judgement were needed by the landlord'. As such, the occupation became more professional – like a branch of the Engineering Surveyors' Institution – an irony given the fact that land purchase at the turn of the century destroyed the profession and the livelihood of the Irish land agent.[8]

Sacking a land agent was a dangerous move on the part of any landlord, for the former knew the goings-on, the intricacies and contradictions of life on the estate – who was stubborn, who was lazy and who was down because of misfortune. In 1844, it was said of one tenant on the Annesley estate near Castlewellan in County Down, 'old McC[racken], like many of his class, was quite immoveable and would do nothing but *talk*'.[9] A land agent had to be able to talk too, but equally had to know instinctively how far matters could be pressed before action was taken. This, of course, frequently left the land agent sandwiched between tenant and landlord. This problem was intensified with many estates in debt.

The Irish land agent bore the brunt of the abuse levelled at the landed property class, and if there was a breath of fraudulent mismanagement, the threatening letters came in thick and fast.[10] Robert Nugent, the long-serving land agent of Rev. Henry King (1799–1857) of the Ferbane estate in King's County, received many threatening letters and was denounced to his employer in what today would be termed whistle-blowing. Generally, of course, a land agent did occasionally fall foul of the law,[11] while the landlord might at times be perceived in the popular mind to have been misled by the Iago-type figure who ran his estate or estates. In the early 1830s, the following notice was posted on a gate near Slane:

This is a caution to the Baron [Hussey] not to continue any longer in his English practice of pounding cattle and charging trespass to the great annoyance of his poor tenantry but the Baron is not entirely to blame, but the set of villains he keeps about him – the first is Cooper Carney who was banished from Louth, who was a stag and got many an innocent man hung at Wildgoose Lodge ...[12]

In fact, the landlord might well be far more devious than the land agent, pushing off onto his employee the unpleasant task of raising as much revenue as possible from a poor or sometimes impoverished tenantry. As a result, *in extremis*, there were often cases of the messenger, literally, being shot.

The three most hated land agents
Three Irish land agents in particular have become famous in history. William Steuart Trench (1808–1872) wrote *Realities of Irish life*, which came out in 1868. Samuel Murray Hussey (1824–1913) produced *The reminiscences of an Irish land agent* a generation later in 1904. The latter was, in fact, a compilation by Home Gordon of Hussey's earlier writings. Both volumes are well written with the occasional instance of dry humour, but they are not always accurate and are somewhat hotchpotch, especially in the case of Hussey who has a tendency to rant at times about his particular *bêtes noirs*. Hussey was a grander figure than Trench and this comes out in his *bons mots* style, which speaks of the gentry class, whereas Trench's tales speak of a man closer to the ground and with a sharpness absent in the urbane Hussey. In this respect, Hussey was more in the league of William Blacker (1776–1850) a generation earlier, who was essentially northern-based and whose publications on agricultural improvements won him a gold medal from the Royal Dublin Society and membership of the Royal Irish Academy.[13]

Trench had experience as a land agent on four substantial estates: the Shirley estate in County Monaghan (1841–5); the Lansdowne estate in County Kerry (1845–50); the Bath estate in County Monaghan (1850–1); and the Digby estate in King's County (1857–72). Gerard Lyne, who gives a very balanced appraisal of Trench in the *Dictionary of Irish Biography*, also noted, 'He is loathed equally in the folklore of Monaghan and Kerry, while his grave at Donaghmoyne, near Carrickmacross, Co. Monaghan, has been repeatedly vandalised'.[14]

Another Trench of the time was no less unpopular. Dr Mark Ryan recalled how when Captain William Le Poer Trench took on Captain J.P. Nolan in the 1872 County Galway parliamentary contest, an anonymous ballad of the time contained the following verse:

There's grace in the pulpit,
There's wit on the bench,
But there's nothing but dirt
To be found in a Trench.[15]

The contradictions in William Steuart Trench's life – the harshness versus the progressive attempts at modernisation – are themes of much of nineteenth-century rural Ireland. Monoculture, subdivision, population growth and squatting by paupers created an impossible situation for any land agent in many areas. He was caught in the middle between landlord (absent or not) and a peasantry, sections of which were disgruntled. Anyone with a grievance or a grudge had little hesitation in threatening the land agent, who, in turn, had little choice but to endure threatening letters. Trench was accurate enough when he wrote in the late 1860s:

> I have known frequent instances of landlords receiving threatening notices for evicting tenants, although these tenants had refused to pay any rent whatever, and of tenants receiving similar notices for taking the land of the evicted occupiers. I have also seen a notice, announcing certain death to a respectable farmer, because he dismissed a careless ploughman; and a friend who lived near me was threatened with death, because he refused to hire a shepherd who had been recommended to him, and who was supposed to be approved of by the local Ribbon Lodge. I myself received a letter, with death's head and cross bones, threatening the most frightful consequences to myself and family, if I did not continue to employ a young profligate carpenter, whom I had discharged for idleness and vice![16]

Trench's policy of providing free passage to America for those tenants in destitution was severely criticised as a form of land clearance which, in a way, it was. Equally, though, it provided some hope for the young and the adventurous who left.

Samuel Hussey was perhaps the most famous land agent in the United Kingdom, and also said to be 'the most abused'. Not only was he agent to various Irish estates, including the Colthurst estate at Ballyvourney and the Kenmare estates, but, for a time, he also ran a land agency administering, it is said, no fewer than 88 estates.[17] From 1866, he lived in a substantial residence called Edenburn, with a 100-acre demesne and arboretum, near

Tralee and Castleisland. Hussey freely admitted, 'mere threatening letters count for nothing. I have had over one hundred in my time, yet I'll die in my bed for all that'. As it happened, he was correct. What was significant about Hussey was that he was not afraid of the opposition. The famous incidents of his ordering the burning of empty houses from which tenants had been evicted, to prevent reoccupation, was portrayed as a scorched-earth policy. In fact, Hussey was merely playing the opposition at their own game and many was the empty house burnt by the moonlighters to prevent occupation by land-grabbers.

Be this as it may, Hussey had a bad reputation and in the early hours of 28 November 1884, a bomb exploded at the back of his home at Edenburn. Though 16 people, including three RIC constables were in the house, no one was injured.[18] Four years earlier, a dynamite attack had been made on the Galway home of the Strokestown land agent John Ross Mahon. It, too, failed in its purpose.[19]

The third famous Irish land agent is the hapless and somewhat limited Captain Charles Cunningham Boycott, who *Vanity Fair* summed up as 'a just man, if a trifle obstinate and imperious'.[20] Unlike Trench and Hussey, Boycott showed no interest in publishing a biography. He found himself the victim of circumstances and he clearly found the whole boycott episode an irritation and inconvenience. Joyce Marlow has commented, 'one thing of which Boycott could not be accused was verbal excess'.[21] He neither requested nor encouraged the recruitment of the Ulster contingent of workers who arrived as his saviours.

Despite his later infamy, at the time, Boycott was not looked upon by most as being particularly evil, in the same way Trench and other land agents were. Ironically, unlike Trench or Hussey, Boycott was not an Irishman.

Boycott's troubles at Lough Mask House, near Ballinrobe, began on 1 August 1879, when a threatening notice was attached to the iron gates of the entrance. This, complete with a sketch of a coffin, warned Boycott to give a reduction of 20 to 25 per cent in rents.[22] There followed an 'escritoire' full of threatening letters, one of which is quoted in Marlow's life of Boycott:

Sir, –You have caused a great deal of disturbance in the County Mayo this last five months about your crops. Sir, you need not give yourself any trouble about the affairs of this world, for if you had all the police and soldiers in Her Majesty's Government you shall fail, you will not have protection at hand at all times to call on. You need not leave Ireland to go to London. There is too many of your countrymen there. The best thing you can do is to pray for your soul for there is no mercy in this side of the grave for you. I main to let you know that their is one of the Leitrim heros on the banks of the Tyne, and I hope in Providence that him and me will have happiness of seeing you some time, and will put a crop in the ground that will yield no fruit. None of us is belongs to the weast of Ireland. We belong to the north of Ireland, but we don't like tirney. So no more at present.

RORY OF THE HILLS.

The letter also had a drawing of a coffin with the following words written in it: 'Here lies the body of the tirant Captain Boycott'.[23]

The Parnell Commission of 1888 also quoted a threatening notice directed at Captain Boycott, which incongruously concluded, 'I have heard in my travel that Lord Erne [whose land agent Boycott was] is about one of the best landlords in Ireland'.[24]

Anthony Trollope, after his visits to Ireland at the height of the Land War, wrote that boycotting had:

become an exact science, and was exactly obeyed. It must be acknowledged that throughout the south and west of Ireland the quickness and perfection with which this science was understood and practiced was very much to the credit of the intelligence of the people.[25]

Boycotting, of course, affected more than the targeted person. In many instances, it cost his servants and labourers their jobs and livelihoods in the same manner that many people were put out of work when the big houses of the Anglo-Irish were burnt in Ireland in the early 1920s. In the Captain Boycott instances, the servants and labourers left early on in the dispute, whether under coercion or willingly is not clear. On the other hand, some employees did hold out longer; for example, the herdsman at Kilmaine, a farm Boycott rented, left his position only after having received threatening letters.[26]

Some Irish land agents were tough enough, but many were genuinely shocked at what was happening on their patch. One such agent in Monaghan, during the Land War, recorded:

We had a very unpleasant business here. We ejected a tenant some months ago. Another tenant took the farm. A threatening notice was posted on the premises and a threatening letter sent to the new tenant but he did not mind them. Yesterday morning when we went to Chapel he found a gravestone he had placed over his father and mother maliciously broken to pieces. His family have resided upon the property for generations and are very respectable quiet people. They are all Roman Catholics. Jammie [Crossle] has had the police here today but I fear they won't find out anything. It is apparently a trifling matter but a bad thing to commence upon the estate.[27]

The Irish landlords

The bloody European retreat from empire in the second half of the twentieth century frequently painted a similar picture, especially in Africa. In reality, the situation was not dramatically different from that in parts of Ireland in the early 1880s. Samuel Hussey was by no means unique when he admitted:

I never travelled without a revolver, and occasionally was accompanied by a Winchester rifle. I used to place my revolver as regularly beside my fork on the dinner-table, either in my own or in anybody else's house, as I spread my napkin on my knees.

Hussey also recounted that once in Tralee, he escaped attack by the simple device of waving his revolver out of his carriage window.[28]

Illustrations appeared in the *Illustrated London News* of landlords with shotguns or rifles under their arms attended by RIC men, by loyal retainers or by the dreaded Emergency men. This hysteria was produced by a mixture of the impact of threatening letters and notices, together with press reports of assaults and the occasional murder of landlords and their land agents and bailiffs. In the most disturbed parts of Ireland, all these also reinforced an atmosphere combining colonialism with the excitement of the nonconformity and danger (real or imaginary) of frontier society – which, it has to be said, well suited the Anglo-Irish mentality. As will be seen, in the 1880s, a threatening letter arriving at the big house invariably led to police involvement in one form or another. Most notably constables may have been stationed on the premises or in the famous police huts which were strategically erected nearby, often at crossroads.

The combination of a public display of formidable firearms (frequently double-barrelled), deterred all but the most daring or the foolhardy, not least because the Irish landed classes were no strangers to the effective use of guns.

They had shot snipe for many years on the boglands and a great deal had seen military duty in the British or Indian armies, or at the very least, in an Irish militia corps. They understood how guns should be maintained and they knew how guns were used, something that their opponents recognised. The Irish landed class also had access to the new revolutionised generation of firearms from the late 1850s onwards, unlike their opponents who too often had to rely on the blunderbuss and the flintlock.

Gun-ownership legislation was, in times of coercion, generally tight, however. In October 1880, one journalist recorded:

> Since the expiration of the Peace Preservation Act the purchase of firearms has been incessant. At the stores in Westport, where carbines are sold, more have been disposed of in the last five months than in the previous ten years, and revolvers are also in great demand. The favourite weapon of the peasantry, on account of its low price and other good qualities, is the old Enfield rifle bought out of the Government stores, shortened and rebored to get rid of the rifling.[29]

Occasionally, the landlord or land agent got the better of an ambush and managed to kill the would-be assassin. The son of the marquis of Sligo's agent returned fire when he and his father were attacked and killed the attacker. As things were rarely simple in rural Ireland, this was invariably greeted with general approval by the tenantry on the grounds that it had been a fair fight and the best man had won. Such Irish idiosyncrasies were frequently lost on the British press.

A landlord's duty

Though the Anglo-Irish were to become famed for their literary endeavours, there are surprisingly few readable Victorian Irish landlord memoirs. Perhaps the most quoted is that of William Bence Jones, who was born in England but was not an absentee landlord; he lived on his estate Lisselan in County Cork for 37 years, during which time he attempted to introduce new farming practices. He had graduated from Oxford and became a lawyer. He fell foul of the Land League and was boycotted, but showed more spirit in opposing them than Captain Boycott had done. In 1880, in London, Macmillan published his rather sadly named biography, *The life's work in Ireland of a landlord who tried to do his duty*; it was largely an anthology of magazine articles he had previously published. Historians have tended to focus on his

154

indiscreet and ridiculous sweeping statements regarding the supposed Irish character, written perhaps late in the evening when some whiskey had been taken and a deadline loomed. These included 'Drink, indolence, debt, and scheming, with ignorance and want of self-reliance as consequences'.[30] Despite such rants, the book is a good source on landlord attitudes in the troubled parts of the country at the time.

An example of a threatening letter to a landlord in the early 1850s was that written to Meredith Chambré, magistrate of Killeavy, County Armagh:

> To all this concerns, and Beware of General Avenger. I am not Fools. I am giving you timely warning, all Tyants and oppressors of the Poor. Its like the Thief of the Gallows, its over you particular landlords, particularly in the seed time, if they don't give their tenants Seed Oats to put in their land, and lower their rents, it will be measured with their corpse. And their is Mr Chambrie, a Beggarman, he had better keep close, for if he does not, he may have his coffin ready; but we will bury him when he will neither have coffin or shroud around him, for its too Good for an oppressor of the Poor, as an idle-hearted rascal; besides, who prides in the downfall of his country men, we need not wonder – he is no Irishman ... I am General Vengence.[31]

Interestingly, this letter changes from the first person to the third, implying perhaps more than one author, or at least a gap in times between the writing of the first section and the second. The preface to Bence Jones' book contains the following:

> Threatening notices were also stuck up about the town of Clonakilty, denouncing all sorts of injuries to any of my tenants who paid more than Griffith's valuation ... These threatening notices, I am told, are all written by a shoemaker ... The 7th [December 1880] was my rent-day. Some men posted themselves in the ruins of an old house, a mile off (not on my land), and, as any tenant came near, ran out and thrust before his eyes a threatening notice ... From first to last the whole thing was intimidation practised by the Land League, and fear on the part of the tenants.[32]

But for all his defiance against the Land League, 'the maverick' Bence Jones took his family away from Ireland in 1881, and died in London the following June.[33]

Informers

One of the most successful informers the police had was connected to the Kenmare estate in Kerry. The pleasantly spoken 5th earl of Kenmare, though a Catholic and, for lengthy periods, residential on his extensive Kerry estate, was not immune to receiving threatening notices and letters. As *Vanity Fair* put it, 'He voted [in the British parliament] for the Disturbance Bill, and received the gratitude of his tenants in the shape of a refusal to pay rent'.[34] The truth was that Kenmare behaved not so differently from his Protestant neighbours in the manner he treated his estate. Improving the estate was regarded with little, if any, excitement by many tenants. However, the earl's religion was by no means a negative factor and on one occasion, a protest march was held through the town of Kenmare by tenants protesting against threatening letters the earl had received. The irony of this situation is that the earl of Kenmare was much more part of the English establishment, being a member of several of Gladstone's governments, than were many Anglo-Irish Protestant landlords who felt the full weight of the peasant revolt.

The informer to the authorities of goings-on on the Kenmare estate was Mary Sullivan. In 1889, she was awarded £60, a very large sum for an Irish informer, on the basis of information she provided to help combat the Plan of Campaign and boycotting on the estate.[35]

Another woman informer was the wife of a prominent Land Leaguer at Ballyduff. She helped bring to book, albeit via the 1881 coercion act, a farmer's 26-year-old son, Martin Sullivan, for writing the following threatening notice, posted up on the village chapel door during mass on 13 May 1881:

Men of Ballyduff you ought to be ashamed of yourselves for
allowing Edward Herbert [process server] to get on as he is, for he is
a disgrace to this country, for he is foremost in every dirty job for
the Landlords: Let no man woman or child speak to him, or deal
with him, let the Landlords support him as he is mean enough to be
doing their work, let him be fully Boycotted, and you D. carroll is
requested to shun him, and not to work any more for him, and also
shun Wm Flaherty the Landgrabber, be sure dont to work for him,
and you Houlihan keep out of Flagherty's house, and let all
concerned in this notice be fully aware, that the Ballyduff boys will
keep their eye on them, we have plenty of ammunition as good a
any Buckshot.
Honest Rory[36]

Stopping the hunt

If you wanted to annoy the Anglo-Irish, you interfered with their hunting. It was a clever if petty manoeuvre on the part of the Land Leaguers. Attempts, often successful, to disrupt hunts, especially in Connaught in the 1880s and indeed into the 1890s, were invariably associated with threatening notices nailed to trees or attached to gateposts. Actions to disrupt hunting were as much acts of intimidation as the occasional standoff confrontation which received much publicity. More sinister were anonymous threats to set poison in fox coverts or in hounds' kennels. This campaign had nothing to do with any moral objection to fox hunting (the Land League organised its own hunts) but was part of the wider campaign to make life as unpleasant as possible for landlords and their class.[37]

A St Stephen's Day hunt meeting of the Galway Blazers was held at the Kilcornan demesne. At the gates of the estate, which was blocked with rocks, a crowd of about 500 people had gathered and on the gate itself was attached a notice which read:

> I hereby give notice to Mr Persee and all the club gentry not to dare venture Kilcornan woods to chase Reynard [the fox], because the country at large is appointed to stop ye all. N.B. We are fully determined to deprive ye of rents and pleasure from henceforth, Hurrah for Parnell and the Land League. We are all united.

The reference to Mr Persee was to Burton Persee of Moyode Castle whence the hounds and huntsmen had come. Persee later received a letter part of which read:

> Honoured Sir, take notice that all the coverts are to be poisoned ... If you run the risk your hounds will be destroyed, as there is as much deadly poison bought for them as would poison all the justices of the peace and hounds in the Co. Galway.[38]

Such threats could be effective. Also out in the far west, the redoubtable Dick Stacpoole was galvanised after his dog-feeder at Edenvale had been 'warned' to fear for his life if he gave the hounds 'bite and sup'. Stacpoole approached the Clare Harriers Hunt Club to buy the pack from him. They declined the offer, 'So the hounds go to England to be sold, and the eviction – of landlords – goes merrily on'.[39] When the American W.H. Hurlbert was in the Kildare Street Club in Dublin, though, he encountered the bravado among the members when the topic of the Land League campaign against hunting was raised:

> They were poisoned, whole packs of them, in the papers, but not a dog really. The stories were printed just to keep up the agitation, and the farmers winked at it so as not to be 'bothered'.[40]

There is an element of truth in this, though the threatening poster campaign and the appearance of large crowds in some areas did, for some time, curtail hunting in parts of the country. In other parts of the country, there was a slightly ridiculous air to the anti-hunting campaign. In Cork, on St Stephen's Day 1887, the hunt of the 4th Hussars was out. This elicited a letter to *The Freeman's Journal* on 5 January 1888 from the celebrated nationalist MP, Dr Charles Tanner, quoting correspondence between Tanner and the regiment. Dr Tanner did not object to the army and navy hunting, but claimed 'persons obnoxious to the people were permitted and encouraged to follow the hounds'. Not surprisingly, this received a curt acknowledgement note from the equally celebrated Captain Ronald Kincaid-Smith, future commanding officer.

This hostility to hunting did not die out with the suppression of the plan of campaign. Until the end of the century, some anti-hunting notices still turned up and there were occasional anti-hunt incidents, showing the matter had not been forgotten. As late as May 1897, a not very successful attempt was made on the marquis of Downshire's land near Blessington in County Wicklow to set fire to a fox covert.[41] The matter, however, deteriorated into farce when an anti-hunt meeting of some 30 or 40 persons gathered at Cloghroe. Of these, about '20 were farmers, the remainder being idlers from the village'. They heard a newspaper reporter impersonate a speech attributed to the East Clare MP J.R. Cox.

As with various other types of threatening letters of a political nature, anti-hunting activity could have an underlying traditional agrarian motivation. The local magistrate believed that a prosecution for poaching was behind the following threatening letter. That may well be so but there are also obvious Land League connections in the fairly well written letter:

> Sir
> We the Invincibles of Reddins & the surrounding locality hereby give you notice beforehand not to come hunting on the lands of Reddins on 14th inst as published in the Chronicle If you don't

ADDRESS OF "MOLLY MAGUIRE," TO HER CHILDREN.

Rec'd 4 July 1845

MY DEAR CHILDREN,

With a heart full of sorrow I am obliged to give you this public warning, from the numerous shabby acts that is daily committing by paltry and vile miscreants, and those acts are left on my Dear Children, who are as innocent of them as those unborn, for I hope I have given you better instruction, than to disgrace myself and Milesian Name, now in my old days. I have, thank God, learned you to bear with christian patience your many privations more than any other children on the face of the earth ; but in the end I have a set of men called *Landlords*, having less regard for you than for their dogs, not caring if you had not enough of Dry Potatoes to Eat, or a Bag to cover you by Night, that a heap of Manure and a Pig was your only property, and a Drink of Water your only beverage. I have lived to see you, so reduced and its now too plain, there is no redress, for even after all the fuss about the *Land Commission*, it now turns out to be the greatest delusion was ever attempted on any people. I am my dear little ones, old enough to see Lord Stanly's Humbug Bill about old ditches, it now lies with yourselves my dear children, not to starve in the midst of plenty, and to obtain that end, and to obtain your fond Mother's Blessing, may I beg of you my Dear Children, to observe the following Rules, viz :—

1—Keep strictly to the Land Question, by allowing no Landlord, more than fair value for his tenure.

2—No Rent to be paid until Harvest.

3—Not even then without an abatement, where the Land is too high.

4—No underminding of Tenants, nor Bailiff's Fees to be Paid.

5—No turning out of Tenants, unless Two Years Rent due before Ejectment served.

6—Assist to the utmost of your power the Good Landlord, in getting his Rents.

7—Cherish and respect the Good Landlord, and Good

YOU ARE DESIRED TO GIVE WELCOME TO

SPENCER

THE MURDERER OF

FRANCIS HYNES

WITH BARRED DOORS and CLOSED BLINDS.

By Order of

"BLOOD AVENGERS"

Above—This rather patronising Molly Maguire threatening notice, dating from a few weeks before the potato blight hit Ireland in 1845, is printed and as such, probably came out of a newspaper works. The tedious details of strictures have all the hallmarks of a Ribbon society. (Courtesy of the National Archives of Ireland: CSORP Outrage papers, 1847)

Left—Printed advice notices ranged from those against Lord Lieutenant Spencer in 1883 to the humble tenant and shopkeeper. (Courtesy of the National Archives of Ireland: CSORP 1883, 3/641/14)

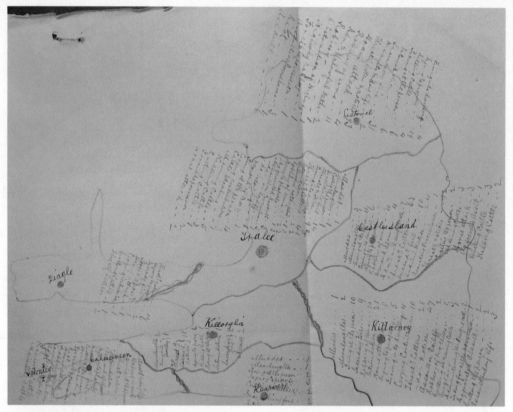

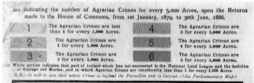

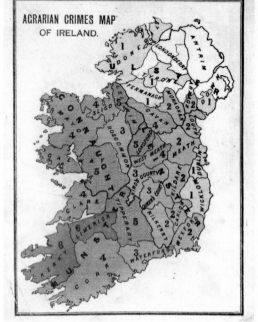

Above–Kerry outrage map, 1881–4. Drawn for Lord Lieutenant Spencer, this hand-sketched map lists the number of different outrages in each division of the county. By far the greatest number relate to threatening letters and threatening notices, Castleisland and Tralee topping the list.
(Courtesy of the National Archives of Ireland: CSORP, 3/644/26, 1884)

Left–Murder map of Ireland. In the 1880s, the Irish Loyalist and Patriotic Union published and distributed millions of political leaflets and tens of thousands of pamphlets. One pamphlet published in 1886 entitled, "'As it was said': Extracts from prominent speeches and writings of the Parnellite Party 1878–1886', contained two maps of Ireland – 'Agrarian Crimes' and 'Parliamentary Map'. Both are remarkably similar, the inference being that agrarian crimes (most of which were threatening letters) were the product of the actions of the Irish parliamentary party in its alliance with the land movement.

The Ribbon Lodge. Threatening notices, as distinct from letters, tended to come from groups, frequently from those secret agrarian organisations collectively referred to as Ribbon societies. Though they could be political in intent, their main concern was land occupancy. They attracted the fervent and the disgruntled, and regarded themselves as quasi-legal groups. Not afraid to use hay burning, cattle maiming, house arson and beatings, the posting of threatening notices, often outside a Catholic church or on gate posts at a farmer's front door, was a particularly common tactic. (Carleton, *Valentine McClutchy, The Irish agent*, 1847, p. 374)

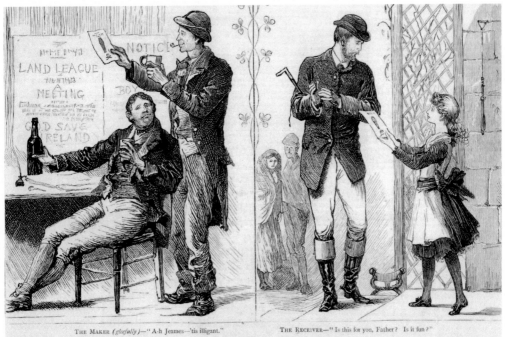

THE MAKER *(gleefully)*—"A-h Jeames—'tis illigant."

THE RECEIVER—"Is this for you, Father? Is it fun?"

ST. VALENTINE'S DAY IN IRELAND

St Valentine's Day in Ireland, 1881. A pro-Irish landlord cartoon portrays the young daughter of a landlord finding a threatening notice complete with a drawn coffin. 'Is it fun?', she asks her father. The hard-drinking authors regard it as 'illigant'. (*The Graphic*, 19 February 1881)

Above left–The hapless Captain Charles Boycott was a land agent and farmer in Galway. He had lived in the area for 26 years and, while 'a trifle obstinate and imperious', was a strange target for the new policy of boycotting. It appears that all the drama which surrounded him, including his 'relief' by the cohort of Ulster labourers, was all rather an annoyance to him. Boycott had a writing desk stuffed with threatening letters that he had received, but sadly none seems to have survived.
(*Vanity Fair*, 29 January 1881)

Above right–Irish Catholic landlord, thorough gentleman and British Liberal cabinet minister, Earl Kenmare, received threatening letters in the 1880s that provoked a group of his tenants to meet and condemn the letters. But the boy-cotting and outrages were too much and he fled to Bel-gravia in London, thereby negatively affecting the livelihoods of many of his former servants and the local tradesmen.
(*Vanity Fair*, 26 February 1881)

Left–John Dillon: *agent provocateur*? Dillon and Davitt did not despatch threatening letters but the ferocity of their language on public platforms laid themselves open to accusations of incitement of outrages, which they stoutly rejected. This caricature of Dillon was sketched on Kildare Street Club notepaper by Dillon's political enemy, the unionist leader, Colonel Sanderson.
(D.P. McCracken)

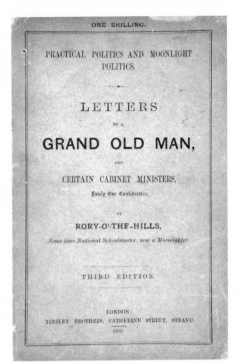

Above left—The penny-dreadful cover belied the serious content of this cheap edition of Lord Ashtown's *The unknown power behind the Irish Nationalist Party: Its present work … and criminal history* (1908).

Above right—The anonymous 64-page satirical pamphlet 'Practical politics and Moonlight politics. Letters to a Grand Old Man, and certain cabinet ministers, lately our confederates, by Rory-O'-the-Hills, some time National Schoolmaster, now a Moonlighter' (1882) was written by the larger-than-life figure, Percy Hetherington Fitzgerald.

The Emergency men were mostly Irishmen, by no means all from the north of Ireland, who were drafted in by Orange and Anglo-Irish societies to counter outrages and boycotting, mainly assisting beleaguered landlords in the 1880s. They served as labourers, servers of summons, escorts of livestock to market and when necessary, as bodyguards. They were not generally thugs, but they were rough and tough and not to be interfered with. (*Illustrated London News*, 15 January 1887)

'I always carry my large-bore revolver … wherever I go, I have a trustworthy man with me carrying a double-barrelled gun. His orders are distinct. If anyone fires at me he is not to look at me, but let me lie, and kill the man who fired the shot'. The psychological impact of the high-profile murder of some landlords and, more often, their land agents and bailiffs was intensified by a dramatic increase in the number of threatening letters, creating a panic among the less level-headed members of the ascendancy class, despite receiving police protection. (*Illustrated London News*, 15 January 1887)

1. Edenburn House, Castleisland, near Tralee.　　2. Mr. Samuel Murray Hussey.　　3. Back of the house, showing effects of the Explosion.

SCENE OF THE DYNAMITE OUTRAGE NEAR TRALEE, IRELAND.

Dynamite attack on Edenburn House in Kerry. Two things strike one about this attack on the home of the infamous land agent Samuel Hussey: first, the size of the mansion he owned and second, the amateur nature of the dynamite attack. (*Illustrated London News*, 6 December 1884)

The Police Gazette,
OR
HUE-AND-CRY.
Published for Ireland on every Wednesday and Saturday.

DUBLIN, SATURDAY, OCTOBER 28, 1854.

Above–*Hue-and-Cry*, the RIC and DMP bi-weekly newssheet, sometimes carried threatening-letter reward advertisements. The problem for the police was not catching threatening-letter writers who had done a runner but proving that an individual in the townlands had written the offending epistle.
(*Hue-and-Cry*, 28 October 1854)

£20
REWARD.

WHEREAS, a Rockite Notice bearing the *Elphin* Post mark, was recently sent to the *Very Rev. Dean Hoare*, of *Achonry*, threatening him:

I HEREBY OFFER A REWARD OF

TWENTY POUNDS

To any Person who shall, within Six Months from the date hereof, give such information as shall lead to the Arrest of the Person or Persons concerned in writing or sending the Notice in question. Payable on conviction.

GEORGE KNOX,
Resident Magistrate.

Tubbercurry, 9th December, 1847.

42,638—G.

Left–Reward notice for £20 for information relating to a threatening letter sent to the dean of the small Church of Ireland cathedral at Achonry in County Sligo. Protestant clergy usually received such letters in relation to land they owned rather than their religious affiliation.
(Courtesy of the National Archives of Ireland, CSORO Outrage papers, 1847)

44 Vic., c. 4.

Protection of Person and Property (Ireland) Act, 1881.

164

MEMORANDUM OF PROCEEDINGS
IN THE CASE OF

Michael Tobin

For whose Arrest a Warrant has been issued.

District *Kilfinane* County *Limerick*

Crime *Causing a threatening letter notice & message to be delivered to one of H. M. subjects.*

Residence *Farmer Kilfinane*

Occupation *Farmer*

Date of Warrant *8 June 1881*

Arrest warrant for farmer Michael Tobin of Kilfinane just north of Mitchelstown, for causing a threatening notice and message to be delivered, June 1881. (Courtesy of the National Archives of Ireland, CSORP 1881, 3/368/4)

T.—No. 32. *Copy*

A $_R^S$

POST OFFICE TELEGRAPHS.

No. of Message { From / To

Prefix { Code / Time } { Office of / Origin } No. of Words ___ No. of Addresses ___

Stamps to be affixed here, and on the back, if necessary.

DEC. 9. 82

FOR INLAND TELEGRAMS WITH MULTIPLE ADDRESSES ONLY.

	SENT			CHARGES
	At	To	By	

FROM *Sub Inspector Talbot. R.I.C. Antrim*

TO
(1)
(2) *John S. Peake Esq.*
(3) *Sessions House*
(4) *Green Street.*
(5) *Dublin*
(6) *Please Telegraph to Antrim stating if it will be*
(7) *sufficient to send you a Summons by post in*
(8) *threatening letter case at Templepatrick against*
(9) *James McSwain*
(10)

G & S [1401] 100,000 2/79 The Text of the Message to be written on the back.

Total } Charge }

John Peake was Dublin Castle's main handwriting expert during the Land War. Whether his fee plus a generous expenses claim justified the expenditure is debatable.
(Courtesy of the National Archives of Ireland, CSORP, 1882)

obey this law and come hunting we the above mentioned society
will stone yourselves and your followers to death and I warn you
again not to come for if you do you wont bring home your life.

Earl Spencer suppressed the meetings so will we deal with the hunt
in like manner we are about to carry out Mr Davitts reolutions &
therefore we wont ever leave a hound or a horse thread on the
surface of reddins for the purpose of hunting we will also warn John
Mulcahy not to entertain you or your followers for if he do we will
shoot him in his parlour so if you come hunting here not only
yourself will be killed but all the huntsmen that will follow you & if
I mulcahy gives you luncheon he will also fall I suppose you are not
aware of the stopping the hounds got here before if you were there
that day you would never come hunting here again we want no
Orangemen amongst us at all enough. Signed
Invincibles[42]

The urge to hunt in some farmers got them into trouble and branches of the
National League had to issue statements naming members who had ridden
out with the local hounds, warning them, in the gravest manner, to stop the
practice.[43]

Taking the bullet

A telling incident illustrates the position of the land agent vis-a-vis the landlord.
In April 1843, Trench arrived on the 26,000-acre Shirley estate. When a rent
reduction was demanded, John Shirley said he would consider the matter and
let the tenants know the following week. Not surprisingly, this was taken as a
nod-and-a-wink of assent by the tenantry who assembled en masse in the
market square in Carrickmacross on the appointed day. Shirley, however, had
no intention of lowering rents and instructed Trench to go out and tell the
crowd. Trench was soon surrounded by a mob which assaulted him and
frogmarched him out of town to the gates of the estate. Like many agents,
Trench was no fool and, being Irish himself and knowing the people, kept his
head, extricating himself much bruised but alive. Ironically, the incident gained
Trench a measure of respect from the local population.[44]

Hussey records a tale which similarly raises a question mark over landlords'
attitudes towards the dispensability of their agents. When receiving letters
threatening to kill his land agent if he did not reduce rents in Kerry, Lord
Derby allegedly stated, 'If you think you will intimidate me by shooting my

agent you are greatly mistaken'.[45] In Ballygawley, James Crossle wrote rather incredulously to Lady Verner, 'You are aware the priests interfered and sent petitions to Sir William [Verner] and the tenants held indignation meetings and I received notices threatening my life and yet Sir William and you seem to think we did not use any pressure upon the tenants at all'.[46]

Threatening letters were not simply an expression of anger and fear of destitution on the part of tenants and labourers. Instead, they were often the first step in an escalating pattern of outrage. If not checked, this built up a momentum of its own. Land agents and sometimes landlords were clear targets, often perceived as being villainous, tyrannical and obnoxious. The fact in many cases that they were not, adds an ironic piquancy to the whole matter. Ciarán Reilly states that between 1830 and 1852 seven land agents were killed in King's County [Offaly].[47] Both Hussey and Trench give the going price for hiring an assassin for such a job as £5.[48] The 1852 commission looking into outrages was told that 'one penny halfpenny per acre, amounting to 50l., was lodged to pay assassins, as far as might be necessary; and that Lord Clermont and his agent were two of the persons who were to be taken off'.[49] This intriguingly amounts to a land-tax assembled by peasantry to create a pot from which to pay hired assassins.

In the 22 years from 1857 to 1878, there were 113 killings (homicides) reported in Ireland.[50] That is about five a year. In 1882 alone, there were 26 murders in Ireland. These were not all landlords or agents, and given the number for both categories, even the 1882 figure was not proportionately great. Of course, it cannot be forgotten that many landlords were shot at and survived, and that estate employees were also assaulted and sometimes killed. The murder of a landlord was a high-profile affair, though, and the impact was magnified by the fascination the Victorian public generally had concerning these murders and their locations. Indeed, even a police tourist guide to Ireland, published in 1893 and entitled *Devia Hibernia: The road and route guide for Ireland*, enterprisingly gave the locations of nine prominent murders – what might be termed outrage tourism.[51]

Trench's successor as land agent on the Shirley estate at Lough Fea, James Morant, was also a tough character. Writing to Rev. James Mulligan in December 1851, he pulled no punches:

What a pity it is that you and your brother do not combine once
and forever to put down that scandal to Ireland, Ribbonism. I
foresee that if it is not exterminated, the people will be, for landlords
must and will get tired of seeing their agents murdered by this

conspiracy and finding it impossible to distinguish the guilty from the innocent will be obliged, in self defence, to purge the country by extermination, doubtless a fearful alternative, but in the present state of affairs almost inevitable.[52]

It is little wonder then that the Irish land agent was no stranger to the threatening letter and notice.

Landlord murders

It was not just land agents who were murdered. Closely allied to evictions and threatening letters was a series of landlord murders which punctuated nineteenth-century Ireland. In terms of numbers, they were not as significant as one might suppose – running into dozens, though the numbers can be doubled if attempted murder is added to the equation. But such landlord murders were important for their impact given that they were occurring in part of the United Kingdom, rather than in distant czarist Russia, where members of the ruling class were being assassinated by peasants. The drama which surrounded landlord murders and ensuing sensational trials did much to maintain public awareness both in Ireland and in Britain of Ireland's land problem and to consolidate in the minds of many, not just the nationalist Irish, the tyrannical Irish landlord and his 'jackal agent'.

Threatening letters were an integral part of this saga. The previously mentioned customary belief was that a threatening letter constituted 'fair warning' prior to killing, especially by one of the secret societies. This seems to have been the case in some instances, but with threatening letters so prevalent when evictions were taking place or threatened, it is impossible to judge whether the practice of giving 'a last chance to get out of the country' really was observed or whether it was simply a rhetorical device to vent frustration. Such warnings sometimes worked, driving out the landlord of a nervous disposition, but an absentee landlord was not necessarily a bad landlord any more than a residential landlord a good one. Then there were those like the Shirleys of Lough Fea who, in the nineteenth century, came and went. Some of the great landlords such as the earls of Kildare or the Downshires had more than one estate so even when they lived in Ireland, they could technically have been classified as absent from their estates in far-flung counties.

Threatening letters were much more likely to be serious in the wake of and capitalising on rural killing, whether addressed to a relative of the deceased, another official on the estate where the murder had occurred, or – more likely – a threatening letter sent to another landlord or agent warning that they were the next on the list. Writing on the famous murder of Major Denis Mahon of Strokestown in November 1847, Peter Duffy highlights this phenomenon. Such letters were received by Mahon's heir, his son, his cousin and a neighbour. As *The Times* reported on 4 December 1847:

> As the son of Major Mahon was going to his father's funeral a man came openly to his carriage window, and handed him a notice, saying that, if he did not alter his conduct to the people, he would be murdered in the same manner as his father had been.[53]

The Mahon murder was even invoked in a warning sent by the Molly Maguires to a Sligo landlord, also quoted by Peter Duffy, insinuating he had embezzled famine relief funds and threatening him with death:

> Molly never takes a mean advantage without due notice, and the exterminator of the tyrant Mahon will dare anything'.[54]

As the Mahon case well illustrated, though, the lot of the unfortunate tenantry of a murdered landlord was worse after the death than before. Vengeance, or at least lack of concern, was uppermost for surviving relatives. In the case of Strokestown, clearance, especially in the 'murder townlands', was pursued by Major Mahon's absentee heir.[55]

The Mahon case was, in fact, followed that same November by the copycat murder of the Rev. John Lloyd, whose clerical vows were obviously no protection when placed beside his alleged tyranny as a local landlord.

This was not the last time that the murder of some local gentry or even of a squire further afield was exploited by a threatening letter writer. Another letter posted in Athlone in November 1868 also alludes to cases beyond the county:

> Do not act the tyrant he done nothing Contery to his agreement he was honest and fathful if you do not like to keep him pay him for his house that cost him twenty five pounds and let him go in pace Hou would you like sir to be threw on the mercy of the waves in the Cold month of November an robed of your owen house a Sir publick Opinion is gone agane you you are tride and found gilty and Sintence is short do not be like Fetherson[56] of mulingar or Sculley of tiperary or any of those Mis-guided men Settle with him Quick and you will not be Sorry I tell you this as a friend

Remain your humble servant a lover of pace and fareplay[57]

Seizing upon a high-profile murder was probably seen as enhancing the threat, though the authenticity of such claims is highly doubtful. Another example was one of the many threatening letters received by Captain Boycott. Posted in far-off Dublin, one such contained the following:

> Captain Boycot if you don't want to have yourself as we did
> Lord Leitrim
> you wont come to collect any more rents, because you are a bloody
> robber or this before he kills, signed Rory. You deserve twice as
> muck you wretch signed Rory of the Hills. We are only waiting for
> to get the chance of your being by yourself and some police and we
> will quiet you.[58]

Vaughan refers to this occurrence of mentioning recent murders as part of the ceremony and trappings of the threatening letter as the recipients of such becoming 'epistolary scarecrows'.[59]

The fight back: The Irish Loyal and Patriotic Union

A London journalist who visited Ireland in December 1880 commented, 'It is impossible to exaggerate the panic prevailing among the landed proprietors of Cork, Kerry, Tipperary, Limerick, and Clare'. Certainly, a number packed up and were driven into being absentee landlords. But a great many stayed on and saw the matter out. In this they were assisted by various factor and bodies, the most influential of which was the Irish Loyal and Patriotic Union (ILPU).

The ILPU has not received the attention it deserves, no doubt because it fairly rapidly became subsumed into the new unionism which emerged in the late 1880s. Established on 1 May 1885, less than a week after the prince and princess of Wales left Ireland following a royal visit,[60] the ILPU was, to all intents and purposes, the Irish branch of the English Primrose League which was established in 1883 and finally dissolved 121 years later in 2004. In the period after the First World War, the league became the symbol of respectable English conservatism exemplified by ladies' tea parties. In its heyday, though, it had been a political force with over two million members by 1910. It was established two years after the death of the Tory statesman Benjamin Disraeli (the earl of Beaconsfield) and was overtly imperial and radically Tory, under the leadership of the maverick Lord Randolph

Churchill. It was the first mainline political organisation in Britain to afford women the same status as men. That the conservative party survived the cataclysm of the first half of the twentieth century and the old Liberal party did not was, in no small part, due to the Primrose League.

The Primrose League had Irish members and had meetings in Ireland. ILPU publications even sometimes carried the league's distinctive emblem of a crown above two sprays of primrose leaves and flowers with the motto 'Imperium et Libertas' [Empire and Liberty].[61] The two organisations shared the same offices in Dublin and London, respectively 109 Grafton Street and 26 Palace Chambers, Westminster.

The figureheads of the ILPU were distinguished aristocracy and gentry. The presidency consisted of the senior peer of the United Kingdom, the duke of Norfolk, followed by two great Irish landlords, the dukes of Devonshire and Leinster. Among the Irish-born and -based were the 2nd duke of Abercorn, Lord Castletown (Barnie FitzGerald), Earl Fitzwilliam, Arthur MacMorrough Kavanagh, Lord Longford and the redoubtable Tipperary-born John Hewitt Jellett, provost of Trinity College Dublin from 1881 until his death in 1888. The vice-presidents of the ILPU were dominated by Irish landlords, most of whom were titled, as well as the land-owning member of parliament, the unionist leader Colonel Edward Saunderson from Monaghan.

The ILPU held over 300 public meetings in Ireland and Great Britain in 1886, which cost them £3,600 to organise. It printed 20,000 posters that year. Given its linkages and patrons, it is little wonder that the ILPU had the substantial funding required for a propaganda drive as well as to employ a staff to mine the Irish nationalist press for any statement which might be taken to reflect disloyalty to Britain or possible incitement to political or agrarian crime.[62] This information was used in the production of a substantial number of leaflets and pamphlets. The magnitude of this ILPU research and publishing enterprise is reflected in the fact that it established a Special Press Bureau. By 1886, the ILPU had published 203 leaflets on various subjects with a total print run of 7,410,100 copies, averaging 37,000 copies per leaflet. To this must be added, 53 pamphlets with a total print run of 573,150 copies, which averaged about 11,000 copies per pamphlet. The largest leaflet print run was *What Home Rule means* (503,000 copies) and the largest pamphlet print run was *England's duty to Ireland* (43,000 copies).[63] This publishing enterprise was costing the ILPU £6,600 a year.

There is uniformity about these ILPU publications, which often followed the scheme contained in a letter that Colonel Sanderson wrote in March 1884:

My Dear Wrench

I have not been able to screw a word out of Lanesborough
[lord lieutenant of County Cavan].

He has not yet made any J.P.s or DLs so I suppose the Chancellor
will make some of the Riff raff & bobtail.

I have been asked to come forward at next election for another
County in the north. If ever I should again enter the House [of
Commons] I should prefer Fermanagh I must say. The only thing
that would ever tempt me to make the attempt would be the case of
an undoubted expression of opinion in a constituency that in the
opinion of the electors I might be of use in the terribly critical times
before us I could be of use to our country. In such a case I should
not feel justified in refusing. I am engaged at present in preparing a
pamphlet in justification of our recent stand in Ulster. This is the
form it will take. In two columns

    Speeches of Leaguers   :   *Crimes and outrages*
                                                      Following speeches

This will make the heathens rage I expect.[64]

The raging heathens had already given the colonel a taste of threatening
letters. As early as March 1879 one such, complete with a drawing of a coffin,
had asserted:

Mr Sanderson I was entend to pay you a visit at the death of Lord
Leitrim but thought it better to give you a nothar chance Now I tell
you to Part with Thos McMahon i have nothing against you only
you have no rite to keep him there after you makin him go to your
Church now I want you to under stand that I will give you and him
a war Resepshon befor yous are very old I shot one tyerint that is
Leitrim I guess he thought when he was a lord that no one Dare
look at him.

I am hear in Philedelphia to day and I want no tyrerents over the
land of Mi fore fathers now over mi Child Eather.

Your Father was a good Man and was respected as a gentlyman so
now I give you this chance If you are a good man we will not have
to go to Belfast for a Membr for the Co. Cavan.

So take mi advice as a frend let Mahon go for the have you as Bad in
this County as Lord Leitrim that is in Hell now som says that your
Wife is the cause of it.

I am one year Back in a America since I Helped to Shoot Leitrim I
Belongin to the Co Cavan I am 28 years of age and Belongin to the
Teening Brothers of America
Good Bt Mr Sanderson and of you do what I tell you are all rite and
if not you are all rong. Yours Truley The F.O. of I[65]

The secretary of the ILPU was Edward Caulfield Houston, described by Alvin
Jackson as a 'recklessly ambitious young Unionist apparatchik'.[66] A journalist
by profession on the Dublin *Daily Express* and a runner for *The Times*,
Houston was the man who purchased the Parnell forged letters from Richard
Pigott and then sold them to *The Times*. He was also the shadowy figure
pushing Captain O'Shea to initiate divorce proceedings against Parnell after
the commission had collapsed in all but name.[67]

If annoying the opposition is a sign of success in Irish politics, the Irish
Loyalist and Patriotic Union, or Loyalist and Patriotic Union as nationalist
politicians tended to refer to the organisation, was a great success. In the
House of Commons, John Dillon even referred to 'these wretched quotations,
which are picked out by the eagle eye of the Loyal and Patriotic Union for
retail to the people of England'.[68] That said, the ILPU was putting up a strong
fight to ensure that William O'Brien's prophecy that 'the sight of a landlord
will be as rare an animal as the wolf' did not come to pass.[69]

The Emergency men
By late 1880, the situation was so tense in rural Ireland that landlords and
conservative groupings in Dublin and Belfast began to take action. This
included the formation by the Grand Orange Lodge of Ireland of an Orange
Emergency Committee. There was also the Property Defence Association and
smaller organisations such as the Land Corporation and the Cork Defence
Union. These were subscription based.[70]

The leading light of the Emergency Committee was John Stopford, 5th
earl of Courtown. The Property Defence Association had as its champion a
young Dublin solicitor called Norris Goddard, who appears to have spent his
days dashing around Ireland trying to subvert and outmanoeuvre the Land
Leaguers, boycotters and anti-land-grabbers. The Emergency Committee and
the Property Defence Association were often subsumed in press coverage as
just 'Emergency men'. The two do seem to have overlapped and at times to
have included the same people. The Grand Orange Lodge of Ireland report
for 1882 recorded that the aim of the Emergency Committee was 'to extend
aid to those of Her Majesty's loyal subjects in Ireland, who were suffering

persecution at the hands of the illegal organisation known as the Land League'. Both Catholic and Protestant were assisted.

After the Peace Preservation Act expired, there was a great rush to buy firearms. It was said in Westport that more carbines were sold in five months than in the previous ten years. Revolvers also were in great demand.[71] The committee provided firearms to those they believed to be under threat, spending £3,500 on this by the end of 1885, 15 per cent of the £22,000 total expended by then. The committee also:[72]

- Provided boycotted farmers and landlords with labour. By mid-1881 nearly 300 labourers had been despatched to boycotted farms in 19 counties of Ireland, commencing with Colonel O'Callaghan's County Clare estate;
- Provided armed Emergency men to occupy and hold, frequently with RIC support, the houses from which tenants had been evicted;
- Provided armed personal protection to those who had been threatened, sometimes using former soldiers or policemen;
- Provided landlords with Emergency men to serve writs;
- Purchased or bid at auctions for boycotted livestock;
- Used Emergency men to act as bailiffs;
- Used the Emergency men as cattle drivers;
- Established and manned Emergency posts (a form of blockhouse, harking back to the plantation and ahead to the Anglo-Boer war).

The aims and actions of the loyalist groupings are clear enough. They offered a physical presence to counter the unrest which following in the wake of the Land League. They offered labour to those boycotted; they occupied farms from which tenants had been evicted; they served writs where necessary on the landlord's behalf; they bought boycotted livestock at markets and auctions; and they offered armed support for those under threat. They did not all come from Ulster, but from other parts of Ireland, too, as well as some from England. The emergency men became the generic name for both the Orange Emergency Committee and the Property Defence Association, but also for smaller enterprises organised by landlords around the country. By 1882, the Property Defence Association had branches in Cork, Monaghan, Queen's County [Laois], Sligo, Wexford and Wicklow.[73] However, the situation of placing loyal hands (and sometimes loyal guns) on property could not be a long-term solution, especially if the landlord had to pay – or pay eventually – as it might cost a landlord £2-10-0 a week.

Even so, by 1881, the Emergency men were, for landlords, an important line of defence against the threatening letter and notice and what followed from them. Not surprisingly, the Emergency men were boycotted. They do not seem to have been thugs, or at least not most of them, nor were they vigilantes, but they were certainly men not to be interfered with. On more than one occasion, though, they came off worst when confronted with a Land League crowd.[74] They were a lifeline to many a landlord, taking on heavy work around the farm and acting as a deterrent against any attack on the property. Generally, they were feared – perhaps because they tended not to show fear – and were therefore abused where possible. They certainly both received threatening letters and were mentioned in threatening letters:

[Tipperary, 1884]
Will you allow this tyrant Bell to trample on your rights – to evict you from your homes and to place in your stead the scrum of society (The Emergency men) no-swear a thousand times by all that's dear to you that he [Bell] must need the death of James Carey unless he ceases at once to act as Agent to Mansergh.
'God save the people'

[Abbeyleix, 1884]
and now I am going to give you a hint before it is too late to work no more for the emergency men or if you do all the Buck Shot that is made wont save you from this [drawing of a gun and a coffin][75]

Sir Thomas Esmonde, the home rule politician and landlord, son-in-law of Henry Grattan, and MP for South Dublin, denounced the Emergency men as lawless in the House of Commons:

A short time ago a party of emergency men were engaged in protecting Park House against no-body at all. These men, after drinking in a public-house, came out and fired off their revolvers in the gaiety of their hearts ... In another case, the emergency men employed on the Brooke estate in County Wexford, whilst in a state of intoxication, threatened to fire their revolvers at unarmed people, for which they were let off on payment of a small fine. Almost all these cases testified to the laxity which prevailed in allowing arming emergency men to go about the country, sometimes in a state of intoxication, to the terror and danger of the people.[76]

Sometimes the occupants of evicted farms were denounced as Emergency men as well as land-grabbers, even when the new tenants had nothing to do with any emergency organisation. Such an accusation appeared in the following threatening notice sent from Althy to Wolf Hill post office in Queens County [Laois] in April 1884:

> I do hereby certify that you James Brennan and your son Pat has come under the notice of the Society for Removing obnoxious individuals And it has been proved before Said Society that you and your Son and Such So now take notice that if after ten days after this notice yous Continue to be Emergency men both your Cases will receive the Most Careful Consideration of this Society and Reward you accordingly
> Take this notice now for what it is worth
> Signed S F R.O.I.[77]

Self-defence

There was a great sense of bravado among many of the landlords, especially in the west of Ireland, which had a reputation by 1881 for being lawless. Four constables with carbines and a sergeant were the usual protection provided where threatening letters and attacks on property suggested violence might follow. Richard Stacpoole of Ballyalla in County Clare chose to have his own retainers as bodyguards. He told Bernard Becker:

> I always carry my large-bore revolver, and I never walk alone, even across the path to look down at the lake. Whenever I go out, and wherever I go, I have a trustworthy man with me carrying a double-barrelled gun. His orders are distinct. If anyone fires at me he is not to look at me, but let me lie, and kill the man who fired the shot.

In Portarlington, the colourful Barnie FitzPatrick, who refused RIC protection in favour of two 'stalwart Northerners' as bodyguards, gave the same instructions as Stacpoole.[78] Of the intrepid Stacpoole, Becker noted, 'There was no appearance of emotion in the speaker [Stacpoole], whose collection of threatening letters is large and curious'.[79]

169

The point, however, has to be made that, as will be seen elsewhere, despite hundreds of landlords accepting police protection, a large number rejected such offers. Indeed, as Becker observed, 'many landlords have an almost invincible repugnance to go everywhere attended by armed police'.[80] Servants and farm hands filling that role, as they sometimes did, was another matter.

Reign of terror

The Major Mahon murder became notorious but even more so did the triple murder of the 3rd earl of Leitrim, his driver and his clerk 30 years later on 2 April 1878 at Cratlagh Wood near his residence at Milford in County Donegal. Perhaps an even more famous murder than either, at least at the time, was that of William Browne, Lord Mountmorres, who lived within or on the boundaries of genteel poverty on a small estate overlooking Lough Corrib in County Galway. He was gunned down while riding home on 25 September 1880. This sparked a series of rural murders in County Galway which culminated in the famous Maamtrasna murders on 17 August 1882. In the police districts of Athenry and Loughrea, there were eight murders relating to land in the 14 months from May 1881 to June 1882 including those of Walter Bourke of Rahasane House and the land agent of the man described by William O'Brien as 'a criminal maniac', Lord Clanricarde.[81]

These were all very high-profile murders. In 1887, Gladstone tried to point out that, in fact, the crime rate in Ireland had declined significantly in the past 55 years, homicides from 248 to 65; attempts to kill ('happily unfulfilled') from 209 to 37; serious offences of all other kinds from 6,014 to 1,057; and the total number of all criminal offences was down from 14,000 to 2,682. He also pointed out that the population of Ireland had declined in this half century.[82]

This was true enough, even taking into account the manner in which crime was recorded or not. However, it ignores two factors. First, that it was in the interests of both sides to portray the country as restless and unruly: the nationalists to show the unjust situation in Ireland and the need for reform, and the British government, to justify the need for the coercive measures necessary to protect the landed classes and retain law and order in unsettled and lawless parts of the kingdom. Secondly, a new dimension had entered Irish politics in the late 1870s/early 1880s: bitterness on various sides had increased to an extreme. The fight for the rights of the rural tenant re-emerged as a key and, for a while, the central focus, blending uneasily existing agrarian feuds and activities to gain a political national platform. Opponents of Irish nationalism made much of the less salubrious activities of the 'men of violence' and what were and had been for many a decade 'outrages'. Samuel Hussey was not alone among the opponents of Irish nationalism in Ireland when he recorded:

> They alone in modern times warred against women and children. Animals were the dumb victims of the inhuman ferocity they in no way tried to check, and they effectively taught the receptive Irish millions that a British Government could be coerced into giving what was demanded provided a sufficient number of crimes created a holocaust large enough to intimidate the weak-kneed at St Stephen's [Westminster] ... Long before this [Mr Gladstone's intervention] the political agitator had set himself to embitter the relations existing between landlord and tenant.[83]

Bence Jones asserted, 'It is these very men who use threats and commit outrages to keep up, as far as possible, a Reign of Terror'.[84] Inevitably such opponents of Irish nationalism believed culpability lay with the Land League and later its successor, the National League. Indeed, in certain parts of the country at certain times it was true enough that 'all law was Land League law'. Michael Davitt – 'the Apostle of outrage' – became a favourite landlord target with the accusation that his words were inciting criminal activity, something he fervently denied. Indeed, Davitt was repelled by the cruelty against animals in this period but that, of course, does not mean that his words – and he did tend to get carried away with what he said on the public platform – did not incite outrages. It is too much of a coincidence that outrages peaked with Land League activity. As W.B. Yeats observed when speaking of the turn of the nineteenth century, 'the Irish people, however lawless, respect a rule founded upon some visible supremacy'.[85] The problem for Dublin Castle in the 1880s was that in certain parts of the country, it was not the RIC but the Land League, and later on the National League, which held that supremacy.

Clifford Lloyd wrote that, 'the gentry in Ireland who remained in the country were loath to believe individually that their doom had been decreed and that the executioners were to be found among their own tenants'. He compared this situation to the time of the 1857 Great Rebellion or Indian Mutiny, when many regimental colonels in the East India Company Bengal Army regiments refused to believe that the troops they had passed their lives with would turn against them. Lloyd was not far wrong. In both Ireland and India, whatever had been the case in the past, self-delusion had set in among the ruling class. With the Mutiny and the Land War, reality had asserted itself and things would not be the same again.

Notes

[1] https://100objects.ie/captain-rock-threatening-letter/ (accessed 25 March 2021).

[2] Becker, *Disturbed Ireland*, pp. 314–15.

[3] Trollope, *The Land Leaguers*, p. 7.

[4] Reilly, *The Irish land agent*, p. 57 (Downshire papers, PRONI, D/671/C/9/410, 25 January 1835).

[5] Akenson, *Small differences: Irish Catholics and Irish Protestants*, p. 162.

[6] *The Times*, 16 August 1859, quoted in Reilly, *The Irish land agent*, p. 155.

[7] *Commission of the Peace (Ireland)*, p. 132.

[8] Hussey, *Reminiscences of an Irish land agent*, pp. 40–1.

[9] PRONI, Annesley papers, Rev. JR Moore to Rev. EP Brookes, D1854/6/5, 8 April 1844.

[10] See for example, Reilly, *The Irish land agent*, p. 49.

[11] Reilly, *The Irish land agent*, pp. 49–50.

[12] Gibbons, *Captain Rock, night errant: The threatening letter in pre-Famine Ireland, 1801–1845*, p. 221, quoted in Dooley, *The murders at Wildgoose Lodge*, p. 57.

[13] C.J. Woods, 'Blacker, William', *Dictionary of Irish Biography*, vol. 1, p. 566.

[14] Gerard Lyne, 'Trench, Richard Steuart ("William Steuart Trench")', *Dictionary of Irish Biography*, vol. 9, pp. 472–3.

[15] Ryan, *Fenian memories*, p. 43. Trench lost the vote but was declared elected on petition after an investigation of electoral malpractice on the part of the Nolan camp.

[16] Hussey, *Reminiscences of an Irish land* agent, p. 227 and Trench, *Realities of Irish life*, p. 49. See also, Duff, 'Emigrants and the estate office in the mid-19th century', pp. 72–4.

[17] C.J. Woods, 'Hussey, Samuel Murray', *Dictionary of Irish Biography*, vol. 4, pp. 860–1.

[18] Hussey, *Reminiscences of an Irish land agent*, p. 61 and Chapter 20; and BBP, *Explosion at Edenburn*, 1885, c. 4285.

[19] Duffy, *The killing of Major Denis Mahon*, p. 309.

[20] *Vanity Fair*, 29 July 1881.

[21] Marlow, *Captain Boycott and the Irish*, p. 147

[22] Ibid., p. 103; *A verbatim copy of the Parnell Commission report with complete index and notes*, Irish Loyal and Patriotic Union, London and Dublin, 1890, p. 51.

[23] Dublin *Daily Express* 18 November 1880, quoted in Marlow, *Captain Boycott and the Irish*, pp. 199–200. The version quoted in this book is that from the Parnell Commission, which has not been corrected as was the newspaper version. See *Special Commission Act*, p. 313.

[24] *Special Commission Act, 1888*, p. 311.

[25] Trollope, *The Land Leaguers*, p. 117.

[26] For this episode see *The Freeman's Journal*, 17 November 1880 and quoted in Marlow, *Captain Boycott and the Irish*, pp. 196–7.

[27] PRONI, Verner papers, letter book, D236/488/2, p. 101, 2 May 1881.

[28] Hussey, *Reminiscences of an Irish land agent*, pp. 67 and 214–15.

[29] Becker, *Disturbed Ireland*, p. 43.

[30] Bence Jones, *A life's work in Ireland*, pp. 86–8. See also pp. v, 20–1, 27.

[31] Madden, *Forkhill Protestants and Forkhill Catholics*, p. 110.

[32] Bence Jones, *A life's work in Ireland*, pp. vii–xii.

[33] Desmond McCabe, 'Jones, William Bence', *Dictionary of Irish Biography*, vol. 4, pp. 1046–8.

[34] *Vanity Fair*, 26 February 1881.

[35] NAI, Crime Branch Special, box 2, S/1416, Return of informants employed in 1889. South West Kerry and Clare Division.

[36] NAI, CSO RP, 1884, 3/644/26.

[37] See Trollope, *The Land Leaguers*, pp. 61, 67 and 119.

[38] Finnegan, *Loughrea*, pp. 43–4.

[39] Becker, *Disturbed Ireland*, p. 165.

[40] Hurlbert, *Ireland under coercion*, I. 50. See also Bence-Jones, *Twilight of the ascendancy*, p. 39; TNA, CO 903/2 (*Leinster Leader*, 17 December 1887).

[41] TNA, CO 903/6, E2.

[42] NAI, CSORP 1884, 3/664/27, Reddins, County Tipperary, 27 January 1884.

[43] See for example, *Ireland in 1887*, pp. 269–70.

[44] Trench, *Realities of Irish life*, Chapter 5.

[45] Ibid., p. 40.

[46] PRONI, Verner papers, D236/488/3, letter book p. 287, 6 September 1882.

[47] Reilly, *The Irish land agent*, p. 9.

[48] Trench, *Realities of Irish life*, p. 54.

[49] *Report from the select committee on outrages (Ireland)*, 1852, p. 548.

[50] Vaughan, *Landlords and tenants in mid-Victorian Ireland*, p. 142.

[51] Edwin, *Devia Hibernia*, pp. 91, 122, 145, 193, 249, 275, 294 and 297.

[52] PRONI, James Morant to Rev. James Mulligan, 16 December 1851, DIORC/1/10/B/46.

[53] Quoted along with other examples in Duffy, *The killing of Major Denis Mahon*, pp. 166–7.

[54] Duffy, *The killing of Major Denis Mahon*, p.167. See also pp. 300–301.

[55] Ibid., pp. 198–9.

[56] James Fetherston was a justice of the peace who was shot dead late at night returning to Westmeath from Dublin in 1868. He was said to be raising levels of tenants' rents. http://www.igp-web.com/IGPArchives/ire/westmeath/xmisc/murders1848-1870.txt (accessed 25 March 2021).

[57] Threatening letter dated November 1868 to Captain Tarleton Creggan, NAI: CSO Library. Threatening letters, 1869–1872, 3/719/5 or 21 [both numbers are on the carton].

[58] *Special Commission Act, 1888*, p. 314.

[59] Vaughan, *Landlords and tenants in mid-Victorian Ireland*, p. 150.

[60] Bence-Jones, *Twilight of the ascendancy*, p. 65.

[61] See for example, *'As it was said.' Extracts from prominent speeches and writings of the Parnellite party 1879–1886*, ILPU, Dublin and London, October 1886, 154 pp.

[62] See for example NAI, Crime Branch Special, carton 9, 29 April 1891, 2345 regarding detective presence at Primrose League meeting at Leinster Hall in Dublin. The Primrose League emerged in its own right in the late 1880s with 22 Irish branches and some 6,682 members by 1888, but was subsumed by the growing force of Irish and Ulster unionism. See Sheets, 'British conservatism and the Primrose League: The changing

character of popular politics, 1883–1901', PhD thesis, Columbia University, 1986, pp. 194, 348 and 350.

[63] *Irish Loyal and Patriotic Union: Annual report of the executive committee for the year 1886*, ILPU, Dublin, London and Edinburgh, January 1887, pp. 15–19.

[64] Sanderson to Wrench, Folkstone, 26 March 1884, in the possession of D.P. McCracken. Sanderson had been defeated by Joseph Gillis Biggar in Cavan in 1874, returning to parliament in 1886 for north Armagh, a seat he retained until his death in 1906.

[65] PRONI, Sanderson papers, T2996/4/1, 31 March 1879.

[66] Jackson, *Ireland 1798–1998: War, peace and beyond*, p. 134.

[67] O'Brien, *Parnell and his party*, p. 281.

[68] *Hansard*, House of Commons, John Dillon, 28 March 1887.

[69] *Ireland. No.4. Resistance to evictions*, p. 11.

[70] Clifford Lloyd, *Ireland under the land League*, pp. 119–28 and 151; Pole, 'Sheriffs' sales during the Land War, 1879–82', *Irish Historical Studies*, vol. 34, no. 136, November 2005, pp. 397–9.

[71] Becker, *Disturbed Ireland*, p. 43. It was said also that the peasantry bought obsolete British army Enfield rifles.

[72] Aiken McClelland, 'The later Orange Order', pp. 130–1.

[73] Cant-Wall, *Ireland under the land act*, p. 48.

[74] *Irish Times*, 15 March, 15 August, 17 August 1881 and 19 April 1882,

[75] NAI, CSO RP, 3/644/27, file 292/740, 2 February 1884; and file245/625, 25 January 1884.

[76] *Hansard*, House of Commons, 29 March 1887.

[77] NAI, CSORP 1884, 21003, 16 September 1884, 3/644/27.

[78] Bence-Jones, *Twilight of the ascendancy*, p. 30.

[79] Becker, *Disturbed Ireland*, pp. 55 and 156.

[80] Ibid., p. 44.

[81] Finnegan, *Loughrea*, p. 11 and O'Brien, *Evening memories*, p. 193.

[82] *Hansard*, House of Commons, 29 March 1887.

[83] Hussey, *Reminiscences of an Irish land agent*, pp. 195–6 and 260.

[84] Bence-Jones, *A life's work in Ireland*, p. 165.

[85] Yeats, *Dramatis personae*, p. 11.

7. How the authorities responded to threatening letters

Legislation

Sending threatening letters was already regarded as a serious offence well before Victoria ascended the throne. The first legislation to tackle the issue was contained in the 1722 act of parliament known as the 9 George I c.22. This made it illegal to send a letter signed with a fictitious name demanding money. This was considered a felony 'without the benefit of clergy'. That is, first-time offenders could expect no leniency compared to repeat offenders. The 27 George II c.15 of 1754 extended the crime to threatening someone with death in a letter, even if no financial demand was made. This was also ranked as without benefit of clergy. Further acts of parliament dealt with workers in specific industries – textiles, iron and leather – sending threatening letters to employers and it carried a sentence of transportation. The 32 George II c.24 for 1758 stipulated the death penalty in certain circumstances.[1] In 1823, benefit of clergy was granted to crimes relating to threatening letters and the death penalty was replaced with transportation or hard labour.

In the early Victorian era, serious incidents of threatening letters and notices were dealt with under the provisions of the Tumultuous Rising (Ireland) Act of 1831: c. 44. [15 October 1831]. Part of this ran:

> And be it enacted, That if any Person or Persons shall knowingly print, write, post, publish, circulate, send, or deliver, or cause or procure to be printed, written, posted, published, circulated, sent, or delivered, any Notice, Letter, or Message exciting or tending to excite any Riot, tumultuous or unlawful Meeting or Assembly, or unlawful Combination or Confederacy, or threatening any Violence, Injury, or Damage, upon any Condition or in any Event, or otherwise, to the Person, or Property, Real or Personal, of any Person whatever, or demanding any Money, Arms, Weapons or Weapon, Ammunition, or other Matter or Thing whatsoever, or directing or requiring any Person to do or not to do any Act, or to quit the Service or Employment of any Person, or to set or to give

out any Land, every Person so offending shall be liable to be transported beyond the Seas for the Term of Seven Years, or to be imprisoned, with or without Hard Labour, for any Term not exceeding Three Years, and, if a Male, to be once, twice, or thrice publicly or privately whipped, if the Court shall think fit, in addition to such Imprisonment.[2]

From the early 1860s, threatening letters were dealt with under the Act to Consolidate and Amend the Statute Law of England and Ireland Relating to Offences against the Person [6th August 1861]. Section c.16 stated:

Whosoever shall maliciously send, deliver, or utter, or directly or indirectly cause to be received, knowing the contents thereof, any letter or writing threatening to kill or murder any person, shall be guilty of felony, and being convicted thereof shall be liable, at the discretion of the court, to be kept in penal servitude for any term not exceeding ten years, ... or to be imprisoned, ... and, if a male under the age of sixteen years, with or without whipping.[3]

Coercion acts

Between 1847 and 1875, 28 acts of coercive legistation were passed – but as Vaughan has pointed out, a great many of them were renews. He also observes, 'Their temporary character suggests not only a solicitude for the freedom of the subject, but also a curious optimism that regarded Irish disorder as recurrent rather than endemic and permanent'.[4] Had Victorian Ireland been a police state, dealing with the extended agrarian unrest, including the epidemic of threatening letters, would have been a much simpler matter.

It also has to be said that these coercion acts were neither enforced uniformly nor had a uniform impact. In Dublin, for instance, Superintendent Mallon tried whenever possible to disguise the date of implementation. As a result and because these coercive measures did not apply to Great Britain, there was a speedy exodus of advanced men out of Ireland to the sanctuary of London, Liverpool and Glasgow when such legislation was about to come into force. The trick for the RIC and particularly the DMP was to swoop the moment the coercive legislation became law and fill the net with the erstwhile runners. For it is one of the extraordinary facts of Irish Victorian society that its police forces were better informed about political crime and who did what than probably any other of the police forces in the United Kingdom at the time.

Between July 1879 and June 1880, the authorities recorded 127 meetings advocating land agitation in four counties alone: Donegal 3; Sligo 16; Galway 46; and Mayo 62.[5] That very severe winter of 1879/1880 assisted in the emergence of the Land League and the consequent dramatic rise of instances of outrage. On 2 March 1881, the Protection of Persons and Property (Ireland) Act (44 Vic, c.4) was passed. It was usually referred to simply as the PPP act. Persons convicted under this 'catch-all' legislation were not treated as ordinary criminals. These included a large number who had been arrested under warrants issued relating to the writing and the delivery or posting up of threatening letters or notices.[6] The PPP was followed up three weeks later with an anti-arms measure, the Peace Preservation (Ireland) Act. The PPP Act became the benchmark by which the authorities, and certainly the police, judged coercion acts. As a result, they regarded later successors as watered down and poor versions of this catch-all measure.

The introduction of the Prevention of Crime in Ireland Act made provision for detaining persons without trial, as will be seen below. There followed the suppression of the Land League on 20 October 1881. Despite the 1881 Land Act and the establishment of the land commission, agrarian violence continued. Then, on Sunday 6 May 1882, the Phoenix Park murders occurred. In July following these murders, more coercion followed with the Prevention of Crime (Ireland) Act, referred to as the Crimes Act. Section 13 of this allowed for the seizure of copies of newspapers which incited treason, violence or intimidation, as has been discussed. Section 14 allowed for the searching of property in proclaimed districts, not only for suspects and arms, but also for documents if they were regarded as connected with secret societies existing for criminal purposes.

Increased coercion and greater security measures in Ireland were not received with much enthusiasm by most of Gladstone's Liberal cabinet and were considered, hopefully, a temporary necessity. Joseph Chamberlain was distinctly cynical about the path being trod. Writing to Gladstone, then prime minister, in November 1880, he had asserted:

> It is really impossible to suppose that the arrest of thirty subordinate
> agents, as proposed by Mr. Forster, would immediately stop
> threatening letters and the assaults on life and property which are
> rife all over the country. It would be like firing with a rifle at a
> swarm of gnats.[7]

The impact of coercive legislation was seen in the dramatic fall in instances of intimidation recorded in monthly constabulary reports. A report for Ballinasloe, dated 30 September 1884, noted:

> Neither Boycotting or intimidation is resorted to in any part of the District. This is due in a great measure to the C.P. Act (82) sec 7 – which has a very salutary effect on those parties who might be disposed to carry on this system of lawlessness – [8]

When this act came up for renewal in 1885, Earl Spencer observed of section 7:

> This is the only check on boycotting and intimidation. The dropping of the clause would give an impetus to the operations of the League and it would be represented to the members that boycotting was no longer a crime.[9]

Between 19 July 1887 and 31 December 1887, 373 people were imprisoned under the Crimes Act.[10] But the 1887 Criminal Law and Procedure Act was considered 'a poor imitation' of the original 1882 act. Under the 1882 act, only two counties (Clare and Kerry) had been proclaimed (allowing for suppression of the Land League in those areas) with only parishes or baronies of nine other counties (Cork, Donegal, Galway, Mayo, Queen's, Roscommon, Tipperary, Waterford and Wexford) being affected.[11]

Enforcement

The problem of enforcement was highlighted in a case concerning a man named F.J. Askin who, in January 1881, had received a threatening letter from 'this silent messenger', Captain Moonlight. The postmark on the letter was Edgeworthstown in Longford. Askin was land agent to a man named Booker, who lived in Westmeath at Lickclay and who held land from a man named Dease near Finea in the same county. The police file was opened at Ballyjamesduff in County Cavan. As Longford, Cavan and Westmeath all converge at Lough Kinale, this was not particularly unusual – but it was problematic in this case.

Constable Patrick McCarney (23159) suspected that the letter had been written by a man named Thomas Deneny. He was an interesting character who appears to have scratched a living writing letters for people. He had attended a college in his youth but had had to leave because of a 'softening of the brain'. He was subsequently employed as a book keeper in the Dublin offices of the Wicklow and Wexford Railway but was also forced to leave there, apparently for the same reason that he gave up his education. Though Deneny had no personal motive for writing the threatening letter, McCarney believed that he had done so for men named Reilly and Cullen.

The constable made contact with a woman called Mary Jackson and learnt from her that Deneny would write a letter for her relating to a bill she had received from Dublin. McCarney called at the Jackson house when Deneny was there doing this job and criticised the letter he composed as having too strong language. Mary Jackson agreed with the policeman and a modified letter was written by Deneny, the constable pocketing the original letter. Subsequently, the ubiquitous handwriting expert, Mr Peake, gave his opinion that the writing in Mary Jackson's letter 'resembled' that in the threatening letter which Askin had received.

This, however, in the eyes of the legal adviser was regarded as insufficient evidence for a normal conviction. The problem now was that the only alternative was to take the matter through the PPP Act, where evidence need not be so stringent. But Cavan, unlike Westmeath, was not a proclaimed county. Furthermore, though the envelope clearly carried an Edgeworthstown post mark, it was suggested that the letter was actually posted in Carrickakillen, which is in Cavan – as 'I believe there is no dating stamp used at Finea Post Office'. It was suggested to send the file from Ballyjamesduff down to Castlepollard police station, which no doubt pleased the inspector in the former. It was argued that Mr Askin's home was in Westmeath as were the lands he controlled.

No doubt to everyone's relief, the matter seems to have petered out at this point as Mr Booker gave up his lands at Finea and they reverted to Mr Dease, who was known to give abatements. It was reported that the tenants lit, 'small bonfires to Exhibit their joy in again becoming Mr Dease's tenants'.[12]

In many respects, the demand for rent abatements, which were frequently granted though not always to the percentage demanded, was little different from the campaign back in the 1820s to have abatements granted on tithes.[13]

Magistrates and the police

The authorities on the ground took threatening letters very seriously, not least because they could lead to acts of violence or accompany acts of violence.[14] In a telling postscript to Under-Secretary Burke, one resident magistrate demanded that the threatening letters he had sent to Dublin Castle be returned to him:

> Every possible plan has been for the past five years & a half tried to
> detect the writer, night watchmen, searching houses, comparing
> writing, watching the Post Office etc etc without success.[15]

As one might expect, if a threatening letter was found by the RIC they
informed the person threatened in it. Inspector Thomas Barry in Monaghan
had his hands full in the 1860s and did much to quieten a volatile part of the
country at a time when 'threatening notices and warnings became numerous'.
Inspector Barry sent on to William Trench one such notice which advised,
'Trench may look out, for he will get the same as Beatson with Gun and
Bludgeon'. Barry also added the following note, 'The above is a copy, and I
am happy to say everything is quiet since the notice was found'.[16]

If the Irish land agent was in the front line in terms of dealing with
outrages, members of the judiciary and especially the resident magistrate and
county and borough magistrate were not far behind. Captain Warburton, a
magistrate from troubled south Armagh, commented that he had known
magistrates to receive threatening notices themselves, but on account of land
matters rather than their position.[17]

The relationship between the judiciary and the Irish police was not always
the happiest. Judges were not slow to criticise where they saw fit. In the 1860s,
they were particularly concerned at the lack of success in bringing to trial
perpetrators of threatening letters and notices. In a report to the lord
lieutenant in 1864, the inspector-general of the Irish Constabulary, Sir Henry
Brownrigg, quoted from several circuit judges and chairmen of quarter
sessions on the subject, including those from Cavan, Kildare, Limerick,
Kilkenny, Longford, Meath and Tipperary. In addressing the grand jury at
Limerick, the judge was frankly spoken:

> There is one offence in particular which I regard as next to actual
> assassination, and as heinous as any known to our laws – that of
> writing threatening letters. A number of those have been written
> and sent, yet I perceive that without a single exception, not one
> individual has been made amenable.[18]

It was, however, the magistrates rather than the judges who dealt with
most of the threatening letter cases. And the most rigorous and notorious of
these magistrates in the 1880s was Charles Clifford Lloyd (1844–1891),
grandson of a provost of Trinity College Dublin, but largely a self-made man
with extensive colonial experience. He became a resident magistrate in Belfast

in 1874 and from there moved to Longford and then Limerick. In 1881, at the height of the crisis in Ireland, Lloyd was one of five (and later six) special resident magistrates. His area of authority, which included the control of troops and the RIC, was Limerick, Clare and Galway. As with the more energetic land agents, Clifford Lloyd and such fellow magistrates as Major Robert Gayer Traill (1839–1908) and John Adye Curran became the subject of opprobrium in advanced nationalist ranks. Lloyd in particular has gained a reputation for impulsiveness and authoritarianism, even joining the ranks of those ridiculed in the satirical Irish nationalist cartoons of the day.[19] Lloyd's reputation was not assisted by his appearance, which was somewhat haggard and later corpulent; even his way of walking did not assist his image. He prowled with his head down, 'He appears very nervous and looks to the right and left when walking, like a hyena'.[20] And like a hyena, Clifford Lloyd was dangerous.

Though much was made of Clifford Lloyd's harsh approach to silencing dissent, he had attributes which, at that time, Dublin Castle needed. He had both police and military experience. He was trained in the law, unlike most Irish magistrates. Instead of being easy going or indolent, he was pugnacious and stubborn. When posted to Kilmallock in County Limerick in May 1881, he soon began asserting his authority. Equally soon, he was singled out for assassination. Later Clifford Lloyd recorded:

each post brought me scores of anonymous letters from all parts, couched in the most gross language, but all telling me to make my peace with God, for my days were numbered. Even some of the parcels I received by railway had death's-heads and cross-bones drawn on the labels. I received also warnings and directions from the Government to adequately protect myself, and a private letter from poor Mr Burke, the Under Secretary, telling me to 'spare no precaution.' Poor Burke! I wish he had acted up to the advice he so thoughtfully gave me.[21]

Lloyd took problems head on. In Kilmallock in June 1881, a farmer called Berklery was a prime target for boycotting and threatening notices sent by the local and particularly virulent branch of the Land League, with at least one fervent cleric in support. Condemned by a Land League court, Berklery's servants were beaten up, his farm gates pulled down, and an attempt was made to use his land as commonage. The public house he owned near the farm was also boycotted. Even an ex-policeman who ran a bakery was too afraid to deliver bread to Berklery: 'my horses would be killed and my drivers too, and my carts broken on the road. I might as well leave the country'.

The farmer left his home for a while but returned again and refused to be browbeaten or intimidated further. Lloyd, too, was up to the fight and stationed armed constabulary in the farm house. He then collected sufficient evidence, including a few witness statements, to justify the arrest of three surrounding and fairly well-off farmers, all he believed to be Fenians: Thomas O'Donnell, aged 35; Patrick McCormick, aged 40; and John Slattery, aged 44. A younger farmer's son, aged 21, was also rounded up to put a stop to the campaign. It is little wonder that Clifford Lloyd himself had 10 men with rifles close to him whenever he went out – 'my faithful and brave-hearted protectors, Irishmen to the core, brave, noble, and unselfish'. But such a life could be maintained only for so long. Lloyd saw the immediate crisis through and by 1883, he was able to escape to Egypt, returning briefly to Ireland as resident magistrate for Derry before again resuming colonial duty, which proved as controversial as his Irish sojourn.[22]

Even after he left Ireland, Clifford Lloyd was not forgotten there. Writing in *United Ireland* on 24 November 1883, Tim Healy sneered, 'Shortly after going to Egypt he [Clifford Lloyd] was attacked by cholera, but the cholera got the worst of it, because there was so much venom in him the cholera could not get a grip on him'.

The special magistrates were particularly involved in dealing with threats to landlords and protection. Though they held great authority in their regions they differed in approach, very often as a result of character. If Clifford Lloyd had an iron fist, Major R.G. Traill's was in a silken glove. Traill had seen service on the north-west frontier of India, where trouble was endemic. Yet both there and in the Lough Mask area, he maintained a cultured existence in India and Ireland. He was the younger brother of the celebrated future provost of Trinity College Dublin, Dr Anthony Traill (1838–1914), and like him was an enthusiastic sportsman, being an accomplished cricketer. His family held regular musical evenings or were part of an amateur dramatic group, with printed programmes for performances in whatever Irish big house they occupied or had access to.[23] Yet Traill was as astute as Clifford Lloyd and perhaps more thoughtful in his reactions.

In 1882, Traill had to deal with a threatening letter aimed at three men in a land agency office in Ballinarobe: George J. Darley, William Burke and William H. Good. In apparently friendly terms, Traill dismissed the story of the arrival of the dynamitards, but regarded the letter addressed to George Darley as a threatening communication:

Sir,

There was too men came over here from ingland and are to go
to Ballinarobe and long to night the have dimamite to put under the
window where you sleep and mind or you will be bloed up yourself
and your mate [Mr Burke?] You done my father a good turn and I
wood like to same you I am an old tenant of yours on Clarks estate

Another threatening letter to Darley had very different wording and, at 164
words, was more than twice as long:

Notice
Mr Darley this is to let you know that there are forty ground tenants
of the landlords and Agents marked out in the County Mayo that is
driving poor starving creatures to the workhouse to the Immegrante
ships And to the grave
Take notice that the land was not created for a few landlords that is
it was created for the whole human race Now you are reckoned to
be the third worse on that number

I do now warn you to through up your Agency at once and leave it
between the Landlord and Tenant You are reckoned to be a good
Agent by the Landlord But we reckon you to be the devils Agent &
remember if you don't through up all your agencies that we will give
you the contents of the revolver and skatter your brains the same as
we would to a mad dog There is many a man waiting the
opportunity You are getting fair chance.

William Burke received an even longer 234-word threatening letter. This
one began, 'How dare you have the impertinent audacity to continuing the
course you have so long pursued ...' and concluded:

This will your last warning and by my oath if it does not have the
desired effect you wont see no other Christmas day until you be in
your Kingdom come notwithstanding all the protection you get
from the R.I.C. Rory of the Hill.

When this arrived, on 3 August 1880, William Burke was in Dublin and the
mischievous letter was opened by Mrs Burke. Not surprisingly she was distressed
and the constabulary were summoned. This was another side of such activity –

the impact on the victim's family. To the credit of Inspector Law, immediate action was taken and two armed constables were installed in the house when Mr Burke arrived home the following evening. It was reported that the police had 'comfortable quarters' in Mrs Burke's back premises.

William Good lived and worked in town, so could be easily protected, but the other two land agents had to travel. So Traill set out in some detail the protective measures to be taken, including the use of a second police vehicle when in the countryside; irregular days for excursions and instructions as to which roads should be patrolled; and that one of the RIC men have only ball in his carbine, the other two being loaded with the wider-spreading buckshot. He also advocated police to go ahead of the person being protected and reconnoitre 'every likely wood, or place of ambush'. He instructed, 'Spare no expense to secure the safety of these gentlemen'.[24]

As well as such cases where the magistrates had to ensure specific personal protection, additional police were, at the local magistrate's request, drafted in to proclaimed districts and areas where trouble had dramatically increased. For example, between 1879 and 1888, the RIC presence in County Clare increased by 43 per cent from 328 men to 572. In the same period in Kerry, the increase was 56 per cent, from 603 to 1,361.[25] There followed a great increase in the number of police patrols especially at night.

Police response

The front line in the fight against outrages, including threatening letters and notices, was the RIC. This paramilitary and largely Irish-recruited force was the vehicle for maintaining stability and law and order in the country. Numbers within the force fluctuated from about 10,000 to 12,000, with the number of stations and barracks well exceeding 1,000.

There was also the British army presence in Ireland, by 1896 numbering some 25,000 men. But the authorities were very reluctant to use the military in anything which did not signal outright rebellion or the prospect of that. So, in 1868 and again in 1880, Dublin Castle issued *General orders for the guidance of the troops in affording aid to the civil power in Ireland*.[26] But even in times of crisis, such as during the Captain Boycott episode, the military were primarily used for guarding and escorting. In the case of civil unrest, such as riot, they were under the overall direction of a magistrate.

Moreover, the concentration of British troops was in greater Dublin/The Curragh region where nearly 45 per cent of troops were stationed.[27] If to that one adds the cities of Belfast, Cork (including Cork harbour) and Limerick, these areas accounted for two-thirds of the Irish garrison. As Figure 29 shows, rural Ireland was not a priority when it came to the army. Indeed, an argument can be made that the regiments were garrisoned in Ireland just as they were elsewhere in the United Kingdom, as much for logistical purposes as security. It is also noteworthy that when the Invincibles were terrorising Dublin in the early 1880s, it was not the garrison troops who were primarily deployed in the Irish capital but imported elite Royal Marines.

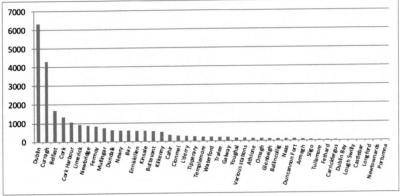

Fig. 29—Size of military garrison in Ireland, 1896

In the Irish countryside, 'outrage terrorism' fell on the shoulders of the local constabulary and the magistrates, albeit in the worst districts augmented by additional draconian powers. What is extraordinary about this situation is how successful the RIC was at keeping matters in check. Equally extraordinary was the fact that until the Anglo-Irish War or the second decade of the twentieth-century, the police were well respected in the communities. That is not to say they were loved. They were not, and come 1922 and independence, there were nasty incidents of RIC men being driven out of their homes.[28] During the Irish War of Independence, between 1919 and 1922, 534 RIC men were killed.[29] That said, the force, which in the ranks was predominately Catholic, had an integrity which carried it through the darkest of days.

In the 1860s, perhaps because of the veiled attack on the police by the judiciary, relating to their failure to bring writers of threatening letters to book, the police did respond and sometimes quite forcefully. The county inspector in Cavan asserted:

In respect to threatening letters, I beg respectfully to submit that, except in a rare case, and where some fortuitous circumstance

185

presents itself to aid in the detection of the offender, it is most difficult, if not altogether impossible, to detect the guilty party. The Ribbon system has generally, I believe, something to do with threatening letters, which may be concocted in the locality,

The county inspector for Roscommon concurred:

It is true that there are people in this county who may have been displeased with their landlords or agents, and have caused to be written and sent anonymous threatening letters to them; but as that offence can be effected in such a private manner, it is almost impossible for the Constabulary to discover who the offenders are. I am sure that, though unsuccessful, they have used every means in their power to do so.

And five years earlier, in 1859, the senior police officer in King's County had asserted:

unless some person in the secret will turn approver; and although the police in all these cases visited the scene, and exerted themselves to discover the offenders, their efforts proved abortive, since the threatened parties could not or would not afford any clue.[30]

Even the under-secretary's department at Dublin Castle, under whom the constabulary fell, was quick to dismiss many threatening letter cases, sometimes with the meaningless and certainly misleading catch-all: 'This case may be regarded as completed. Nothing further is likely to transpire about it'.[31]

Both the *Irish Constabulary Guide* and the *Royal Irish Constabulary Manual* covered threatening letters, the former dealing with legislation relating to the matter and the latter laying out procedure to be followed in threatening letter cases. The latter laid out that the policeman should initial and date the back of both the letter and the envelope. With the turn of the century, finger printing was employed with threatening letters, and recipients were advised not to open any other letter which arrived with the same or similar handwriting. The constabulary members were also advised that they were not to obtain samples of a suspect's handwriting by 'inducing him by any trick or artifice to write something for the purpose of comparison'. This last regulation was frequently ignored.[32]

Police protection and the armed compound

During the 1880s, a considerable sum was spent on giving armed protection to those whose lives were thought by the authorities to be in danger because of outrages. In 1884, in Dublin, the DMP provided three inspectors, six sergeants and 99 constables as personal protection for senior high-profile Dublin Castle officials as well as for judges and police magistrates. As most of these dignitaries lived close to each other in Merrion Square, Fitzwilliam Square, Baggot Street or Lesson Street, that part of Dublin just south of Leinster House must have been awash with policemen. It is noteworthy that in the capital, none of those protected might be termed private individuals, a statement in itself on the different circumstances relating to rural Ireland.

In the countryside, the situation was very different. It is true that large numbers of magistrates had constabulary protection as did some landlords, but so too did others less elevated. Table 8 illustrates the situation which existed in the quarter ending 30 June 1884.

Where protection was granted outside Dublin, up to seven constabulary men were either housed with the victim or in a small wooden hut erected nearby in which two, three or four constables lived a dull and cramped

Table 8–Protection given by RIC, 1884

Division	Number of special police huts or posts	Number of police employed on police protection	Number of persons under protection
Midland	42	126	49
Western	119	487	100
South-western	102	387	122
South-eastern	10	21	14
12 counties directly under the Inspector General of the RIC	20	106	17
RIC districts total	*293* (96%)	*1,127* (92%)	*302* (95%)
Dublin Metropolitan Police district	*13* (4%)	*96* (8%)	*17* (5%)
Grand total	306	1,223	319

existence. Most of these postings were made because of attempted murder or serious arson attacks. Those who were boycotted and groups of Emergency men were also sometimes given police protection. Invariably, threatening letters and notices preceded the decision of the authorities that a genuine threat of attack existed. In 1884, the following were cases in point:

- S.D. Cahil of Ballard, Ennistymon, Galway:
  Hut with 5 police.
- W.P. & P. Lambert of Castle Ellen, Athenry, Galway:
  House with 7 policemen.
- W. Seymour of Ballymore, Ballinalloe, Galway:
  Hut with 4 policemen.
- Dr B. Cogan (& Ml White, herd) Kilkittare, Woodford, Galway:
  House with 3 policemen.
- George J. Darley of Lakeview, Ballinrobe, Mayo:
  House with 3 policemen.
- William Burke, J.P., of Lisloughery, Ballinrobe, Mayo:
  House with 3 policemen.
- Michael Molloy of Bunmore East, Newport, Mayo:
  House with 2 policemen.
- James McGoohan & Mr Benison, Aghoo, Ballinamore, Leitrim:
  House with 2 policemen.
- Col. R.A. Dopping-Hepenstal, Derrycassan, Granard, Longford:
  House with 3 policemen.[33]

In fact, the number of persons receiving protection from the police far exceeded anything recorded. If a landlord received the protection of two or three constables, for example, they were protecting the whole household, too. This might include a wife and children as well as hapless servants trapped in the invidious position of having to choose between loyalty to their employer and loss of their livelihood.

During the Famine years, the Church of Ireland dean of a Sligo parish received a threatening letter dated from Strokestown and posted in Elphin. In his appeal for police protection he observed that if he, as a clergyman, carried a gun and used it on an attacker, it might cause an outcry from the public and give an erroneous impression of his character. He was given the protection he sought and the resident magistrate had a notice printed offering £20 for information received which resulted in a conviction over the secret society Rockite notice.[34] Occasionally the recipient of a threatening letter was permitted a licence by the police to carry a firearm. This occurred in the Ballyjamesduff case quoted elsewhere when a gombeenman called O'Reilly found that he had taken on more than he could handle when trying to get a tenant farmer to pay his debt.[35] Issuing gun licences to those perceived to be under possible threat in times of agrarian unrest was common enough. One auctioneer's advertising poster in March 1847 mentioned:

> Whereas many evil disposed persons avail themselves of the present scarcity of Food, as a pretext to commit acts of Violence against property, and otherwise disturbing the peace of the Country, his Excellency the Lord Lieutenant is pleased to grant all her Majesty's peaceable and loyal subjects without distinction, the power to have and to keep any description of Firearms, for the protection of the public peace and likewise their own homes and property, without restriction, except an invoice or Certificate of the person from whom the Arms are purchased.

While the landed classes freely carried revolvers, often in a cavalier fashion, there are only one or two instances where these were actually used to fend off an attacker.

During the 1880s, there was a correlation between areas where threatening letters were prevalent, the provision of additional constabulary patrols and the provision of full-time special protections to individuals. As Figure 30 illustrates for 1887, Munster had most police intervention, followed by Leinster, then Connaught and finally Ulster, with Antrim and Tyrone having no such constabulary protection at all. The only divergence in pattern was that Connaught fell behind Leinster in overall special patrols provided by the RIC with totals of 180 and 233 respectively. For instances of constant protection, Connaught actually exceeded Leinster, the numbers being 65 for Connaught and 27 for Leinster. Overall, in 1887, the total number of patrols and special protection situations stood at 1,001. In 1888, it was 910 and by 1892, it had fallen to 645, a decline in five years of 36 per cent. This trend was echoed in the same five years by a 22 per cent decline in recorded threatening letters.[36]

All the extra constabulary patrols and personal security provided to those under threat of violence had to be paid for. The practice was to add an extra

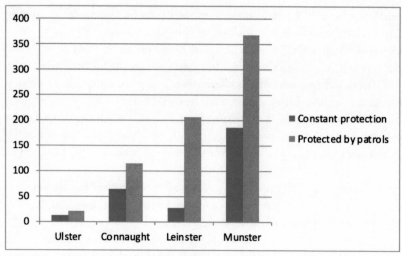

Fig. 30–Number of persons receiving special police protection, 1887

tax or cess to the local rates, something which became so unpopular that this in itself became the subject of outrages, in particular threatening letters. In December 1851, in Newtownhamilton in County Armagh, a cess collector called McClean was given police protection when he received a threatening notice ordering him to cease collecting the extra cess in the village of Creggan, near Crossmaglen. A reward of £50 for information leading to a conviction in the case was offered.[37]

The police newspaper
A useful source for the historian of crime in Victorian Ireland is the official Irish police newspaper, entitled *The Police Gazette* or *Hue-and-Cry*. This was published in Dublin every Wednesday and Saturday and was circulated to all police barracks and stations. It covered both the jurisdiction of the RIC as well as the DMP, and frequently also featured notices from police forces in Great Britain. It was essentially a list of the most wanted, whether criminals or deserters from the armed forces. Its columns are mostly taken up with notices concerning crimes such as assault, indecent assault, larceny, manslaughter, murder or attempted murder, rape and theft. Sometimes, there were notices relating to absconding, arson, embezzlement, firing at an individual and fraud. Very occasionally, a pick-pocket might make the pages. For lengthy periods, though, threatening letters or notices were not a feature of the *Hue-and-Cry*.

190

The reason for this lacuna was not that threatening letters or notices were not regarded as a crime or were not prevalent but that police tended to view such actions as less serious than other crimes. But there was another factor. Invariably the notices in the *Hue-and-Cry* specifically sought named individuals who were either suspects or who had fled justice. Very rarely did the police have anyone who was suspected of composing or posting a threatening communication who was on the run. For this reason, in some editions of the *Hue-and-Cry*, notices were published, such as the one below, usually offering a £20 reward in relation to tracing the authors of secret society 'rockite' letters or notices.[38]

Galway

Twenty Pounds Reward.

Wheras, on the night of the 14th instant, a rockite notice was posted on Mr William Roberston's gate at Roundstone, co. Galway, threatening his life should he not give up the lands of Letterdiffe to its former tenants:
I hereby offer a reward of £20 to any person who shall, within six months from the date hereof, give such information as shall lead to the arrest of the party concerne in writing or posting the notice in question. Payable on conviction.
Robt. McKim, Head-Constable
Roundstone, 20th Dec, 1854.[39]

The sending of threatening letters to the clergy seems to have been more likely to elicit a reward notice in the *Hue-and-Cry* than such threats sent to an ordinary landlord. One example is as follows:

Waterford

Twenty Pounds Reward.

Whereas, a rockite notice was recently sent, by a party unknown, to the Rev. David Alfred Doudney, of Bonmahon, in the county of Waterford, warning him 'have his coffin made and his grave dug.'
I hereby offer a reward of £20 to any person who shall, within six months from the date hereof, give such information as shall lead to the arrest of the party concerned in writing or sending the notice in question. Payable on conviction.
Edward Orme, Resident Magistrate
Dungarvan, 3rd June, 1857.[40]

As already mentioned, threatening letters to Protestant clergy invariably centred on land ownership rather than naked sectarianism.[41]

Sending threatening letters to judges in Ireland is a timeless occupation which transcends the centuries and the judicial dispensation. In 1880, it was said of Judge Fitzgerald of the Munster assizes:

> The Judge himself received many threatening letters, written in the hope of intimidating him. One of these, exceptionally vindictive in tone, he read from the Bench. The writer swore that worms would have their Christmas dinner off the Judge's bones, if he attempted to bring convictions against certain prisoners.[42]

This was not likely to be a helpful move on the part of the associates of the accused person.

Jurors were also sometimes targeted for threatening letters as Judge 'Peter the Packer' O'Brien observed, no doubt this was because they were not as tough as the Victorian Irish assize judge.

The famous Dublin magistrate and later county court judge, John Adye Curran, recounted a threatening letter case which came before Chief Baron Pigot in the 1860s. The defendant was a Maryborough schoolmaster. 'An expert', a bank manager and an RIC district inspector all swore that the writing in the threatening letter was that of the accused. The defending barrister was Curran's father, Curran junior assisting. The latter knowing he had handwriting similar to his father, wrote 'John Adye Curran' three times on a sheet of paper and then asked his father to write the same name on the same sheet of paper. The result was predictable. The handwriting expert was recalled and shown the sheet of paper. He requested time to consider whether one or more hands had written the name on the sheet. He, in turn, consulted a second expert. It very much underlined the verdict of William O'Brien, the nationalist politician, on the mumbling of the abracadabra of the handwriting expert.[43]

In the end, neither expert agreed with the other as to how many hands had written the name. The case against the schoolmaster was dismissed, with Curran senior recalling the words of Judge Keogh that 'he would not hang a dog on the evidence of an expert'.[44] This is a good anecdote, but it also highlights the near impossibility facing the authorities in achieving a conviction on a threatening letter charge.

The law became more amenable to the matter of handwriting as the Victorian era progressed, compared to the early 1850s. Initially, a magistrate could not, in theory, raid premises just for the purpose of obtaining an example of the handwriting of a suspected threatening-letter writer. Nor were juries permitted to inspect a threatening letter with any example of the handwriting of the accused.[45]

Low prosecution rates

During the 1850s, although threatening letters were not as major a feature of rural Irish society as they had been or would become again later, the conviction rate for outrage crimes remained low. Take, for example, the troubled Kilmacrenan region of west Donegal. Between 1851 and 1861, 385 crimes were reported for Kilmacrenan. Of these only 133, or 35 per cent, went to trial and there were 46 convictions. Of these 385 cases, 43 or 11 per cent related to threatening letters, and only six cases went to court. Of those six cases, one accused fled to the United States, one was granted bail, three were acquitted and in only one case was there a conviction, involving four people.[46]

In March 1886, it was said that before the grand jury in Kerry were:

- 2 cases of murder
- 39 cases of cattle, horse and sheep stealing
- 11 cases of arson
- 18 cases of maiming cattle
- 52 cases of seizing arms
- 18 cases of letters threatening to murder
- 72 cases of sending threatening letters
- 24 cases of intimidation

That is 90 cases of threatening letters, or nearly 40 per cent of the 236 cases tabled.[47] Overall, in the seven years from 1886 until 1892, the authorities claimed to have 'successfully grappled' with 54 cases of 'Persecution and intimidation'. But that was less than 2 per cent of the total of 2,859 threatening letters recorded for that period, and some of those 54 cases would not have involved threatening letters or notices.[48]

Low conviction rates

Even when the authorities brought a threatening-letter case to court, their chances of gaining a conviction were slim. This was sometimes in part because of partisan juries but also because of other factors. One of these was the attitude judges had to handwriting experts. In 1933, Dr Robert Saudek quoted a London evening newspaper:

when the experts were called upon to testify as to the genuineness or otherwise of the disputed document, they disagreed as they always do ...[49]

Mention has already been made of the authorities making use of handwriting experts in threatening-letter cases. As early as the 1860s, the authorities were using these experts in such criminal cases.

In the threatening letter trial of John Gillick of Cavan, a Mr Craig was paid £6-4-0 for his expert opinion. These opinions were not always satisfactory and the local magistrates were not always convinced their fees were worth the trouble, especially if someone local could identify an accused's handwriting without charge. In one instance in Gort, County Galway, the magistrate and the police had to deal with shooting into a house and posting of a threatening letter, as well a possible suicide by one of the suspects and the receipt of a threatening letter by the other, whose bail was paid by the victim's tenants. As the local constable stoically observed, 'I beg leave to say that it is very difficult and I believe almost impossible to carry out the administration of justice in this threatening notice transaction'.[50]

To make matters worse, the handwriting expert submitted a claim for £10-18-0, for which the fee itself was only two guineas. The balance of the claim consisted of six guineas to attend the Gort petty sessions for two days and £2-10-0 for train and jaunting-car travel. The claim went through Samuel Anderson's office to the under-secretary in Dublin Castle, who approved it.

As handwriting evidence was now acceptable if not always successful in gaining a conviction, the natural consequence was, where possible, to seek out examples of a suspect's handwriting in the hope of gaining a conviction. But raiding private premises could not be undertaken without a warrant. In 1864, a senior RIC officer commented:

> The Constabulary frequently search suspected houses for writing, for the sake of comparison with the threatening letter; but that course is not strictly legal, the Law Officers having decided that we cannot search a man's house for writing or papers with that object. A search warrant to do so cannot be obtained; a Magistrate will not issue a warrant for any such purpose; and I believe that if a Police Officer were to search houses in the way I have now described, he would do so at his peril; and were an action to be taken against him, the jury might be told he was an unlawful trespasser, and that damages must be given against him.[51]

However, with the passing of the Prevention of Crime Act in 1882, this was permitted under section 14 for the duration of the measure. For example, the property of John O'Sullivan at Rathreale in County Limerick was raided on 20 October 1884 at 6 p.m. with the following result: 'Found and seized documents resembling writing in threats and Boycotting recently posted up about Shanagolden in connection with his Son's late farm.' Another raid at New Pallas in the same county on 17 October, on the home of Michael Nolan, had been less successful: 'Searched for handwriting of Michael Nolan Junr. for comparison with Boycotting notice found posted at Bohm chapel 17 August 1884. None found except his name written in Books.'[52]

Table 9 gives details of convictions in threatening letter cases coming to trial in the mid-to-late 1840s.[53]

Table 9–Convictions for threatening letters, 1844–50

Year	Number of threatening letters reported in year	Number of cases brought to trial	Number of convictions	Convictions as % of total cases brought to trial	Convictions as % of cases reported
1844	863	25	5	20%	0.50%
1845	1944	33	14	42%	0.70%
1846	1773	24	6	25%	0.30%
1847	951	26	11	42%	1.10%
1848	784	19	5	26%	0.60%
1849	645	20	2	10%	0.30%
1850	821	18	3	17%	0.30%
Total	7,781	165	46	28%	0.60%

In 1850, of the 18 cases of threatening letters, 17 of the defendants were male and one was female. Twelve could read and write; four could only read; and the authorities could not ascertain the literacy standard of the remaining two. Fifteen, more than 80 per cent, were discharged or acquitted. The remaining three cases went to trial. All were convicted, with one transported for seven years while the other two received six-month prison sentences each.

A generation later, matters remained unsatisfactory from the point of view of the authorities when it came to convictions for writing or delivering threatening letters and notices, as Tables 10 and 11 show.

According to George Goschen, the chancellor of the exchequer, in 1886, only 6 per cent – 61 convictions – resulted from 1,056 cases of agrarian

Table 10–Conviction rate for threatening letters: April–June 1882[54]

1882	Number of threatening letters reported each month	Arrests made relating to threatening letters	Convictions
April	287	5	1
May	244	1	1
June	155	0	-

Table 11–Convictions for threatening letters, 1883[55]

Year	Number of threatening letter reports in year	Number of cases brought to trial	Number of convictions	Convictions as % of total cases brought to trial	Convictions as % of cases reported
1883	630	37	9	24%	1.40%

outrage. Conviction rates were also low in cases where outrages turned violent. There was only one conviction among six murder cases and also only one conviction among 10 cases of firing at a person.[56] The authorities faced three key problems when trying to secure a conviction. The foremost was that of getting a local jury to convict, even when the evidence of guilt was clear cut. Second was the reluctance of witnesses to expose themselves to what the advanced men in the community regarded at best as a betrayal and at worst as the act of an informer. Jury packing, in one guise or another, was a two-way street in Ireland. The third problem was less of an obstacle than some writers imagined: that of carrying out normal detective work in the countryside. Had the first two problems been resolved, the third would not have been a great issue. Nonetheless, the perception was there. As one writer in the *Quarterly Review* picturesquely phrased it in 1870:

> Detectives can track crime in crowded cities; but these murders are committed in rural districts where every man is known to his neighbour, and where a stranger appearing near the scene would be

himself tracked and watched night and day, and, as soon as his errand was guessed, probably lodged in some bottomless hole in the convenient bog.[57]

Internment without trial

Cases involving threatening letters fell under the famous PPP Act allowing for internment without trial. Samuel Lee Anderson made an analysis of the consequences of the Protection of Persons and Property (Ireland) Act, 1882. By February 1881, Thomas Burke, the under-secretary, had compiled a list of 512 individuals who had been caught in the PPP net. This included

Table 12–Those detained without trial for writing threatening letters, 1880–1[58]

Name	Prison detailed	Suspected grounds for arrest
Timothy Dooling	Limerick	Writing and posting a notice threatening violence and injury to a certain person, for the purpose of deterring him from serving legal process, committed in a prescribed district.
Charles O'Beirne	Galway	Unlawfully causing to be delivered a threatening message requiring persons to desist from following their lawful occupation, committed in a prescribed district.
Edward Barrett	Galway	Writing, and causing to be received, threatening notices, committed in a prescribed district.
Martin Spellman	Galway	Causing to be posted diverse threatening notices requiring others not to deal or hold communication with certain persons, committed in a prescribed district.
Michael Glennon	Galway	Causing to be posted a threatening notice requiring certain persons to quit and give up their employment, committed in a prescribed district.
Patrick Guihan	Galway	Writing and posting threatening notices, committed in a prescribed district.
Michael Watters	Armagh	Writing letters threatening to murder, committed in a prescribed district.

Charles Stewart Parnell, who was incarcerated in some comfort in Kilmainham Jail. Seventy-three per cent of the internees, including Parnell himself, were rounded up for various acts of alleged intimidation. But only seven people, or 1 per cent of the 512, were specified as having been arrested under suspicion of having written threatening letters or notices. These are listed in Table 12.

Given the thousands of threatening letters being written at the time, these seven represent a small haul. Matters did not improve. By the autumn of 1882, the number of people who had been arrested and held for a myriad of outrage crimes under the PPP Act had doubled to nearly a thousand. These included assault and robbery, arson, attacking dwellings and buildings, boycotting, cattle maiming, intimidating against paying rent, malicious wounding, murder, rioting and inciting riots, shooting, treasonable practices, unlawful assembly and involvement in threatening letters and notices. But, as Table 13 illustrates, in the 17 months from April 1881 to August 1882, only 22 or just 2 per cent of the total of 992 arrests related to threatening notices or letters.[59] This shows an interesting reversal from another set of statistics. In the 1881/1882 period, there were 5,600 cases of threatening letters reported to the RIC, an increase of 75 per cent on the previous two years. This total of 5,600 far exceeded any other category of outrage. It indicates the great difficulty the authorities had in even identifying suspects, including Dublin Castle justifying their internment, let alone successfully pursuing a case through the courts.

Sentencing in threatening-letter cases

Sentences handed out to the unfortunate few convicted of writing threatening letters and notices fluctuated over time. On the whole, they were harsher in the early Victorian era than in the late. This is not particularly surprising given the nature of law reform in the nineteenth century. However, the lack of arrests in threatening-letter cases irritated the judiciary. By the 1860s, they made no bones about this frustration. A Cavan judge in 1864, listing various unsolved crimes, concluded:

> ... and twelve *threatening* letters, in which only two persons were made amenable [all crimes including threatening letters]. It is a serious and startling state of things, and one deeply to be deplored, that so large an amount of undiscovered crime should exist in the county. I will offer no opinion on this deplorable state of things, but would impress on you as magistrates and residents, to give the

198

Table 13–Internment under the PPP Act, April 1881 to August 1882

County	Place	Person arrested	Period held	Reason for arrest
Donegal	Dungloe	Edward Coll	7	Sending threatening notice
	Dungloe	Hugh McBride	7	Sending threatening letter
Galway	Athenry	Edward Barrett	14	Sending threatening letter
	Dunmore	Michael Ryan	3.5	Sending threatening notice
	Loughrea	Michael Glennon	7.5	Posting threatening notices
	Portumna	Patrick Larkin	4	Posting threatening notice
Kerry	Listowel	Timothy Dowling	10	Threatening notice
	Listow	Martin Sullivan	5	Posting threatening notice
Leitrim	Ballinamore	Charles O'Beirne	11	Sending threatening letter
	Drumahaire	Patrick Guihan	7.5	Writing threatening notice
Limerick	Kilfinane	Francis Allen	4	Sending threatening notice
	Kilfinane	Thomas Dowling	1.5	Accessory to sending threatening notice
	Kilfinane	Daniel Reardon	3.5	Sending threatening notice
	Kilfinane	Michael Tobin	3	Sending threatening notice
	Kilmallock	James W. Joyce	4	Writing threatening notices
	Kilmallock	Thomas O'Donnell	3	Sending threatening notice
	Kilmallock	John Slattery	3	Sending threatening notice
	Newcastle West	Thomas Wall	2.5	Publishing threatening notice
Longford	Longford	James Fury	1.5	Posting threatening notice
Queens	Mountrath	Martin Delaney	3	Writing threatening letters
West-meath	Delving	James Higgins	5	Writing threatening notices
			Av. 5.2 months	

matter your best consideration, and if possible, apply a practical remedy to so serious an evil.

His counterpart in Longford was similarly direct in asserting that those involved in writing threatening letters, when brought before him, 'would be visited with the severest punishment which he was empowered by Legislature to inflict'.[60] Despite this pressure, many magistrates, and indeed some judges, refused to be bullied into handing out draconian sentences. As a result, there emerged a great disparity of sentencing from one county to the next and one decade to the next.

County Limerick assizes in 1846 included Thomas Maher and also Patrick Ryan, both referred from Murroe petty sessions, and given six months each.[61] In the 1847 spring assizes at Nenagh, there were six convictions for delivering threatening letters. Five of these received seven years' deportation and one got 12 months in prison. At the next summer assizes at Nenagh, there were four convictions for serving threatening notices, with three defendants being sentenced to two years' imprisonment and one to one year.[62] As late as 1865, a man at the Fermanagh assizes was sentenced to five years' penal servitude for sending a threatening letter.

What Judge Curran remarked of those convicted for short-term prison sentences for cattle-driving could as well be said of those convicted for writing and sending threatening letters: 'Sending the guilty parties to prison for a month in default of giving bail was quite futile. Those men went in as martyrs and came out as heroes'.[63] Even so, a large number of convicted threatening letter writers did receive short sentences, especially as the century progressed. The petty sessions tended to hand out sentences of two to six months for the offence. In December 1880, a man received nine months' hard labour 'on extremely flimsy evidence' for sending a threatening letter to his employer, Peter Blake of Hollypark, after allegedly sending the landlord a letter which threatened death if he evicted a woman.[64] Why certain cases were referred to the assizes is not clear. On occasion, it appears to have been on not much more than whim.

Sometimes matters went the way of the authorities, who could then be magnanimous in sentencing, such as in the Rathcahill Creamery case in County Limerick. A sub-manager had been sacked on suspicion of theft. Subsequently a notice was found threatening farmers not to supply milk to the creamery until the manager was restored to his position. Unfortunately for those involved, at 10.30 p.m. at night on 28 July 1897 an RIC patrol caught three of the four men in the act of posting up this notice. The matter went before the Newcastle

Table 14–Rewards offered for information leading to conviction in threatening letter and notice cases, 1836–7

Date	County	Outrage	Reward amount
January 1836	Sligo	Posting a threatening notice	£20
February	Wicklow	Threatening notices served on the lands of Rosshane	£40
March	Sligo	Posting threatening notice	£40
April	Galway	Threatening notice served on Rev. Mr Burke	£40
August	Queen's [Laois]	Sending threatening notice to W.D. Ferrar, Esq.	£40
September	Tipperary	Posting illegal notices and attacking houses in parish of Bally-moreen, barony Eli-ogurty	£50
December	Kilkenny	Threatening notice posted at Gowran against tithes	£30
February 1837	Wexford	Posting illegal notice at Ballyhast	£30
March	Londonderry	Sending threatening notices to Mr McAfee	£40
March	Longford	Leaving threatening notice with J. Atkin-son	£30
April	Donegal	Threatening notices served	£40
December	Leitrim	Pasting threatening notice at Outeragh	£20

petty sessions on 7 August. Meanwhile the defendants' friends had canvassed lifting the boycott and soon normal supplies were arriving at Rathcahill. Sensibly, the magistrate decided that the matter would not go to trial and directed the defendants to find security to keep the peace for 12 months. This was duly procured and the matter closed.[65]

Rewards

There is ample evidence that the authorities, on occasion, were alarmed enough by a threatening letter or notice, or series of such, to offer a reward for information leading to a conviction. Table 14 sets out 11 such in the two-year period 1836/1837 – none of these rewards was claimed.[66]

Several points can be made from this information. The first is that out of 519 rewards offered by the authorities in this two-year period, only 11 or 2 per cent related to threatening notices. Second, the reward varied from £20 to £50 and averaged about £40, a large sum of money in 1837. Finally, the fact that no reward offered was claimed in this period indicates the difficulty in obtaining a conviction in a threatening letter case.

The Staunton threatening letter trial

A summary survives, badly water-stained even after restoration, of a threatening notice case which went for trial to the spring assizes in March 1858 at Naas in County Kildare. The defendant was a man named Thomas Staunton and the case was heard before Chief Justice Monahan and a jury. Sergeant Berwick, Mr Battersby QC, Mr W.H. Grith and Mr Crawford appeared for the crown and Mr Ball QC and Mr J.A. Curran defended the prisoner.[67]

The gist of the case was that Thomas Staunton, a tenant at will of a man named Dobbs, had had an on-going and bitter dispute with the local land agent, Christopher Rynd, and the bailiff, John McDermott. On 1 January 1858, a rambling printed notice had been found at the chapel of Staplestown, just south-west of Maynooth. Other copies were also found by various individuals in the neighbourhood. The notice demanded, on behalf of Mr Dobbs' tenants, that Rynd and McDermott resign and leave the country – 'to hunt these Reptiles off the land'. The notice went on to assert that Rynd had 'vowed to evict every Catholic off the property and supply their place by Protestants'.

There was also an allegation that Rynd had given £110 to the election campaign of Sir Edward Kennedy, 'for the purpose of bribery and perjury'. This sum had, the notice continued, been subsequently levied on the turf banks of the Dobbs' estate. Kennedy had stood for Kildare in the 1852 general election as a conservative and was unsuccessful, coming bottom of the poll with 616 votes, beaten by two liberals.[68]

Staunton was by no means an impoverished tenant, an interesting fact in itself. As well as farming, he ran a shop in the village. He fell under suspicion when a man named Broughton informed the authorities that Staunton had asked him to 'drop a few notices thro' the country'. This Broughton had refused to do. In addition, the authorities learnt that Staunton had made a remark that he would 'let fly a squib of a notice at Mr Rynd'. The search of Staunton's house revealed a locked trunk in the sleeping room. In this trunk, inside a book, was a copy of the printed notice. Downstairs in Staunton's shop the police found a locked drawer in which was a piece of paper. Written on it in blue ink was a 'more malignant' version of the printed threatening notice. This was said to be in Staunton's handwriting. This handwritten version threatened to shoot dead Rynd and McDermott if they did not quit the country. Two other scraps of paper were found with similar writing on them, which the constabulary considered to be drafts of the notice. To cap matters, a pot of blue ink was found in the shop.

It was an interesting case, not least in the verdict, which at seven years' penal servitude was particularly severe for the period. This appears to have been imposed both as a deterrent as well as in recognition that threatening notices were frequently harbingers of more serious offences. In a statement on the case, Sergeant Berwick observed:

> Such offences have generally commenced with threatening Notices; written for the purpose of terrifying the rich, but the fatal effect has been to ruin the poor – Seldom has it occurred that the owner has been the person substantially injured, but almost always the poor and the holders of the land.

He went on to comment:

> For the purpose of meeting this class of cases, a code of law has been invented. The legislature wisely thought that the best course was to nip such proceedings in the bud, and to take care that proceedings, which in order states of society might be passed over in silence and treated with contempt, should be laid hold of in order to prevent those engaged in them from becoming implicated in more serious offences.

Notes

1 Edward Cromwell Brown, 'English law – The threatening letter or writings', *The Imperial Magazine*, March 1827, 7.75, cols 238–9.
2 Tumultuous Rising (Ireland) Act 1831: Cap. 44. [15 October 1831].
3 http://www.irishstatutebook.ie/eli/1861/act/100/enacted/en/print.htmlmrder (accessed 18 June 2016).
4 Vaughan, *Landlords and tenants in mid-Victorian Ireland*, pp. 140–1.
5 BPP: *Agrarian crimes (Ireland). Returns of all agrarian crimes and outages reported by the Royal Irish Constabulary in the Counties of Galway, Mayo, Sligo, and Donegal, from the 1st day of February 1880 to the 30th day of June 1880 ...*, 3 August 1880, p. 2.
6 See, for example, NAI, CSORP 1881, James O'Donnell, 7 July 1881, 3/638/4.
7 Quoted in Townshend, *Political violence in Ireland*, p. 134. BL, Add. MS 44125, ff. 48–9.
8 NAI, CSORP 1884, Western Division, 22141, 30 September 1884, 3/644/28.
9 BL, Spencer papers, Add Ms 77314, memorandum to cabinet, 25 December 1885. Also in Finnegan, *Loughrea*, p. 137.
10 Townshend, *Political violence in Ireland*, p. 210.
11 TNA, CO 903/1.
12 NAI, CSORP 1881, 3/638/ 4, 1881.
13 See, for example, NAI, CSORP 1821, SC, 689.
14 See, for example, CSORP outrage papers, Tipperary 1846, 27/6061, 8 March 1846, 3/704/29.
15 NAI, CSO, RP File 15046 (8–11), Kilbeggan, Reade to Under Secretary, Bilbeggan, 7 October 1870.
16 Trench, *Realities of Irish life*, p. 230.
17 *Report from the select committee on outrages (Ireland)*, 1852, p. 10.
18 Brownrigg, *Examination of some recent allegations concerning the constabulary force of Ireland*, p. 52.
19 See, for example, *History Ireland*, vol. 23, no. 5, September/October 2015, p. 27.
20 *Western News*, 19 August 1882, quoted in Finnegan, *Loughrea*, p. 123.
21 Clifford Lloyd, *Ireland under the Land League*, pp. 91–3.
22 Richard Hawkins, 'Lloyd, Charles Dalton Clifford', *Dictionary of Irish Biography*, vol. 5, pp. 521–2.
23 The author has Traill concert programmes for: Nowshera, Punjab (1867); Rawalpindi, Punjab (1869); Armagh (1882); Clonoe 1882); Heathstown, Alexanra (1885); Ballinlough Castle, Delvin (1886); Kilbride, Co. Meath (1886); Ballinlough Castle (1887); Sylvan Park (1887); and Saint Columba (1888). Also per. com. David Traill to Donal McCracken, 23 June 2021.
24 NAI, CSORP 1882, box 2782, 3/639/1.
25 'Twelve years of Clare and Kerry', leaflet no. 7, fourth series, contained in *Irish Loyal and Patriot Union. Publications issued during the year 1889*, p. 34.
26 *General orders for the guidance of the troops in affording aid to the civil power in Ireland*, Dublin, HMSO, 1880, Z/Ireland/112. A copy can be found in NAI, CSORP, 1880, box 2706.
27 CSORP, 1893, box 3880, 'Distrubution of the army in Ireland, 1st July, 1893, Gs.
28 McCarthy, *The Irish revolution, 1912–23. Waterford*, p. 99.

[29] Herlihy, *The Royal Irish Constabulary*, p. 151.

[30] *Examination of some recent allegations concerning the constabulary force of Ireland*, pp. 65 and 82.

[31] NAI, CSORP 1884, Threatening notice Garrangibbon, 21362, 2 April 1884, 3/644/27.

[32] See, Reed, *The Irish Constable's Guide*, pp. 436–7; Sparrow, *The Royal Irish Constabulary Manual*, pp. 303–5.

[33] NAI, CSORP, 1884, box 2984, 3/644/16.

[34] NAI, CSORP, Outrage papers, Tipperary, Sligo and Roscommon, December 1847.

[35] NAI, CSORP, 1884, 3/644/28.

[36] BPP: *Police Protection (Ireland)*, p. 2.

[37] NAI, CSORP, Outrage papers, Armagh, 1851, 3/705/20.

[38] See for example, *Hue-and-Cry*, 19 October 1847; and 18 and 23 August 1854.

[39] *Hue-and-Cry*, 23 December 1854.

[40] *Hue-and-Cry*, 12 June 1857.

[41] See, for instance, a reward of £40 offered in connection with a threatening letter sent to Rev. D.O. Etough of Oughteragh in County Leitrim and his land agent in *Hue-and-Cry*, 12 July 1854.

[42] O'Brien, *The reminiscences of the Right Hon. Lord O'Brien*, pp. 31–2.

[43] O'Brien, *Evening memories*, p. 30.

[44] Curran, *Reminiscences of John Adye Curran K.C.*, pp. 17–18.

[45] *Report on the select committee on outrages (Ireland)*, 1852, pp. 13 and 15.

[46] *Outrages (Kilmacrenan)*, p. 13.

[47] Hussey, *Reminiscences of an Irish land agent*, pp. 261.

[48] TNA, CO 903/1.

[49] Saudek, *Anonymous letters*, p. 1.

[50] NAI, CSO RP, 1870, 2/630/17, c1783/18593.

[51] *Examination of some recent allegations concerning the constabulary force of Ireland*, p. 63.

[52] NAI, CSO RP, 1884, 3/644/35, file 24995.

[53] Extrapolated from *Ireland. Tables showing the number of criminal offences ... 1850*, pp. 93 and 98–9.

[54] BBP: *Agrarian outrages (Ireland). (Persons made amenable to justice) (No.2)*, pp. 1–3.

[55] *Criminal and judicial statistics. 1883*, pp. 92–5.

[56] *Hansard*, House of Commons, 29 March 1887.

[57] Gregg, 'The Irish cauldron', p. 267.

[58] *Protection of persons and property (Ireland) act, 1881. List of all persons detained in prison under the statute 44 Cict. C. 4.*, House of Commons, 7 February 1882, pp. 2, 4–6, 8 and 26.

[59] British Library, Balfour papers, Papers relating to disturbances in Ireland, 1880–1886, BPP 13/4(8).

[60] *Examination of some recent allegations concerning the constabulary force of Ireland*, pp. 42 and 50.

[61] BBP: *Committals (Limerick)*, 221, House of Commons, 22 April 1846, p. 1.

[62] NAI, CSO RP, outrage papers, Tipperary, 1847.

[63] Curran, *Reminiscences of John Adye Curran*, p. 241.

[64] Finnegan, *Loughrea*, p. 41.

[65] TNA, CO 903/6, 13 927.

[66] BPP: *Outrages (Ireland). A return of all rewards offered by proclamation of the lord*

lieutenant of lords justices of Ireland, for the discovery of the perpetrators of murders and other outrages, from the 1st January 1836 to the 12th December 1837 with the dates of the proclamations; and distinguishing which such rewards (if any) have been claimed and paid by the Irish government, in consequence of information given pursuant to such proclamations, House of Commons, 23 February 1838, pp. 2–7 and 9.

[67] NLI, Mayo papers, *Queen v. Thomas Staunton*, Kildare, Ms 11, 952.

[68] Walker, *Parliamentary election results in Ireland, 1801–1922*, p. 84.

8. Response among nationalists

The political element behind outrages

It is impossible to make a sweeping statement regarding the political influence or motivation behind agrarian outrages in Victorian Ireland. Circumstance and the particular period matter. For instance, it would be difficult to make more than a superficial case for political motivation behind the outrages, including the massive volume of threatening letters, during the era of the Famine. That tough law enforcer Chief Baron Francis Blackburne (1782–1867) was probably not far off the mark in many cases when he asserted that the key cause for such acts was 'the wild justice of revenge'.[1] It is difficult to find much politicking behind agrarian outrages in these years. Where, after all, was the repeal movement during these years?

The same question posed a generation later during the Land War of the late 1870s/early 1880s is more difficult to answer. A few years later, though, the Irish Loyal and Patriotic Union (ILPU) had no doubt that outrages of all descriptions emanated from the National League. The ILPU's pamphlet blitz in the late 1880s and early 1890s set out to prove this.

Statistics of outrage crimes fed into the ILPU's campaign against the National League by supporting their claim of lawlessness in parts of Ireland. Figure 30 well illustrates how threatening letters greatly inflated the total number of outrages reported to the authorities. In 1881, threatening letters doubled the figures, with 2,195 threatening letters compared to 2,098 other reported outrages, giving a total of 4,293.

Establishment nationalists, however, had become quite twitchy over the threatening-letter phenomenon. They saw threatening-letter statistics as harming the nationalist cause in two ways. This was due first to the phenomenon being seen as encouraged by nationalist platform rhetoric. Secondly, more seriously, threatening letters and notices were viewed as the prelude to other violent crimes which harmed the home rule cause. Threatening letters also magnified the whole outrage phenomenon, literally doubling it in the public mind. The nationalist establishment had reason to be concerned. Many threatening letters originated, in one form or another,

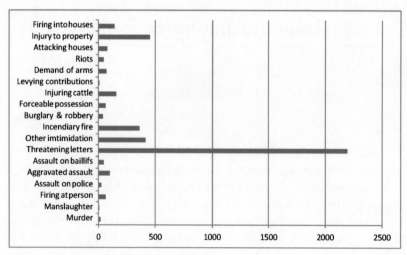

Fig. 31–Chart of reported outrages, 1881

from rural Ribbonism, that most nebulous and mercurial of secret societies and certainly a phenomenon over which the Irish Parliamentary Party had no control.

As well as playing down the importance of threatening letters, therefore, nationalist leaders tried to separate threatening letters from other outrages in the public mind. When the Protection of Person and Property (Ireland) Bill came before the House of Commons in February 1881, Dr Gommins, member for Roscommon, tabled an amendment seeking to omit 'threatening letters, attacking houses, firing into dwellings, or assault on police'. The Irish attorney general, Hugh Law (1818–1883), would have none of this:

> Probably the hon. and learned Gentleman meant only to exclude
> threatening letters; but as the Amendment runs, it seemed also to
> exclude firing houses. No doubt, the hon. and learned Gentleman
> did not intend to exclude that class of crime. As regards threatening
> letters also, my opinion is that they are about the most mischievous
> form of intimidation that can be used – the most effective and most
> cowardly – and, certainly, the Government are not disposed to
> accept any form of the clause which would exclude the power of
> proceeding against those who were suspected of manufacturing
> those terrorizing documents. We cannot accept the Amendment.

Irish MPs Joseph Biggar and Edmund Dwyer Gray confirmed that the amendment was intended to exclude threatening letters. Before going to the vote, which was lost by 113 votes to 73, the Irish attorney general observed:

> He (Mr. Callan) did not think that a man should be liable to 18 months' imprisonment without trial on the mere suspicion of having sent a threatening letter. The detection of handwriting was a matter upon which there was the greatest diversity of opinion, even among experts. The man was a coward who would send a threatening letter. He had himself received threatening letters, even in that House; but was he, on a mere suspicion conveyed to a detective, as to the writer, to have a particular man arrested? He only wished in some cases that he could discover the writer, not in order to denounce him to a detective, but that he might inflict summary punishment upon him for his cowardly act.[2]

Again, in October, John Redmond in the House of Commons pulled up Chief Secretary Trevelyan on the issue of including threatening letters in outrage figures he was quoting.[3]

Six years later, in March 1887, an interesting exchange on the subject of threatening letters occurred in the House of Commons. Arthur Balfour, the new chief secretary of Ireland, was denouncing the lawlessness, especially in the west of Ireland, and the difficulties that the authorities faced in the workings of the courts. Thomas Sexton, then member of parliament for west Belfast, interjected, 'We want the particulars'. To this 'Bloody Balfour' asserted that of 755 offences reported since the previous summer's assizes, the number of cases where the authorities had no idea of the offenders was 536. That is 70 per cent. To this, M.J. Kenny, member for mid-Tyrone, interjected, 'How many [of the 755 offences were] threatening letters?'. Balfour's reponse was, 'The figures I am giving have no reference to threatening letters'.[4]

William Gladstone, who in the past had brought both reform and coercion to Ireland, was with the Irish nationalists on the matter of threatening letters, or at least he was now that he was in opposition:

> Now, Sir, with respect to threatening letters, they are a social inconvenience – a social mischief; but it would be ridiculous to speak of them in connection with such a question as the legislative restraint of the liberties of the people.[5]

This was all well and good were it not for the fact that the threatening notice was perceived to be the precursor of the act of violence, or to use the chronologically not too distantly coined axiom of King Cetshwayo kaMpande of the Zulus: 'First the trader, next the missionary and then the red soldier'. In Ireland's case, the dictum might run: First the threatening letter, next the maimed cow and then the lead ball.

The government was not completely insensitive to accusations that threatening-letter statistics distorted the outrage picture. In 1888, it published a short parliamentary paper listing Irish agrarian offences exclusive of threatening letters and notices and comparing the number of offences during the first six months of 1882 with the second six months of 1887. The respective numbers were 1,040 against 306.[6]

In some districts, the Land League might well have incited agrarian violence, intentionally or not, but that was certainly not its policy. On occasions, the Land League branch also spoke out against specific crimes. Even in that hotbed of trouble, Loughrea in County Galway, in August 1881, the local Land League branch passed a resolution roundly condemning the murder of Constable Linton, the local constable of 20 years' standing:

> Adhering to the principles enunciated by Davitt, and constantly followed by the Land League we ... condemn the employment of threats and violence, for we cannot see that crime and outrage, no matter by whom or for what motive committed, furnish a weapon unscrupulously used by able and influential enemies to asperse and discredit our columns and organisation.[7]

Both Davitt and Joseph Biggar, two renowned rabble-rousers, were equally strong in their denunciation of the maiming of cattle, the latter describing it as 'a frightfully cruel and sinful thing to do'. As far as threatening letters were concerned, on 13 December 1880, in a memorandum of instructions to organisers and officers of Land League branches, Davitt stated:

> Threatening letters are as unnecessary as they are stupidly criminal and unjust; and we feel assured that no member of our organisation has resorted to such a method of making just demands which invites the stigma of cowardice and clumsily plays into the hands of the landlords.[8]

Generally, there is no reason to doubt the sincerity of the Land League in this, naive as it appears from a distance of over 140 years. But the wild men in its ranks bowed the knee to no chief.

The IPLU, through their series of pamphlets, did a fairly comprehensive job of illustrating that where the Land League was active, there was agrarian trouble. But that is not the same as proving that the League promoted outrage. That some of its grass-root members were extremists is hard to deny, and a case can be made for politicians, consciously or not, inciting the populace to acts of outrage. Equally, the Land League was actually a restraining influence, as believed by the lord lieutenant, Earl Cowper.[9]

Examples of nationalist politicians receiving threatening letters were not as common as earlier in the century. Writing to his son Morgan on 25 May 1840, Daniel O'Connell stated:

> I have been in the habit of receiving anonymus intonations of a
> somewhat similar description varying only as to the mode of death
> but also threatening my life ... I have become so accustomed to
> them that I scarcely read them.[10]

By the 1880s, the volume received by the Irish parliamentary leadership seems to have decreased. But quite what Charles Steward Parnell thought of the following couplet he received while in the comfort of his room in Kilmainham Jail in 1881 is not known. It was more admonitory than threatening, but irritating nonetheless:

> O Mr Parnell, O Mr Parnell
> Cease to do evil, and learn to do well[11]

The numbers of threatening letters received by nationalist politicians, and more likely, Land League or National League members, is hard to estimate. Not surprisingly, few if any were handed to the police. Michael Davitt was receiving threatening letters as late as the Anglo-Boer War period.[12] He touched on the subject when discussing the failed prosecution of him in Sligo in 1880 in *The fall of feudalism in Ireland*:

> Mr. Parnell and other prominent Land-Leaguers were in daily
> receipt of threatening letters at this time. All kinds of violence were
> to be resorted to by 'a landlord's son,' 'the son of an agent,' 'an anti-
> communist,' 'a hater of rogues and vagabonds,' and others who were
> careful, like all writers of sanguinary epistles, to conceal their names.

For every landlord fired at one of us was to experience the sensation of being made a human target of in retaliation. This was not altogether fair, seeing that our attacks were not made upon landlords personally, but upon rents, which were a violation of all laws except those passed expressly by a landlord-ridden Parliament for the selfish interests of the class. But threatening letters are not concerned with nice distinctions between the sanctity of rent and the worth of a life, and we were constrained to purchase revolvers, and to be on the defensive against possible assaults in Dublin and other places where there were comparatively large pro-landlord partisans and pro-British minorities.[13]

In fact, Davitt's revolver had been given to him for his protection (one suspects against sections of the advanced nationalists rather than any vengeful landlord's son or Orange-supporting thug) by the police.[14]

William O'Brien's leaders in his *United Ireland* frequently had little restraint in attacking opponents and consequently, he was himself the recipient of threatening letters while a member of parliament. Writing of the period just after the 1882 Phoenix Park murders, O'Brien recorded:

Then also commenced a series of anonymous threatening letters which continued for many months to come from a variety of worthy English lunatics, menacing me in terms of irrelevant obscenity with every penalty from a horsewhipping to bloody murder. The most considerable success of the writers was their ingenuity in leaving their letters unstamped and compelling my greenhorn self to pay double postage on them. Even this little comfort, however, was soon cut off from them by the excellent postmaster in the Lobby [of the House of Commons] who used to hold up a packet of unstamped missives to me with a grin, as he remarked: 'They are only some more of those cracked threatening letters, Mr O'Brien,' and cast into the waste-paper basket a mass of sanguinary literature which in the hands of a practised Dublin Castle official would have sufficed for the indictment of a nation.[15]

Given the reticence of the English to send threatening letters on the Irish scale, it might be more reasonable to assume the authors to be ardent Irish unionists.

The satirical response: *The threatening letter-writer*

In 1889, during the excitement of the Parnell Commission, the Dublin publisher M.H. Gill brought out a 46-page satirical pamphlet entitled *The threatening letter-writer and Irish loyalist companion*.[16] It was written by the 38-year old Derry poet, story-writer and humourist Patrick O'Conor MacLoughlin and sold at the price of sixpence. The stated purpose of the 'little book' was:

> to supply a long-felt want. i.e., to afford landlords, and others, a ready means of framing minatory letters to tenants and popular persons, and acquiring arguments which the limited education and intelligence of the 'intelligent and educated Minority' prevent them doing by themselves.

The pamphlet was divided into two parts. The first contained 19 fictitious letters between prominent persons such as landlords, magistrates and other persons whom they threaten. These basically consisted of people in power bullying and threatening. One exchange ran as follows:

–Henry Cahirbeg J.P. to his tenant Dermot Hurley
Hurley, – My son Reginald is standing for the Dunbeg Division of Cahirbeg Union. You and I were always friends, Hurley, and I hope your voting against my son will not make us enemies. You and your forefathers have lived for generations on my property (derived by my ancestors from His Excellency Lord Protector Cromwell, who took it from the O'Hurleys), and during that period you and yours have, no doubt, heard of such things as ejectments. Henry Cahirbeg, J.P.

–Dermot Hurley to Henry Cahirbeg The Big House
Honoured Sir, – I would rather vote for Mr. O'Neill, but, God's will be done, I'll vote for young Master Reginald. I've five childe'. Your humble servant, Dermot Hurley.

–Parish Priest, Dunbeg, to Lord Chancellor of Ireland
My Lord, – I enclose a copy of a letter addressed by Mr. Henry Cahirbeg, J.P., of Cahir House, in this county, to his tenant (and my parishioner), Dermot Hurley. I beg to respectively inquire if your lordship considers Mr. Cahirbeg a proper person to hold the

Commission of the Peace after the threat contained in that
communication? I am, my lord, Your obedient servant, _____P.P.

—Lord Chancellor's secretary to Parish Priest, Dunbeg
Rev. Sir, – I submitted your letter and the enclosure to the Lord
Chancellor, and am commanded by his lordship to express his
surprise that either you or Hurley should considered Mr. Cahirbeg's
letter to contain a threat. On the contrary, I am directed to point
out to you that Mr Cahirbeg expresses a desire (under certain
conditions) for Hurley's friendship – the allusion to an ejectment
being evidently intended to remind Hurley that he had not been
evicted. His lordship cannot avoid saying that your innuendo
concerning Mr, Cahirbeg is quite unfounded, as is proved by his
appointment to a Deputy Lieutenancy of your county since your
letter was received. I am, Rev. Sir, Your obedient servant

—Henry Cahirbeg to Messrs Droit and Droit
Dear Droit – I believe that your head clerk is a rebel in disguise, and
is delaying my ejectment against Hurley, who, after all, did not vote
for my son. In keeping my business in your office, I hope I shall not
be put to the pain of meeting the fellow. Yours faithfully, Henry
Cahirbeg.

—Droit and Droit, solicitors to their chief clerk, T. O'Connor
Dear Sir – We regret to say that, owing to the decrease of our
business, which, you must have perceived, is caused by the lawless
state of the country, we must dispense with your services from the
1st proxo.

We enclose cheque for salary to that date and (by the way) will
thank you to push on the case of Cahirbeg v. Hurley. Hurley is a
notoriously bad character. Yours faithfully, Droit and Droit.

Part two of MacLoughlin's pamphlet was made up of 'Containing useful
calculations, samples for forged letters, how to pack a jury, and other items
of information never before compiled or published, and which no loyalist
should be without'. This included examples of the signatures of Parnell, Joe
Egan, Patrick Egan, Tim Healy, and T.D. Sullivan, as well as examples of
drawings of threatening art such as a coffin, a sword and four pistols above

an anonymous letter which read: 'National League Office. Dear Captain Moonlight – Find £1 5s 0d. enclosed. Murder us 25s. worth of landlords.'

Apart from the Captain Moonlight note, the humour deteriorates somewhat in quality in this section, irony giving way to schoolboy humour and wry comment, with such sections as:

How to pack a jury
- Scale of sentences in inferior courts [Such as: girl under 10 years weeping at eviction ... one month imprisonment]
- Punishment for murder and felony [guilty or not]
- Table of rewards to loyalists
- Table showing Chief Secretary veracity [Philosophic doubt ... 99; Truth ... 1]
- Analysis of Ulster 'Loyalty' [Ignorance ... 10; Bigotry ... 25; Civil and religious liberty ... 0; Self-interest ... 60; and Hatred of the pope ...5].
- Chart of pedigree showing Mr Parnell's descent from Satan
- How to burn your house
- How to obtain compensation off the county for a 'dry' cow

This was all very well but after a decade of William O'Brien's biting sarcasm and ridicule in the weekly *United Ireland*, this was hardly a new line of attack. The concept that an eviction notice or open act of landlord bullying was as much a threatening letter as those reported annually in their thousands to the police was a word game which impressed few in Ireland in 1889, not least when landlords were a minority of those who actually received anonymous threatening letters and notices.

This was all rather different in tone and substance from the tenacious, if rather monotonous, pamphlets of the Irish Loyalist and Patriotic Union; though packed with quotations, these tend to hammer home a single point too much, namely, that Irish nationalists were by their speeches and articles encouraging outrages. Occasionally there were interesting observations, such that in some areas, Parnell medals and/or rewards were handed out, by whom is not clear, for services to moonlighting. Certainly, Parnell medals did exist, but whether some found their way by nefarious means into the hands of threatening-letter writers is impossible to prove.[17]

Fenians
It is difficult to comment upon the Fenian movement and threatening letters

as, in the cities, there was certainly no organised tradition of threatening-letter writing, unlike in the market towns and countryside. This is not to say that IRB members did not send threatening letters, but it was not a major focus. Charles Kickman had little time for the more unsavoury methods employed in the agrarian outrages. But as Superintendent John Mallon of the Dublin police well knew, a core of hard men in the Fenian tradition could be found within the Land League and were not beyond doing some incitement of their own.

Tenants

Outside of Ulster, the majority of tenants were Catholic, as well as nationalist by inclination. It needs to be said that even in those regions where threatening-letter writing was endemic, most tenant farmers did not get involved in such activity. Indeed, many tenants found themselves squeezed from both sides. The landlord wanted his rent, come rain or sun. The nationalist politician looked for their political support, especially as the franchise was extended. Tenants were also subject to O'Connell's repeal rent, to donations to the local priest and later, during the Land War days, whether they liked it or not, they had to toe the nationalist line and subscribe to the Land League or find themselves targeted. Like many mass movements, its masses had to be kept in line, but occasionally there was a silent protest. On 5 January 1848, the *King's County Chronicle* carried a report of a threatening letter having been sent to the wife of Colonel Westenra, the local landlord at Sharavogue. An address signed by 60 tenants deplored this threatening letter and spoke of the Westenras' 'many acts of kindness to the poor of your neighbourhood'.[18]

A generation later, a similar silent rebellion took place in Kerry – the most politically active and agitated region in the country.[19] As mentioned previously, some of Earl Kenmare's tenants marched through Kenmare in protest at threatening letters which had been sent to their landlord. The clean-cut picture created, and still popularly held, of Ireland divided between landlord and tenant is superficial and ignores the reality of the relationships and respect which built up across divides of faith, culture and race when people worked daily together, in this instance albeit in a paternalistic situation.

The clergy

The clergy were not immune from threatening letters. In the case of Protestants, though, there tended to be a link with land when such missives were received, be it in the early days over tithes, or later and where a cleric was also a landlord. For the Catholic priest, the situation was more complicated as they were not generally landlords. While there is no shortage of examples of priests being involved in radical rural politics, it should not be forgotten that they were also a restraining influence in many areas, and were not slow to denounce atrocities in the early 1880s. S.J. Connolly has observed:

> In the 1820s and 1830s ... direct assault on the Catholic clergy or even on their property appears to have been rare. Anticlerical agitation was largely confined to threatening letters or to the sort of mass protest employed in Mayo and Sligo in 1842–43.[20]

There were occasional examples of priests who got dragged into a threatening-letter saga. One example occurred in Leighlinbridge in County Carlow in March 1884. A shouting match between two members of the McDonald clan of Johnduffswood, who were next-door neighbours, got out of hand. The widow McDonald used 'very abusive language' towards Thomas McDonald. He threatened to take her to court over this. The result was that he received the following threatening letter:

> Dear Sir, i am informed that you are gone to law with the widow McDonald and if it is a thing that you have any thing to do with that woman or her children you will have to get out of this country, and another thing if you go to Bagenatstown [Bagenalstown or Muine Bheag] you will never Bring yourself out of it the day that you will go to the Court it will be a sore day you have better stay home.

Thomas McDonald received this on 21 March, the day he attended a funeral. There he met James Maher, to whom he showed the threatening letter and whose advice he asked. Maher said he must take it to the police. However, a few days later, Maher went to confession and told Father Delany of Leighlinbridge about the letter. To Maher's surprise, the priest said he had no right to have told McDonald:

> to go to the police and directed Maher to go at once & tell Mrs McDonald the supposed writer & sender of the letter to at once destroy any papers or material that would connect her with the

threatening letter and go and tell McDonald not to attempt
reporting anything about the threatening letter to the Police.

In fact, Thomas McDonald had already done so, and RIC Sergeant J.M.
Ballard soon had the saga of the priest also. The district inspector was,
however, a wiser man, and the matter was quietly allowed to drop.[21]

Questioning the statistics

The Irish nationalist approach to threatening letters and notices did not stop
at them playing down the phenomenon and at times treating it as a joke.
They also questioned the accuracy of all the outrage statistics.[22] The colourful
Irish MP for Liverpool, T.P. O'Connor, took up this long-standing point with
great gusto. As late as 1909, Henry Cleary, editor of the *New Zealand Tablet*,
devoted a section in his book *An impeached nation being a study of Irish
outrages* to 'The official exaggeration of Irish crime'. In it he wrote of 'Mr.
Forster's method of manufacturing manufactured "outrages" out of rather
flimsy material'.[23]

Long before that, though, such attacks and assertions had led Arthur
Balfour, himself no stranger to the Irish threatening letter, to sit down in
the Irish Office in 17/18 Great Queens Street, London, and draft a curious
parliamentary paper entitled 'Agrarian outrages (Ireland), Memorandum
as to the principle upon which outrages are recorded as Agrarian, and
included as such in the returns laid before parliament' on the day he was
appointed chief secretary of Ireland. The gist of this two-pager was that
the divide between agrarian and ordinary crime was problematic and had
been severely criticised. It stated that the authorities in Ireland 'have been
more and more strict in their requirements, before they permitted any
crime to be classified as agrarian'. He went on to say that for a crime to be
deemed agrarian it:

> must be directly traceable to some specific motive connected with
> land. So that a large number of crimes specifically characteristic of
> Irish disorder, such as maiming of cattle, firing into houses,
> moonlighting, and raiding for arms, may never appear in the Return
> of Agrarian Outrages at all.

Balfour then proceeded to look at the time of the Westmeath bubble when
Chichester Fortescue, later Lord Carlingford, was chief secretary when a new
method of counting outrage offences was adopted. This greatly increased

numbers. He gave several examples, one of which was specifically related to threatening letters:

> Again 22 threatening notices were posted on the night of the 13th of January 1870 on the houses of 22 persons living on the one townland, in the County Mayo, threatening with death any person who paid any more than the Government valuation, and these cases were shown as 22 threatening notices. In 1871, the previous system was again brought into operation, namely, to record similar cases as only one of each kind, when the outrages were perpetrated by the same party on the one occasion.

No doubt there is some truth in the accusation that outrage crime statistics were exaggerated, whether by design or compilation methods. However, as discussed elsewhere, that cannot be said for the number of threatening letters recorded. What is beyond dispute, however, is the impact and public perception of threatening letters and notices, especially among the nationalist population.

Notes

[1] Woodham-Smith, *The great hunger, Ireland 1845–9*, p. 329.
[2] *Hansard*, House of Commons, 14 February 1881, cols 798–811.
[3] *Ibid.*, 31 October 1881, cols 462–3.
[4] *Ibid.*, 28 March 1887.
[5] *Ibid.*, 29 March 1887.
[6] BBP: 'Agrarian offences (Ireland): Returns of agrarian offences, exclusive of threatening letters and notices', Parliamentary paper 117, session 1888, LXXXIII, p. 411.
[7] Finnegan, *Loughrea*, p. 93.
[8] Quoted in *A verbatim copy of the Parnell Commission report with complete index and notes*, Irish Loyal and Patriotic Union, London and Dublin, 1890, p. 106.
[9] Townshend, *Political violence in Ireland*, p. 149.
[10] NLI, O'Connell papers, Ms 40 021, Daniel O'Connell to Morgan O'Connell, 25 May 1840.
[11] McCracken, *Inspector Mallon*, p. 57.
[12] King, *Michael Davitt after the Land League*, p. 469.
[13] Davitt, *The fall of feudalism in Ireland*, pp. 188–9.
[14] Bussy, *Irish conspiracies*, p. 31.
[15] O'Brien, *Evening memories*, p. 10.
[16] Patrick O'Conor MacLaughlin, *The threatening letter-writer and Irish loyalist companion*, M.H. Gill, Dublin, 1889, 46 pp. London School of Economics, available at http://www.jstor.org/stable/60213855?seq=1#page_scan_tab_contents (accessed 4 May

2016).
17 'As it was said', 1886, p. 92.
18 Quoted in Reilly, *The Irish land agent*, p. 142.
19 Lucey, *Land, popular politics and agrarian violence in Ireland*, p. 6.
20 Connolly, *Priests and people in pre-famine Ireland 1780–1845*, p. 241.
21 NAI, CSORP 1884, 21454, 3/644/27.
22 Connolly, *Priests and people in pre-Famine Ireland 1780–1845*, pp. 241 and 254.
23 Cleary, *An impeached nation*, pp. 256–77.

9. The lingering threatening-letter tradition

The great age of the Irish threatening letter largely fizzled out after the Land War and plan of campaign in the 1880s, followed by the advent of tenant proprietorship in the 1890s and early 1900s. By then there had, for some time, been rising expectations in the Irish farming community. The American journalist William Henry Hurlbert (1827–1895) believed that the increasing sums invested in Irish provincial savings banks were an indication of growing wealth, and by extension, it might be argued that this fact gave a lie to the established truth that tenants could not afford to pay their rents. Though to that might be added the caveat that in some circumstances, they may have been unable to pay full rents because of their debts to shopkeepers and dues to the church. Hurlbert, in his *Ireland under coercion*, gives the following examples of increased savings in Post Office savings accounts, summarised in Table 15.[1]

Table 15–Amounts in various PO savings accounts, 1880/1887

Post Office savings account	Total amount in 1880	Total amount in 1887	Percentage increase
Six-Mile-Bridge, County Clare	£382	£934	245%
Killorglin, County Kerry	£282	£1,299	460%
Inch & Gore, County Wexford	£3,699	£5,308	143%
Youghal, County Cork	£3031	£7,038	232%

The irony of the situation was that, even in the 1880s, a great number of landlords were giving reductions in rents, or abatements, as a matter of course, which is more than the shopkeepers in the towns were offering tenants who fell into debt with them. Of the rise in expectations, William Hurlbert quotes one tenant farmer to illustrate how circumstances which had been accepted by a previous generation were no longer considered good enough as time went by:

> My father could pay the rent, and did pay the rent ... because he was content to live so that he could pay it. He sat on a boss of straw, and ate out of a bowl. He lived in a way in which I don't intend to live, and so he could pay the rent. Now, I must have, and I mean to have, out of the land, before I pay the rent, the means of living as I wish to live; and if I can't have it, I'll sell out and go away; but I'll to _____ if I don't fight before I do the same![2]

Hurlbert also recalls a visit to Wybrants Olphert's estate, Ballyconnell House, in northern Donegal. He comments on how curious it was to see the young Mr Olphert come in and throw down his belt and his revolver on the hall table 'like his gloves and his umbrella'. Olphert senior commented to Hurlbert that personally, he had always been on the best of terms with the people of the nearby village of Falcarragh and added:

> The older tenants, even now, if he met them walking in the fields when no one was in sight, would come up and salute him, and say how 'disgusted' they were with what was going on. It was the younger generation who were troublesome – more troublesome, he added, to their priest than they were to him.[3]

As far as threatening letters were concerned, by the turn of the century, their heyday had gone. The inspector-general of the Royal Irish Constabulary (RIC) noted confidentially in January 1900, 'Intimidation by threatening letters and minor outrage is still resorted to in a very few instances but no really serious case has occurred'.[4]

There was a slight upturn in the number of threatening letters recorded in the late Edwardian era, as Figure 31 illustrates, but the figures were low in comparison to earlier periods, even though the proportion of agrarian instances within the general category remained largely the same. The chief justice, addressing the grand jury in County Clare in early March 1908, remarked that 'There had been a very considerable increase under the heading of intimidation, the sending of threatening letters and notices, and the firing into houses'.[5]

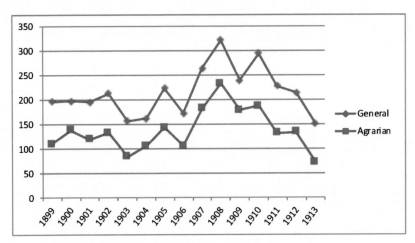

Figure 32–Threatening letters recorded in the Edwardian era

Needless to say, as seen in Table 16, the conviction rate for sending threatening letters and notices remained very low.

Table 16–Threatening letters or notices convictions, 1905–7

Date	Reported	Amenable but not convicted	Conviction
1905	142	8	2
1906	105	0	0
1907	182	2	0
1908	233	0	0

The Ulster unionist threatening letter

Ironically, the threatening letter in politics and among the judiciary continued as before, although there had always been far fewer of these than in rural areas of Ireland. Indeed, it has not stopped to this day. In the late Edwardian and pre-First World War period, a largely new category of threatening letter emerged out of the Liberal government's attempt to introduce a home rule bill. These letters had a harshness about them and lacked the stylistic form of their nationalist and rural counterparts. This is not to say that they were never colourful and dramatic. The Liberal politician Lloyd George was no stranger to receiving threatening letters. In 1914, when chancellor of the exchequer, he received the following:

It has been decided by the committee of our league that in the event of 'Home Rule' being granted within a few days of the passing of the bill, you will be assassinated and your head will be thrown into Picadilly. So be warned.
From
Those who are determined

In a similar vein, another such read:

IT WAS YOU WHO HASTENED THE DEATH OF KING EDWARD –
YOU AND YOU ALONE ARE RESPONSIBLE FOR THE BLOODSHED THAT WILL TAKE PLACE IN ULSTER –
THE FIRST SHOT FIRED WILL MEAN THE DESTR-UCTION OF YOURSELF AND FAMILY.
    W.SPU

Part of another, threatening to kill the whole British government cabinet, King George V and John Redmond if home rule was forced on Ulster, read:

WE ARE ALL GOOD SHOT WITH RIFLES AT LONG RANGE SO POLICE GUARDS WONT SAVE YOU. WE WONT MIND HANGING IF CAUGHT ... WE WONT BE RULED BY ROMAN PRIESTS BY PROXY FROM DUBLIN ... FIFTY ULSTERMEN WILLING TO DIE TO SAVE THEIR PEOPLE'S LIBERTY.[6]

It is important, though, not to exaggerate the impact of these letters out of all proportion to their volume.

British politicians, of course, had received Irish-related threatening letters before, especially and perhaps not surprisingly, William Gladstone. At the time he was pushing his second home rule bill through the house of commons in 1893, he received, on 5 July, the following unsigned note, in a neat hand. It can hardly be classified within the canon of Irish threatening letters in terms of style, language and neatness, and it is most likely, therefore, to have been written by an educated Londoner:

This is to warn Mr Gladstone that a party of 'Moonlighters' are now in Ireland who have sworn to blow him up with dynamite along with Mr Morlay, Lord Herschal, Lord Spencer and Sir Wm Harcourt and to shoot every Nationalist Member when he returns to Ireland should the Home Rule Bill pass – [7]

Irish suffragettes

The other new manifestation of the Irish threatening letter in the second decade of the twentieth century related to the suffragettes. The Irish suffragettes, harking back perhaps to the Ladies Land League, were probably ahead of the field in writing threatening letters. The imprisonment of several members also produced a flurry of threatening letters:

BEWARE FOR YOUR OWN SAFETY HOW YOU TREAT THEM!

And:

To day I have put destructive liquid in a letter-box as a protest at the hideous treatment of the Dublin Suffragists, Mary Leigh and Gladys Evans.

Leigh was the first suffragette in Ireland to be force-fed.

Burning of the big houses

Also new were the arson attacks which destroyed over 250 of Ireland's big houses between 1920 and 1923. Terence Dooley, in his pioneering study, *The decline of the big house in Ireland*, has illustrated how the burning of Tubberdaly, King's County [Offaly], on 15 April 1923, was presaged by threatening letters.[8] In several cases, the underpinning reason for the destruction of these mansions was to drive out the old landed class and subdivide the land among the former tenants – ironically a form of land-grabbing.

Return of the old

The Irish agrarian threatening letter and notice survived the home rule drama, the 1916 Rising, the Anglo-Irish war and partition. Indeed, as the dramatic events of the Anglo-Irish war mounted and lawlessness re-emerged in its former haunts in 1920 and 1921, some 700 threatening letters were recorded by the RIC. But there was a major difference from previous times. The Land

War had been won and the social revolution effected. Now the desire of some former tenant farmers was to remove from the land completely those against whom they had fought of old, or alternatively those they just did not like and with whom scores had to be settled. In other words, the resurgence of threatening letters was motivated by revenge and land greed.

The assault on some farmers involved in pasture farming resulted in cattle-driving, the practice of driving livestock off land to intimidate the owners to sell. This had existed in the past, but now became more prominent.[9] In addition, employees of farms wanted or claimed by locals for themselves were threatened, and constant pressure was placed on those who refused to sell their farms and quit, irrespective of gender or age. It was not only the old landlord class who were the victims. Other farmers, and especially farmers from outside a narrow local perimeter, received these threatening letters. Into the fray also came those who had, for whatever reason, been evicted sometimes decades earlier and who now had no farms. The summary police reports tell their own tale as these examples illustrate:

> Notices posted warning people having anything to do with Major
> Persse. The latters land is wanted for division.
> (Loughrea, Coorheen, County Galway, 25 May 1920)

> Threatening letters were received by four workmen to cease working
> for G.R. Cooke, Esq., J.P., and a threatening notice was chalked on
> the gate of one of his farms, from which his horses, cattle and sheep
> were driven. The farm is wanted by the landless people who are
> agitating for it.
> (Templemore. Borrisland S. & Mount, Tipperary, 21 October 1920)

> A man received a threatening letter with the object of deterring him
> from bidding for a farm to be sold by public auction. It was sold to
> another man who was the only person that bid for it.
> (Mullingar, Westmeath, 2 November 1920)

> Thomas Murphy, Cattle-dealer & Publican, received a threatening
> letter not to purchase or take on the 11-months system grazing
> lands at Doneraile. A notice warning graziers was also posted up.
> Motive – to secure lands for division amongst local people.
> (Mallow, Doneraile, Cork, 14 November 1920)

226

Letter received by A. Rathburne warning him to surrender a farm wanted for division.
(Kesh. Belleek. County Fermanagh, 10 December 1920)

Threatening letters were received by Lord Inchiquin and two ex-soldiers. Motive – to prevent the division of land amongst ex-soldiers.
(Sixmilebridge, Newmarket & Doomoland, Clare, 4 February 1921)

Three employees of Mrs Shawe Taylor received threatening letters to leave their employment. There is a continuous agitation to compel this lady to sell her land for division.
(Athenry, Moorpark, Galway, 9 February 1921)

Wm. A. Dobbyn, Clerk of Crown and Peace, received a threatening letter. Motive – to compel [him] to sell his Estate to his tenants on favourable terms.[10]
(Newtown, County Waterford, 30 March 1921)

A threatening notice was posted up on the gate pier of a farm of John Minahan and his son-in-law's cattle and sheep were driven off the farm. Local people want the farm for division amongst themselves.
(Tiermaclane, outside Ennis, County Clare, 19/20 May 1921)

Time and time again, the police reports relating to the many forms of agrarian outrage ended, 'This land is wanted for division'. While the burning of the big ascendancy houses was happening, on another level, land agitation continued apace.

But these attempts to divide the spoils of the defeated landed class and pre-empt the coming expropriation work of the land commission over the next two generations are part of a different saga. There was, however, one RIC report of a threatening letter which had nothing to do with the new 40-acre landed proprietors, one which might as well have been written in 1820 as 1920. Some things in the threatening letter business had not changed:

A turf bank belonging to T. O'Connell was damaged by letting water into it; and letters received by O'Connell and his labourer warning them to let Maloney's turf alone. Maloney claims this turf bank.[11]

Notes

1   Hurlbert, *Ireland under coercion*, vol. 2, pp. 5, 12, 66n and 248.
2   *Ibid.*, p. 193.
3   *Ibid.*, pp. 114–15.
4   TNA, CO 904/69, f.577.
5   *Intellingence Notes. Assizes. Spring assizes, 1908. Chief Secretary's Office, Judicial Division. Confidential.*
6   TNA, MEPO 3/2767, Special Branch letter book.
7   TNA, MEOP, 3/2767, threatening letter to Gladstone, 5 July 1893, 2920/124.
8   Dooley, *The decline of the big house in Ireland*, pp. 175–7.
9   *Hansard*, House of Lords, 18 March 1909, vol. 1, cols 495–502.
10 TNA, CO 904/121, Précis of agrarian outrages reported this day, 1921.
11 Graystown, Cashel, County Tipperary, 27 May 1920.

Select bibliography

Primary sources

British Library
Balfour papers, Add Ms 49 808.

National Archives, Kew, London
Home Office papers: Threatening letters to Her Majesty, 1882–1939, HO 144/99/A17173.
Irish Crimes Records: CO 903 (1885–1892); CO 904 (1893–1897); CO 904 (Outrages).
London Metropolitan Police papers: Officer of the commissioner, Special Branch letter book, 1892–1918, MEPO 3/2767.
Treasury papers: DMP, T1/12860.

National Archives of Ireland
Chief Secretary's Office Registered papers.
Crime Branch Special papers.
Famine Relief Commission papers.
Fenian papers 'R' series.
Outrage reports (counties) (CSO).
Police and Crime (Crimes Act 1882).

National Library of Ireland
Clonbrock papers, Ms 35,758.
Crown Solicitor's Office, 1867–1885, Ms 5970.
Considine papers, Ms 43,080 and 43,081.
Conyngham papers, Ms 25,346.
De Vesci papers, Ms 38,968.
Headfort papers, Ms 48,989.
Larcom papers, Ms 7519.
Lismore papers, Ms 43,382; 43,439; 43,446; 42,456.

Mayo papers (Staunton), Ms 11,952.
Joseph McCarrity papers, Ms 17,574.
O'Connell papers, Ms 40,021.
Poe (magistrate), Ms 15,349.
Sweetman, Ms 47,590.
Westport collection, Ms 41,029.
Wicklow papers, Ms 38,603.

Public Record Office of Northern Ireland
Coopershill papers, D4031.
Downshire papers, D671.
Charlemont papers, D266.
Clandeboye estate, D1071.
Crossmaglen Conspiracy Trial, T3194/1.
Earl of Erne's papers, D1939.
Estrange, Sligo, T3905/5.
Johnston, Downpatrick, D3815/A/108.
John Kerr, Enniskillen, D1163.
Saunders papers, T2996.
Shirley papers, D3531.
Verner estate (Agents: James and Henry Crossle), D236.

In author's possession
Ink pen sketch of John Dillon on Kildare Street, notepaper by Colonel
    Sanderson, n.d.
Letter from Edward Sanderson to ___ Wrench, 24 March 1884.
Remains of scrapbook belonging to Major R.G. Traill, *c.*1868–90.

Newspapers
The Cork Examiner
Daily Express (Dublin)
The Freeman's Journal
The Irish Times
Limerick Leader
Kerry Sentinel
Newry Telegraph
The Nation
The Police Gazette or Hue-and-Cry
Roscommon & Leitrim Gazette and Carrick-on-Shannon & Boyle Advertiser

The Suspect
The Times
United Ireland

British Parliamentary Papers (BBP) and official publications
Note: Not listed here are the large number of returns of general and of agrarian outrages published as British parliamentary papers during the Victorian era generally under the title of *Return 'of outrages reported to the Constabulary Office during the year _____ '.* There were also lists published under the title *Agrarian offences (Provinces) (Ireland). Return 'by provinces of agrarian offences throughout Ireland reported to the Inspector-general of the Royal Irish Constabulary, between the 1st day of January _____, and the 31st day of December _____ ...'.* All these lists were usually published annually, although there were also some monthly returns in the beginning of the period and quarterly returns in the opening years of the twentieth century. Many of these outrage reports are bound in volumes on the open shelves of the National Archives of Ireland. They are also available online from the National Archives of Ireland website: http://www.nationalarchives.ie/search-the-archives/. Their reference numbers are:

CSO/ICR/1 (1848–1878)
CSO/ICR/2 (1879–1893)
CSO/ICR/4 (1877–1882: monthly and annual returns)

The Documenting Ireland: Parliament, People and Migration is also a useful source (http://www.dippam.ac.uk/eppi/) as is the University of Southampton's Library Digitalisation Unit website (https://archive.org/details/@library_digitisation_unit_university_of_southampton). There is also the proQuest collection of British parliamentary papers online.

Hansard parliamentary debates: 1881, 1882, 1886, 1887, 1888, 1900.

Abstracts of police reports of some of the principal outrages in the counties of Tipperary, Clare, Limerick, Leitrim, and Roscommon in the year 1845, Command paper, 1846.

Agrarian crimes (Ireland). Returns of all agrarian crimes and outages reported by the Royal Irish Constabulary in the Counties of Galway, Mayo, Sligo, and

Donegal, from the 1st day of February 1880 to the 30th day of June 1880, of the number of meetings called for the purpose of promoting land agitation reported by the constabulary within the same counties since the 30th day of June 1879: Of the number of cases reported by the constabulary in which resistance was offered to the police when protecting process servers, bailiffs, and others in the execution of their duty: And of the number of police engaged in each case on protection duty, and total number so engaged, (Mr. Tottenham), House of Commons, 327 – series 2, 3 August 1880.

Agrarian offences (Ireland): Returns of agrarian offences, exclusive of threatening letters and notices, for first six months of 1882: Of agrarian offences, exclusive of threatening letters and notices, for first six months of 1887; and of analysis of returns during first and second six months 1882 and 1887 respectively, 117, session 1888, LXXXIII, p. 411.

Agrarian outrages (Ireland), Memorandum as to the principle upon which outrages are recorded as Agrarian, and included as such in the returns laid before parliament (Mr. Arthur Balfour), 140, House of Commons, 9 May 1887.

Agrarian outrages (Ireland). (Persons made amenable to justice) (No.2), 281, House of Commons, 14 July 1882.

Commission of the Peace (Ireland), 2 – sess.2., House of Commons, 27 August 1886.

Committals (Limerick), 221, House of Commons, 22 April 1846.

Copies of secret official reports made by officers of the Dublin Metropolitan Police between December 1880 and March 1883 on the subject of secret societies and the nationalist movement in Ireland. Together with a memorandum by Mr. E.G. Jenkinson and others on the same subject. Printed for the use of the Cabinet. April 1889, p. 49 [TNA, CAB 37/24].

Crime and Outrage Act, etc. (Ireland), 195, House of Commons, 31 March 1860.

Criminal and Judicial Statistics. 1883. Ireland. Part I. Police – Criminal proceedings – Prisons. Part II. Civil proceedings in central and larger and smaller district courts, c. 4181, Houses of Parliament, Dublin, 1884.

Evidence taken before Her Majesty's commission of inquiry into the state of law and practice in respect to the occupation of land in Ireland. Part III.i, Houses of Parliament, Dublin, 1845.

Examination of some recent allegations concerning the constabulary force of Ireland in a report to His Excellency the Lord Lieutenant. By Sir Henry John Brownrigg, C.B., Inspector-General, Dublin, HMSO, 1864.

Explosion at Edenburn. Report to the Right Honorable the Secretary of State for the Home Department on the circumstances attending an explosion which occurred at Edenburn, the private residence of Mr S.M. Hussey, in the County of Kerry on the morning of the 28th November, 1884; By Colonel A. Ford, H.M. Inspector of Explosives. Presented to both houses of parliament by command of Her Majesty, London, 1885, c. 4285.

General orders for the guidance of the troops in affording aid to the civil power in Ireland, Dublin, HMSO, 1880, Z/Ireland/112.

House of Lords. [Bill 129.] Protection of Life and Property in certain parts of Ireland [H.L.], brought from the Lord's 5 May 1871, ordered by the House of Commons to be printed, 8 May 1871.

Ireland. Tables showing the number of criminal offenders committed for trial or bailed for appearance at the assizes and sessions in each county in the year 1850, and the result of the proceedings. Chief Secretary's Office, Dublin Castle, Houses of Parliament, Dublin 1851.

Outrage and intimidation (Ireland). Return of certain cases of outrage and intimidation referred to by the chief secretary for Ireland in a speech in the House of Commons on 13th February 1890, 85, House of Commons, 4 March 1890.

Outrages (Ireland). A return of all rewards offered by proclamation of the lord lieutenant of lords justices of Ireland, for the discovery of the perpetrators of murders and other outrages, from the 1st January 1836 to the 12th December 1837 with the dates of the proclamations; and distinguishing which such rewards (if any) have been claimed and paid by the Irish government, in

233

consequence of information given pursuant to such proclamations, House of Commons, 23 February 1838.

Outrages (Ireland). Return of the nature of outrages reported to the Constabulary Office, within the barony of Owneybeg. House of Commons, 342, 22 May 1846.

Outrages (Kilmacrenan). A return 'of the Outrages specially reported by the Constabulary as committed within the Barony of Kilmacrenan, County Donegal, during the last Ten Years; specifying the Nature of each Offence, the Number of Parties Arrested on Suspicion, and whether Conviction had or not.' (Mr. Conolly.), House of Commons, 5 July 1861.

Papers relating to the state of Ireland. House of Commons, 7 July 1834, command paper 459.

Police Protection (Ireland). Return showing by provinces and counties, the number of persons specially protected by the Royal Irish Constabulary, on 31st day of July 1887, and on the 31st day of January, 1888, respectively, both Houses of Parliament, Dublin, 1888. See also NAI, CSORP, 1894, box 3/6557/4.

Protection of persons and property (Ireland) act, 1881. List of all persons detained in prison under the statute 44 Cict. C. 4., House of Commons, 7 February 1882.

Report from the select committee on outrages (Ireland); together with proceedings of the committee, minutes of evidence, appendix and index, 438, House of Commons, 4 June 1852.

Special Commission Act, 1888. Reprint of the shorthand notes of the speeches, proceedings, and evidence taken before the commissioners appointed under the above-named act. Vol. 3, HMSO, London, 1890.

Statistical tables of the Dublin Metropolitan Police, for the year 1865, Alexander Thom, Dublin, 1862. Also, for the years 1861, 1869 and 1870. Copies in the National Library of Ireland.

Acts of parliament relating to or relevant to the writing and sending of threatening letters

For laws relating to the writing and sending of threatening letters see:
http://www.lawreform.ie/_fileupload/Reports/rNonFatalOffences.htm
http://www.irishstatutebook.ie/eli/1861/act/100/enacted/en/print.html
(both accessed 3 November 2016).

1825: *An act for the amendment of the Law as to the Offence of sending Threatening Letters* [6 Geo IV].

1847: *An Act for the better Prevention of Crime and outrage in certain Parts of Ireland until the First Day of December One thousand eight hundred and forty-nine, and to the End of the then next Session of parliament. [20th December 1847]* [11 Vict c. 2].

1871: *Protection of Life and property in certain Parts of Ireland* [34 Vict].

1881: *Protection of Persons and Property (Ireland) Act* [44 Vic, c. 4].

1882: *Prevention of Crime (Ireland) Act, 1882* [45 & 46 Vict. c. 25].

Irish Loyal and Patriotic Union and Property Defence Association pamphlets

ANONYMOUS, *A verbatim copy of the Parnell Commission report with complete index and notes*, ILPU, London and Dublin, 1890.

ANONYMOUS, *Annual report of the executive committee for the year 1886. With appendices*, ILPU, Dublin, London and Edinburgh, January 1887.

ANONYMOUS, *'As it was said.' Extracts from prominent speeches and writings of the Parnellite party 1879–1886: with classification and index and a sketch of the separatist movement illustrated with agrarian crimes' map, and parliamentary map of Ireland*, ILPU, Dublin and London, October 1886, 154 pp. [Contains 'Agrarians crimes map of Ireland'].

ANONYMOUS, *Ireland in 1887. Part I. Proceedings at assizes. Part II. Extracts from proceedings of National League branches. March 31, 1887*, ILPU, Dublin and Westminster.

ANONYMOUS, *Ireland. No.1. The truth about the Irish elections of 1885. By the defeated candidates. With an introduction*, ILPU, London and Dublin, n.d.

ANONYMOUS, *Ireland. No.4. Resistance to evictions*, ILPU, Dublin, n.d.

ANONYMOUS, *Ireland. No.6. The National League and outrages*, ILPU, Dublin and London, 1886.

ANONYMOUS, *Irish Loyal and Patriotic Union. Publications issued during the year 1889*, ILPU, Dublin and London, n.d.

ANONYMOUS, *Statement submitted to the prime minister by the Irish Loyal and Patriotic Union. Part I. Social order in Ireland under the National League*, ILPU, Dublin and London, 1886.

ANONYMOUS, 'Threatening Letters', *The London Journal*, 6 March 1897, p. 218.

FOSTER, Arnold, *The truth about the Land League, its leaders and its teaching*, PDA, Dublin 1883.

Contemporary works

ADDISON, Henry Robert, *Recollections of an Irish police magistrate and other reminiscences of the south of Ireland*, Ward and Lock, London, 1862.

ANONYMOUS [F.E.R.], *Historical reminiscences of Dublin Castle from 849 to 1904*, 6th ed., Sealy, Bryers and Walker, Dublin, 1904.

ANONYMOUS, 'Lord Roden's committee on Irish crime', *Edinburgh Review*, vol. 70, no. 142, January 1840, pp. 503–44.

ANONYMOUS, 'Outrages in Ireland', *The Leader*, 16 October 1852.

ANONYMOUS [Percy Fitzgerald], *Practical politics and Moonlight politics. Letters to a Grand Old Man, and certain cabinet ministers, lately our confederates, by Rory-O'-the-Hills, some time National Schoolmaster, now a Moonlighter*. Tinsley Brothers, London, 1882.

ANONYMOUS [Percy Fitzgerald], *Recollections of Dublin Castle and Dublin society by a native*, Chatto and Windus, London, 1902.

ANNONYMOUS, *The social revolution: Agitate! Educate!! Organize!!! To the members of the P.P.A.S.* [Political Prisoners' Aid Society] *by an humble follower of Michael Davitt*, n.d., 8 pp.

ASHTOWN, Rt Hon. Lord, *The unknown power behind the Irish nationalist party: Its present work and criminal history*, Swan Soonnenschein, London, 1908.

BECKER, Bernard H., *Disturbed Ireland: Being the letters written during the winter of 1880–81*, Macmillan, London, 1881.

BENCE JONES of Lisselan, W., *The life's work in Ireland of a landlord who tried to do his duty*, Macmillan, London, 1880.

BUSSY, Frederick Moir, *Irish conspiracies: Recollections of John Mallon (The great detective) and other reminiscences*, Everett, London, 1910.

BROWN, Edward Cromwell, 'English law – The threatening letter or writings', *The Imperial Magazine*, March 1827, 7.75, cols 238–9.

CARLETON, William, *Valentine McClutchy, the Irish land agent; or, the chronicles of Castle Cumber; together with the pious aspirations, permissions, vouchsafements, and other sanctified privileges of Solomon McSlime, a religious attorney*, James Duffy, Dublin, 1847.

CASHMAN, D.B., *Life of Michael Davitt, founder of the national Land League, with selections from his speeches, by D.B. Cashman. To which is added the secret history of the Land League, by Michael Davitt. Cameron & Ferguson edition*, R. & T. Washbourne, Glasgow, n.d.

CLEARY, D.D., Henry W., *An impeached nation being a study of Irish outrages*, New Zealand Tablet, Dunedin, 1909.

COLLES, Ramsay, *In castle and court house: Being reminiscences of 30 years in Ireland*, T. Werner Laurie, London, *c.* 1911.

CANT-WALL, E., *Ireland under the Land Act: Letters contributed to the 'Standard' newspaper; with an appendix of leading cases under the act, giving the evidence in full, judicial dicta, etc.*, Chatto and Windus, London, 1882.

CURRAN, John Adye, *Reminiscences of John Adye Curran K.C. late county court judge and chairman of quarter sessions*, Edward Arnold, London, 1915.

DAGG, D.I., George A. De M. Edwin, *Devia Hibernia: The road and route guide for Ireland of the Royal Irish Constabulary*, Hodges, Figgis & Co., Dublin, 1893.

DAVITT, Michael, *The fall of feudalism in Ireland or the story of the Land League revolution*, Harper, London and New York, May 1904.

GREG, W.R., 'The Irish cauldron', *Quarterly Review*, vol. 128, 1870, pp. 251–300.

HEAD, Sir Francis B., *Fortnight in Ireland*, 2nd ed., John Murray, London, 1852.

JESSOP, George H., 'The emergency men', in [Anon] *Stories by English authors: Ireland*, Charles Scribner's Sons, New York, 1902, pp. 23–63.

LEWIS, George Cornewall, *On local disturbances in Ireland*, B. Fellowes, London, 1836.

LLOYD, Clifford, *Ireland under the Land League: A narrative of personal experiences*, William Blackwood, Edinburgh and London, 1892.

MACLAUGHLIN, Patrick O'Conor, *The threatening letter-writer and Irish loyalist companion*, M.H. Gill, Dublin, 1889, 46 pp. London School of Economics, available at http://www.jstor.org/stable/60213855?seq=1#page_scan_tab_contents (accessed 4 May 2016).

O'BRIEN, Hon. Georgina, *The reminiscences of the Right Hon. Lord O'Brien (of Kilfenora) lord chief justice of Ireland*, Edward Arnold, London, 1916.

O'BRIEN, William, *Evening memories: Being a continuation of Recollections by the same author*, Maunsel, Dublin and London, 1920.

O'BRIEN, R. Barry, *The life of Lord Russell of Killowen*, Thomas Nelson, London, Edinburgh, Dublin and New York, n.d.

O'CONNOR, James, *Recollections of Richard Pigott*, M.H. Gill, Dublin, 1889.

O'MEARA, Barry E., *Napoleon in Exile: Or, A voice from St. Helena: the opinions and reflections of Napoleon on the most important events of his life and government, in his own words*, 2 vols, W. Simpkin and R. Marshall, London, 1822.

'PRESTER JOHN', 'Terrorism in Ireland', *Dublin University Magazine*, March 1889, pp. 390–5.

REED, Sir Andrew, *The Irish Constable's Guide*, 7th ed., by Hume R. Jones, Alex. Thom, Dublin, 1918.

RONAN, Barry, *Forty South African years: Journalist, political, social, theatrical and pioneering*, Heath Cranton, London, 1919.

ROXTON, George W., *The methods of the Parnellites*, reprinted from the *Dublin University Review* for November 1885, Dublin, 1885.

RUSSELL, Sir Charles, 'Ireland's vindication before the special commission appointed by parliament to inquire into the charges and allegations formulated by The Times against Mr. Parnell and his colleagues. Speeches by Sir Charles Russell (extending over six days) in opening the defence', *The Freeman's Journal*, 1889.

RYAN, Dr Mark, *Fenian memories*, M.H. Gill, Dublin, 1945.

SAUDEK, Robert, *Anonymous letters: A study in crime and handwriting*, Methuen, London, 1933.

SPARROW, R., *The Royal Irish Constabulary Manual or Guide to the discharge of police duties*, 6th ed., Alex. Thom, Dublin, 1909.

Threatening letter cartoon 'A magnificent class!', *Weekly Freeman's*, 30 July 1881.

TRENCH, W. Steuart, *Realities of Irish life*, Longmans, Green and Co.,

London, *c.* 1870.

TROLLOPE, Anthony, *The Land Leaguers*, Penguin edition, London, 1993 (first published 1884).

WILSON, Edward D.J., 'The present anarchy', *The nineteenth century*, January 1881, pp. 37–52.

Later works

AKENSON, Donald Harman, *Small differences: Irish Catholics and Irish Protestants*, McGill-Queen's University Press, Kingston and Montreal, 1988.

BALL, Stephen (ed.), *A policeman's Ireland: Recollections of Samuel Waters, RIC*, Cork University Press, Cork, 1999.

BEAMES, Michael, *Peasants and power: The Whiteboy movements and their control in pre-Famine Ireland*, Harvester Press, Sussex, 1983.

BENCE-JONES, Mark, *A guide to Irish country houses*, Constable, London, 1988.

BENCE-JONES, Mark, *Twilight of the ascendancy*, Constable, London, 1987.

BEW, Paul, *Land and the national question in Ireland*, M.H. Gill, Dublin, 1978.

BOWEN, Elizabeth, *Bowen's Court*, Collins Press, Cork, 1998.

CAMPBELL, Christy, *Fenian fire: The British government plot to assassinate Queen Victoria*, Harper Collins, London, 2002.

COMERFORD, R.V., 'Churchmen, tenants, and independent opposition, 1850–56', in W.E. Vaughan (ed.), *A new history of Ireland: V Ireland under the union I 1801–70*, Clarendon, Oxford, 1989, pp. 396–414.

COMERFORD, R.V., 'The land war and the politics of distress, 1877–82', in W.E. Vaughan (ed.), *A new history of Ireland: VI Ireland under the union II 1870–1921*, Clarendon, Oxford, 1996, pp. 26–52.

CONNOLLY, S.J. *Priests and people in pre-famine Ireland 1780–1845*, Gill and Macmillan, Dublin, 1985.

CRONIN, Denis A., *Who killed the Franks family? Agrarian violence in pre-Famine Cork*, Maynooth Studies in Local History: Number 83, Four Courts Press, Dublin, 2009.

DOHERTY, Gillian M., *The Irish ordnance survey: History, culture and memory*, Four Courts Press, Dublin, 2006.

DONNELLY, James S. Jr, *The great Irish potato famine*, History Press, Stroud, 2001.

DONNELLY, James S., *The land and the people of nineteenth-century Cork*, Routledge and Kegan Paul, London and Boston, 1975.

DONOGHUE, Fergal, *Crime in the city: Kilkenny in 1845*, Four Courts Press, Dublin, 2015.

DOOLEY, Terence, *The decline of the big house in Ireland*, Wolfhound, Dublin, 2001.

DOOLEY, Terence, *The murders at Wildgoose Lodge: Agrarian crime in pre-Famine Ireland*, Four Courts Press, Dublin, 2007.

DUFF, Patrick J., 'Emigrants and the estate office in the mid-nineteenth century: A compassionate relationship', in E. Margaret Crawford (ed.), *The hungry stream: Essays on emigration and famine*, Ulster-American Folk Park and Queen's University Belfast, Belfast, 1997, pp. 71–86.

DUFFY, Peter, *The killing of Major Denis Mahon: A mystery of old Ireland*, Harper, New York, 2007.

DUNGAN, Myles, *Mr Parnell's Rottweiler: Censorship and the United Irishman newspaper, 1881–1891*, Irish Academic Press, Sallins, 2014.

DUNNE, Terry, 'The agrarian movement of 1920: "Cattle drivers, marauders, terrorists and hooligans"', *History Ireland*, 28.4, 2020, pp. 30–3.

FERGUSON, Stephen, *The Post Office in Ireland: An illustrated history*, Irish Academic Press, Dublin, 2016.

FINNEGAN, Pat, *Loughrea, 'that den of infamy' during the Land War in Co. Galway, 1879–82*, Four Courts Press, Dublin, 2014.

GIBBONS, Stephen Randolph, *Captain Rock, night errant: The threatening letter in pre-Famine Ireland, 1801–1845*, Four Courts Press, Dublin, 2004.

GRIFFIN, Brian, *Sources for the study of crime in Ireland, 1801–1921*, Maynooth research guides for local history: Number 9, Four Courts Press, Dublin, 2005.

HERLIHY, Jim, *The Dublin Metropolitan Police: A short history and genealogical guide with notes on medals and casualties, and lists of members connected with the London Metropolitan Police, the Irish Revenue Police, the (Royal) Irish Constabulary and the British Army*, Four Courts Press, Dublin, 2001.

HERLIHY, Jim, *The Royal Irish Constabulary: A short history and genealogical guide with a select list of medal awards and casualties*, Four Courts Press, Dublin, 1997.

IRISH STATUTES: http://www.irishstatutebook.ie/eli/1861/act/100/enacted/en/print.htmlmrder

(accessed 18 June 2016).

JACKSON, Alvin, *Ireland 1798–1998: War, peace and beyond*, Blackwell, Oxford, 1999.

JOHNSON, Dr J. Stafford, 'The Dublin Penny Post – 1773–1840', *Dublin Historical Review*, vol. iv, no. 3, March–May 1942, pp. 81–95.

KELLY, Michael, *Struggle and strife on a Mayo estate, 1833–1903: The Nolans of Logboy and their tenants*, Four Courts Press, Dublin, 2014.

KOLBERT, C.F. and O'BRIEN, T., *Land reform in Ireland: A legal history of the Irish land problem and its settlement*, Occasional paper no.3, University of Cambridge Department of Land Economy, Cambridge,1975.

LEWIS, Colin A., *Hunting in Ireland: An historical and geographical analysis*, J.A. Allen, London, 1975.

LUCEY, Donnacha Seán, *Land, popular politics and agrarian violence in Ireland: The case of County Kerry, 1872–86*, University College Dublin Press, Dublin, 2011.

LYNE, Gerard J., *The Lansdowne estate in Kerry under the stewardship of William Steuart Trench, 1849–72*, Geography Publications, Dublin, 2001.

LYONS, F.S.L., *Charles Stewart Parnell*, Collins, London, 1977.

McCLELLAND, Aiken, 'The later Orange Order', in T. Desmond Williams (ed.), *Secret societies in Ireland*, Gill and Macmillan, Dublin, 1973, pp. 126–37.

McCRACKEN, Donal P., *Forgotten Protest: Ireland and the Anglo-Boer War*, Ulster Historical Foundation, Belfast, 2003.

McCRACKEN, Donal P., *Inspector Mallon: Buying Irish patriotism for a five-pound note*, Irish Academic Press, Dublin, 2009.

McCRACKEN, Donal P., *Saving the Zululand wilderness: An early struggle for nature conservation*, Jacana media, Johannesburg, 2008.

McCRACKEN, Donal P., 'The imperial British newspaper, with special reference to South Africa, India and the "Irish model"', *Critical Arts*, 29.1, 2015, pp. 5–25.

McCRACKEN, Donal P., 'The troublemakers', in Donal P. McCracken (ed.), *The Irish in southern Africa, 1795–1910*, *Southern African-Irish Studies*, vol. 2, 1992, pp. 39–53.

McCRACKEN, J.L., 'The death of the informer: James Carey: A Fenian revenge killing?', *Southern African-Irish Studies*, vol. 3, 1996, pp. 190–9.

McCRACKEN, J.L., 'The fate of an infamous informer', *History Ireland*, vol. 9, no. 2, summer 2001, pp. 26–30.

McGEE, Owen, *The IRB: The Irish Republican Brotherhood from the Land*

League to Sinn Féin, Four Courts Press, Dublin, 2005.

McKEOWN, Thomas, and McMAHON, Kevin, 'Agrarian disturbances around Crossmaglen. Part x: The Shooting of Meredith Chambre', *Seanchas Ardmhacha: Journal of the Armagh Diocesan Historical Society*, 19, no. 2 (2003), pp. 206–24.

MAC SUIBHNE, Brendán, *The end of outrage: Post-famine adjustment in rural Ireland*, Oxford University Press, Oxford, 2017.

MADDEN, Kyla, *Forkhill Protestants and Forkhill Catholics, 1787–1858*, Liverpool University Press, Liverpool, 2006.

MALCOLM, Elizabeth, 'The reign of terror in Carlow': The politics of policing Ireland in the late 1830s, *Irish Historical Studies*, vol. xxxii, no. 125, May 2000, pp. 59–74.

MALCOMSON, A.P.W., *Virtues of a wicked earl: The life and legend of William Sydney Clements, 3rd earl of Leitrim (1806–78)*, Four Courts Press, Dublin, 2009.

MARLOW, Joyce, *Captain Boycott and the Irish*, History Book Club, London, 1973.

MARLEY, Laurence, *Michael Davitt: Freelance radical and frondeur*, Four Courts Press, Dublin, 2007.

MILLER, David W. (ed.), *Peep O' Day and defenders: Selected documents on the disturbances in County Armagh, 1784–1796*, PRONI, Belfast, 1990.

MOLONY, Senan, *The Phoenix Park murders: Conspiracy, betrayal and retribution*, Mercier Press, Cork, 2006.

MOODY, T.W., *Davitt and Irish revolution 1846–82*, Clarendon Press, Oxford, 1982.

MOODY, T.W., MARTIN, F.X., BYRNE, F.J. (eds), *A new history of Ireland: VIII, A chronology of Irish history to 1976: A companion to Irish history part I*, Clarendon Press, Oxford, 1982.

MOODY, T.W., MARTIN, F.X., BYRNE, F.J. (eds), *A new history of Ireland: IX, maps, genealogies, lists: A companion to Irish history part II*, Clarendon Press, Oxford, 1984.

MORAN, Gerard, 'The land war, urban destitution and town tenant protest, 1879–1882', *Saothar: Journal of the Irish Labour History Society*, vol. 20, 1995, pp. 17–31.

MURRAY, A.C., 'Nationality and local politics in late nineteenth-century Ireland: The case of County Westmeath', *Irish Historical Studies*, xxv, no. 98, (November 1986), pp. 144–58.

O'BRIEN, Conor Cruise, *Parnell and his party 1880–90*, Clarendon Press, Oxford, 1957.

O'CALLAGHAN family of Maryfort, County Clare: http://www.clarelibrary.ie/eolas/coclare/history/bodyke_evictions/maryfort_house.htm (accessed 12 January 2017).

O'CONNOR, Michael M. and O'CONNOR, James R., *When crowbar and bayonet ruled: The Land War on the Balarra estate of Heather Gardiner and Susanna Pringle 1879–1910*, Original Writing, Dublin, 2013. See also: http://www.ouririshheritage.org/page/harriet_gardiner_b1821_d1892 (accessed 19 June 2021).

O'TOOLE, Fintan, *A history of Ireland in 100 objects*, Royal Irish Academy, Dublin, 2013.

POLE, Adam, 'Sheriffs' sales during the Land War, 1879–82', *Irish Historical Studies*, vol. xxxiv, no. 136, November 2005, pp. 386–402.

REILLY, Ciarán, *The Irish land agent, 1830–60: The case of King's County*, Four Courts Press, Dublin, 2014.

SHEEL, Diane Elaine, 'British conservatism and the primrose league: The changing character of popular politics, 1883–1901', unpublished PhD thesis, Columbia University, 1986.

SMITH, Cathal, *Thomas Bermingham: Nineteenth-century land agent and 'improver'*, Four Courts Press, Dublin, 2018.

TOWNSHEND, Charles, *Political violence in Ireland: Government and resistance since 1848*, Clarendon, Oxford, 1983.

TRAVERS, Pauric and McCARTNEY, Donal (eds), *Parnell reconsidered*, Dublin University College Press, Dublin, 2013.

VAUGHAN, W.E., *Landlords and tenants in mid-Victorian Ireland*, Oxford University Press, Oxford, 1994.

VAN ONSELEN, Charles, *Masked raiders: Irish banditry in southern Africa 1880–1899*, Zebra Press, Cape Town, 2010.

VAUGHAN, W.E. (ed.), *A new history of Ireland: V Ireland under the union I 1801–70*, Clarendon Press, Oxford, 1989.

VAUGHAN, W.E. (ed.), *A new history of Ireland: VI Ireland under the union, II 1870–1921*, Clarendon Press, Oxford, 1996.

VAUGHAN, W.E., *Landlords and tenants in Ireland 1848–1904*, Economic and Social History Society of Ireland, Dundalgan, 1985 reprint.

VAUGHAN, W.E., *Sin, sheep and Scotsmen: John George Adair and Derryveagh evictions, 1861*, Appletree Press and Ulster Society for Irish Historical Studies, Belfast, 1983.

VESSEY, *The murder of Major Mahon, Stokestown, County Roscommon, 1847*, Maynooth Studies in Local History: Number 80, Four Courts Press, Dublin, 2008.

WALDRON, Jarlath, *Maamtrasna: The murders and the mystery*, De Burca, Dublin, 2004.

WALKER, B.M., *Ulster politics: The formative years,1868–86*, Ulster Historical Foundation and Institute of Irish Studies, Belfast, 1989.

WALKER, Brian (ed.), *Parliamentary election results in Ireland, 1801–1922*, New History of Ireland ancillary publication IV, Royal Irish Academy, Dublin, 1978.

WEATLEY, Michael, *Nationalism and the Irish party: Provincial Ireland, 1910–1916*, Oxford University Press, Oxford, 2005.

Whyte's history and literature Sunday 13 March 2016 (catalogue), Whyte and Sons, Dublin, 2016.

WINSTANLEY, Michael J., *Ireland and the land question, 1800–1922*, Methuen, London and New York, 1984.

Waterloo directory of Irish newspapers and periodicals, 1800–1900, available at http://irish.victorianperiodicals.com/series3/ (accessed 6 January 2017).

WOODHAM-SMITH, Cecil, *The great hunger, Ireland 1845–9*, Hamish Hamilton, London, 1962.

Entries in the *Dictionary of Irish Biography: From the earliest times to the year 2002*, James McGuire and James Quinn (eds), 9 vols, Royal Irish Academy and Cambridge University Press, Cambridge, 2009 (https://www.dib.ie/):

Francis Blackburn (1782–1867), by James Quinn, vol. 1, pp. 564–6.

William Carleton (1794–1869), by Clíona Ó Gallchoir, vol. 2, pp. 347–9.

Percy Hetherington Fitzgerald (1830–1925), by Frances Clarke, vol. 3, p. 907.

Edward Harrington (*c.* 1852–1902), by Marie-Louise Legg, vol. 4, p. 473.

Hugh Holmes (1840–1916), by Bridget Hourican, vol. 4, pp. 760–1.

Hugh Law (1818–1883), by Patrick M. Geoghegan, vol. 5, pp. 349–50.

Maurice Lenihan (1811–1895), by Liam Irwin, vol. 5, pp. 448–9.

Edward Martyn (1859–1923), by William Murphy, vol. 6, pp. 405–7.

Thomas Nicholas Reddington (1815–1862), by James Quinn, vol. 8, pp. 407–9.

Frederick Oliver Trench (1868–1946), by Patrick Maume, vol. 9, pp. 462–3.

Index

Curran, Judge J.A. viii, 181, 192, 200, 202
Cusack, A. 86

Daecon, John 100
Dalton, Mrs xii
Daly, Charles 86
Daly, Martha 8
Darby, Jonathan 147
Darley, George 182, 188
Davies, Inspt. 121
Davitt, Michael 35, 67, 80, 96-97, 114, 132-133, 159, 171, 210-212
Daylight, Captain 135
De Andrade, R.J.L. xii
De Freyne estate 99
De Salis, Count 23
De Valera, Eamon 28
De Vesci, Viscount 66-67, 71
Dease, __ 179
Delaney, Martin 199
Delany, Father 217
Delany, William 8
Delving 199
Delworth, William 41
Deneny, Thomas 178
Derby, Lord 159
Derry/Londonderry 15-16, 59, 182, 201, 213
Derrycassan 188
Devia Hibernia 160
Devine, Thomas 41
Digby estate 149
Dillon estate 99
Dillon, John 35, 166
Dingle 103
Disney, Kate 100
Disney, Lambert 115
Dobbs, __ 202
Dobbyn, William 227
Dodvilla, __ 54
Doherty, Patrick 36
Donaghmoyne 149
Donegal 15-16, 66, 85, 99, 121, 170, 177-178, 193, 199, 201, 222
Donnelly, James S. 98

Doocastle 26
Doolaghty, James 116
Doolan, __ 29
Dooley, Terence 225
Dooling, Timothy 197
Doomoland 227
Dopping-Hepenstal, Col. R.A. 188
Doudney, Rev. David 191
Dowling, Thomas 199
Dowling, Timothy 199
Down 15-16, 23, 28, 58-59, 85, 148
Downshire estate 158, 161
Doyle, Bernard 130
Doyle, Constable Thomas 33
Drimmin 75
Drogheda 62
Dromoland Castle 47
Drumahaire 199
Drumilly 80-81
Drunkenness 10, 31, 39-40, 64, 112, 118, 155, 168
Dublin vi, ix, 6, 9, 10, 15-16, 21-22, 28, 33, 35, 37, 40, 44, 46, 51, 76-77, 81, 83, 88-91, 107, 112, 115-124, 127, 130-131, 157, 163-164, 166, 168, 176, 179, 183-187, 190, 192, 212-213, 216, 224-225, 230
Dublin Castle 77, 90, 127, 132, 136, 198
Dublin Metropolitan Police vi, 9-10, 83, 112, 114, 117-118, 121, 187
Dublin University Magazine 95
Duffy, Peter 162
Dundalk 130
Dungan, Myles 122-123
Dungloe 199
Dunkerrin 129
Dunmore 199
Dunn, John xii
Dunsandle, Lord 127
Durrow 38, 51
Dwyer, __ 62
Dwyer, __ 19-20
Dysert 21

Earlshill 115

Lisnagree 21
Lisselan 154
Listowel 103, 199
Littleboy, __ 64
Lloyd George, David 223
Lloyd, Charles Clifford 25, 106,
    171, 180-182
Lloyd, Rev. John 162
Londonderry (See Derry)
Longford 13, 15-16, 41, 49, 86, 99,
    178, 180-181, 188, 199-201
Lough Iron 78
Loughrea 24, 199, 210, 226
Lourenço Marques xii
Louth 15-16, 86, 99, 107, 130, 149
Lowry, Joseph
Lucey, Donnacha Seán 101
Lucy, Ernest W. xii
Luggacarren estate 99
Lynch, H.B. 128
Lynch, James 116
Lynch, William 65
Lyne, Gerard 149
Lysaght, Sergt. 120

Madden, Kyla 32, 43
Magheraclogher 121
Maguire, Mary 30
Maguire, The Widow 31
Maher, James 217
Maher, Peter 85
Maher, Thomas 200
Mahon, Major Denis 54, 162, 170
Mahon, John Ross 151
Maiming of domestic animals vii, ix,
    7, 47, 193, 198, 210, 218,
Malachy, John 61
Malavery, __ 59
Mallon, John vi, 82-83, 91, 96, 113-
    114, 117, 123-124, 176, 216
Mallow 226
Mallow, John 41
Maloney, __ 227
Manorhamilton 38
Mansergh, __ 36
Marlow, Joyce 151

Marshall, W.G. 86
Martyn, Edward 118
Maryborough (Portlaoise) 192
Maryfort 20
Mask, Lough 151, 182
Massareene estate 99
Mathews, John 130
Mauleverer, Lindsay 48
Maume, Patrick 122
Maxwell, John 135-136
Maxwell, Stewart 58
Mayo xiv, 7, 9, 15-16, 20, 26, 35,
    42, 61-62, 65, 83, 89, 98-99, 114,
    118, 127, 146, 151, 177-178, 183,
    188, 217, 219
MacLoughlin, Patrick O'Connor
    107-108, 213
MacPhilpin, John 128
McAfee, __ 201
McAteer, Henry 114
McBride, Hugh 121, 199
McCabe, John 61
McCaffrey, __ 69
McCanney, Nancy 67
McCarney, Patrick 178
McCarthy, Denis & Timothy 122
McCartney, James 85
McClean, __ 190
McClenaghan, __ 85
McClure, Thomas 85
McClutchy, Col. Val 106
McColgan, __ 85
McCormick, Patrick 182
McCoy, John 84
McCracken, __ 148
McDermott, John 202
McDonald, Father 93
McDonald, Thomas 217-218
McDonnell, Peter 19
McGeough, Robert 67
McGoohan, James 188
McGrew, Peter 45-46
McKenna, James 40
McKim, Robert 191
McKnight, Daniel 26
McMahon, __ 99